AMONG OTHER THINGS

AMONG OTHER THINGS

A Description of the Novel

TERRENCE DOODY

For Jennie and Jill
with all my love
Terry

LOUISIANA STATE UNIVERSITY PRESS
Baton Rouge

Designer: Glynnis Weston
Typeface: Bodoni
Typesetter: Wilsted & Taylor
Printer and binder: Edwards Brothers, Inc.

Library of Congress Cataloging-in-Publication Data:
Doody, Terrence, 1943–
    Among other things : a description of the novel / Terrence Doody.
        p.   cm.
    Includes index.
    ISBN 0-8071-2248-3 (alk. paper)
    1. Fiction—History and criticism.   I. Title.
PN3351.D65   1998
809.3—dc21   98-23621
                                                    CIP

The paper in this book meets the guidelines for permanence and durability
of the Committee on Production Guidelines for Book Longevity of the
Council on Library Resources. ⊗

for
Clare and Robin
Kathleen and Rachelle

CONTENTS

ACKNOWLEDGMENTS

This book has taken some time to write, and I have debts I am happy to acknowledge at last. First, I would like to thank the National Endowment for the Humanities and the Mellon Foundation for grants, administered through Rice University, which supported the initial stages of my research. Allen Matusow, who was dean of humanities at the time, was helpful in securing these grants and was very encouraging of the project. Next, I would like to thank Mark Spilka and the editors of *Novel*. The germ of this book is an essay entitled *"Don Quixote, Ulysses,* and the Idea of Realism," which first appeared in *Novel* and was later republished in *Why the Novel Matters: A Postmodern Perplex*. These were very encouraging developments, and so was the generosity of Richard Pearce. I am grateful as well to the editors of *Contemporary Literature, The Journal of Narrative Technique, Mid-America Review,* and *New Orleans Review* for permission to use material originally published in these journals.

Kit Wallingford, Virginia Carmichael, and Monroe Spears; then Chris Newfield, the late René Fortin, David Day, and Walter Isle; then Andy Hurley, Bob Patten, and Walter Isle, again, read various versions of this argument. Their generosity and intelligence have given this book greater clarity of focus and kept it shorter than it tried to be. And Wes Morris gave my last questions an answer.

For typing and word processing through the early stages, I am grateful to Nancy Bosworth, Nancy Dahlberg, and Joy Shaw. Julie Sims Steward helped with the final draft, checking it for errors and reading it for sense. I am also grateful to John Easterly and Gerry Anders of Louisiana State University Press and to my copy editor, Ruth Laney. No one, however, has done more for this book in every way, through all its final visions and revisions, than Terry Munisteri.

I also wish to thank the students I have taught at Rice and at the Women's Institute of Houston, who have helped me understand these novels through their responses, their papers, and their appetite for clarity.

This book is dedicated to my children and my wife. With Kathleen, Clare, and Robin, reading *Charlotte's Web, Little House on the Prairie,* the *Star Wars* books, and *The Jungle Book,* I've learned what is absolute about our need for narrative. My wife, Rachelle, urged me to start this book and urged me to finish it; and never, I'm thankful to say, did she share my doubts about it. I hope they all like being in this book as much as Don Quixote thought he'd like being in his.

AMONG OTHER THINGS

INTRODUCTION

Alas and alack, small things overcome great ones!
A tooth triumphs over a body. The Nile rat kills the crocodile,
the swordfish kills the whale, the book will kill the building!
—VICTOR HUGO, *Notre Dame of Paris*

The sole raison d'être *of a novel is to discover*
what only the novel can discover.
—MILAN KUNDERA, *The Art of the Novel*

THE NOVEL HAS been many things throughout its history, but it has never been just another literary type, like the Pindaric ode or the *roman à clef.* Like the comic sense or the historical sense, the novel's sense of life offers a broadly enabling vision that can be embodied in many ways. Yet whatever embodiment this vision takes, realism has traditionally been the novel's epistemology. Realism links the novel to the empirical science, skeptical philosophy, and newly democratic political thought of the seventeenth century; and as Western society developed, the novel grew with it to become as instrumental as any other human invention in the shaping of modernity. For the novel has helped us take our place, among other things, in the secular physical world; it has taught us to tell time, not *sub specie aeternitatis,* but in plots and stories written during a time of ceaseless, endless change; and it has aided us in the construction, exploration, and critique of psychological individuality, the modes of thought and interpretation necessary to define individual experience and its meanings, and the social institutions built to accommodate that individuality. The novel has been, as Lionel Trilling said, the chief agent of our moral imagination, the form that more than any other has taught us the virtues of understanding and forgiveness.[1] For at least the last century, the novel has been the dominant form of literature in the West. Delmore Schwartz's opinion that the "normal state of affairs occurs when poetry is continually digesting the prose of its time"[2] now seems to apply to *The Prelude* and *The Ring and the Book* as much as it does to *The Waste Land*

---

1. Lionel Trilling, *The Liberal Imagination* (New York, 1978), 209.
2. Quoted in David Lehman, "The Shield of a Greeting," in *Beyond Argument: New Essays on John Ashbery,* ed. David Lehman (Ithaca, 1980), 110.

and the *Cantos.* Any critical theory that alters our sense of the novel, or challenges its utility, is also going to affect our sense of human being.

Linguistics, the structuralist disciplines that developed from it, and the poststructuralist thought that has grown up as a critique of structuralist assumptions have issued fundamental challenges to our traditional understanding of language itself and the literary forms language enables. In brief, structuralism constructs synchronous wholes and focuses on the interrelations of the elements these wholes contain as the basis of meaning (as it denies the positive entity of any single thing in itself), so it has seemed to the novel what the New Criticism once seemed to the lyric poem: the "natural" theoretical approach. Poststructuralist thought has cast doubt on the validity of these structural wholes and encourages us to recover intrinsic, apparently forgotten contradictions that preclude any totalizing unity. Nonetheless, these two modes of thought have both grown from and fostered a critical strategy (which in some cases is also an article of faith) of founding ontology in language alone. This move should not have seemed, at first blush, a devastating blow to literature and literary studies, founded as they are in language. And it should not have seemed particularly disabling of the novel, if we are convinced by Robert Alter's argument for the novel's role in the formulation of modernity: "If modern philosophy can be said to begin with Descartes's methodological skepticism, his making ontology essentially problematic, a whole tradition of the novel, as the paradigmatically modern narrative genre, is informed by that same critical-philosophical awareness, beginning almost half a century before Descartes with Cervantes."[3] But in practice, this idea of a linguistic ontology has proved extremely unsettling because it reduces substance itself to the play of similarity-and-difference; it makes literary characters, and human beings as well, actants or functions in a system of representation rather than autonomous psychological individuals; and it displaces interpretive authority from the author to the reader, who has become a text herself and therefore subject to the discursive forces at work throughout the illimitable field of intertextuality. In doing so, this ontology seems to rob writers of their formal power, to deprive all individuals of their freedom, and to create a higher formalism that amounts to an irremediable fatalism. But we don't have to allow the introduction of uncontrollable discursive forces to define, or even limit, our engagement with the novel. What I want to argue in this book is that although structuralist and poststructuralist ideas promote a rich rereading of the novel and its basic structures—its intrinsic form of narrative, its theory of character, and the ideal of its realism—reducing everything to language

3. Robert Alter, *Partial Magic: The Novel as a Self-Conscious Genre* (Berkeley, 1978), x.

systems and linguistic values costs too much and ignores those aspects of experience, even of the experience of reading, that are outside language.

Among Other Things is, first of all, a book on the novel. Although I use the ideas and example of recent theory to review and refine a sense of the novel's components and their operation, I also use the novel to test the utility and expense of these ideas. Critical theories tend to be exclusive, imperialistic, and centered in a set of values that reduces everything else to itself. The novel still is, as it has always been, more capacious, democratic, and relatively uncentered. Theory has recently reduced the self to a single, usually minimalist, construct, often called "the subject." The novel doesn't offer a single definition of the self but many definitions; and some of the greatest novels, such as *The Sound and the Fury*, offer several definitions, several styles of consciousness and interpretation, in the same book. Moreover, many ideas about subjectivity and authority that theory now brings to bear on the novel, as though from on high, the novel has anticipated in practice for some time. So while theory, even deconstructive theory, ultimately seeks greater purity and internal rigor as *theory*, the novel still entertains an openness to unrecorded experience and to other forms of discourse, including the theory that would constrain it. In my mind and argument the novel comes first, and I try to fit the theoretical ideas I have not only to the novel as a form but to all the novels I discuss.

In my mind, the novel always has capital letters, for "The Novel" has no exact counterpart in discussions of other genres. We do not say The Rise of The Tragedy or The Origins of The English Poetry, perhaps because tragedy and poetry seem timeless and universal. The phrase "The Novel" applies to the genre, but the force of the definite article's particularity is not to be ignored. The novel is less universal than poetry but broader than the sonnet, or even the epic, in its range of reference. It is both a particular object and a general form, just as it is both a physical object and a verbal construct, a book and a text. Characters in a novel are both psychological representations and linguistic signs. And while novels unfold in linear plots, which entail the actions of a narrator, they are also structures of relationships in which the narrator is not necessarily privileged. "The Novel," therefore, is a phrase that keeps reminding us of its own and its components' ambiguities. I hope the reader will come to think of it this way also.

Among Other Things has always been the title I had in mind. It suggests a novel's physical existence in a world of material objects, its physical independence as a thing itself, and its manifold, but not merely linguistic, relationships to other things as well; the phrase has a familiar ring and, I hope, a critical resonance. The subtitle was more difficult to find, because I wanted a single phrase to indicate too many things. The first of these is my debt to Joyce. Almost everything I think about the novel I have learned, in some fashion, from *Ulysses*. *Ulysses* exhibits an extraordinary fidelity to the things of concrete experience, the data of Dublin in 1904, down to the factual accuracy of street addresses, as though Joyce had already committed himself, as Shaun says of Shem, to "writing the mystery of himsel [*sic*] in furniture."[4] Since readers have explored this realistic fidelity and verified all the detail, recent criticism of *Ulysses* has focused on its theoretical dimension. Patrick McGee's *Paperspace: Style as Ideology in Joyce's "Ulysses"* (1988) is a title that exemplifies the way Joyce has become the Shakespeare of the novel, the figure each generation of readers has to appropriate in order to legitimize itself and its reading.[5] I also wanted a subtitle that would reflect a debt to Robbe-Grillet, considerably smaller but still important. His critical essays are no longer required reading, but I have always thought his prescription for a fictional method in "A Future of the Novel" a healthy antidote: "Let it be first of all by their *presence* that objects and gestures establish themselves, and let this presence continue to prevail over whatever explanatory theory that may try to enclose them in a system."[6] This may be an impossible project, but aspiring to it is completely in keeping with the implication that the furniture in a novel is related to the mystery of the self, and that its own mystery is an ontological matter more complex than any merely metonymic ordering of setting or scene.

A subtitle I considered was "Recent Theory and the Structures of the Novel," which expresses some of this book's central concerns but is also misleading. For my thinking on the novel is indebted to older, more traditional critics who are still useful in placing the newest *des nouvelles critiques* in perspective. Nonetheless, newer criticism and theory have taught me to see the novel's traditional components—plot, character, and realism—as structural arrangements themselves, terms in a complex of relationships that can no longer be simply isolated and substantialized. I tried for a long time to formulate a subtitle that would acknowledge the novel's own ongoing, internal theorizing: the way that novelists have thought about things theorists think about, and the fact that they have done it in writing after they too have read novels informed with theories other than their own. Nevertheless, I have settled on "A Description of the Novel," despite its blandness, because as Nietzsche says in *On the Genealogy of Morals,* only those entities that exist outside history can be defined. And, as he insists, there are none.

4. James Joyce, *Finnegans Wake* (Harmondsworth, 1976), 184.

5. See Terrence Doody, "What We Talk About When We Talk About Joyce, Now," *Novel: A Forum on Fiction,* XXIV (1990), 100–107.

6. Alain Robbe-Grillet, *For a New Novel: Essays on Fiction,* trans. Richard Howard (New York, 1965), 21.

Among Other Things is not intended to be an exposition such as Vincent B. Leitch's *Deconstructive Criticism* or Wallace Martin's *Recent Theories of Narrative.* Nor is it a poetics such as Gerard Genette's *Narrative Discourse: An Essay in Method,* which focuses on a single work (although *Remembrance of Things Past* is not just any other novel). In his study of Claude Simon, David Carroll explains the limitations inherent in Genette's approach and his own: "A book analyzing the novels of some other twentieth-century novelist (Joyce, Proust, Faulkner, or Beckett, for example) in connection with these same theoretical questions would be different . . . and the form of the confrontation between the theories and fictions analyzed also different."[7]

What this book will do is insist upon the novel first as a physical object and develop some principles based on this assertion. One is that novels are forms of presence that critical theories point to as the signifier points to a signified. This is an idea, or at least a strategy, that I subscribe to in saying that novels have priority in my argument throughout this book. For although we may now agree that any signified is also a signifier, physical presence cannot be easily or entirely resolved into anything else; and the novel in our hands and the act of reading it in time, under circumstances that remain literally illimitable and perhaps literally unimaginable, resist reduction, even into so universal a category as language. This in turn suggests that the novel's materialism and heterogeneity promote the formalization necessary to talk about all these things as novels, a formalization each of them opposes as an instance of the individual novel that says with *Jacques the Fatalist and His Master,* "That's what would happen in a novel, sooner or later, in this way or some other; however, this is not a novel."[8] This kind of formalization takes place whenever we talk about any literary genre, but the novel, both historically and formally, resists it: historically, because its origins are so disparate and dispersed;[9] formally, because as a signifier itself it points to the world of other things and characters that have their own signifying codes, even their own theories, that the novel tests and is tested by.[10] This give-and-take gives the novel its particular internal tension.

"To master, encompass, and make sense of fiction," says David Carroll, "has

7. David Carroll, *The Subject in Question: The Languages of Theory and the Strategies of Fiction* (Chicago, 1982), 5.

8. Denis Diderot, *Jacques the Fatalist and His Master,* trans. J. Robert Loy (New York, 1978), 37.

9. For an account of how we can describe the novel's origin, see Michael McKeon, *The Origins of the English Novel, 1600–1740* (Baltimore, 1987), 14–19.

10. For a discussion of this testing, see Walter L. Reed, *An Exemplary History of the Novel: The Quixotic Versus the Picaresque* (Chicago, 1981), 1–18.

perhaps always been the goal of theory; but fiction, insomuch as it claims to be fundamentally literary, has a parallel goal: to resist theory, to inscribe theory within itself, to produce its own theory of itself and thus reduce all forms of speculative thought on it."[11] There is a moment in Proust that exemplifies Carroll's claim. Throughout all of *Remembrance of Things Past,* the narrator writes the theories which explain the principles by which he is writing the book, and often these theories arise in discussions of the artists Marcel admires, such as Elstir and Vinteuil; but in a central apologetic moment of *Time Regained,* in assessing critical theories that do not have the kind of dramatic embedding that his have attained, he says flatly:

> Authentic art has no use for proclamations of this kind, it accom-
> plishes its work in silence. Moreover, those who theorised in this
> way used hackneyed phrases which had a curious resemblance to
> those of the idiots whom they denounced. And it is perhaps as much
> by the quality of his language as by the species of aesthetic theory
> which he advances that one may judge of the level to which a writer
> has attained in the moral and intellectual part of his work. Quality
> of language, however, is something the critical theorists think that
> they can do without, and those who admire them are easily persuaded
> that it is no proof of intellectual merit, for this is a thing which they
> cannot infer from the beauty of an image but can recognise only
> when they see it directly expressed. Hence the temptation for the
> writer to write intellectual works—a gross impropriety. A work in
> which there are theories is like an object which still has its price-
> tag on it.[12]

This is a pretty funny punch line: Marcel's narrator is no mere critic, but neither does he work without his own "proclamations" and theoretical indices. Here he does exactly what he says shouldn't be done and, by doing so, points to the novel's characteristic stance both in and against the world. For the novel is a text that is also necessarily a thing, a book. As a thing, it resists any reduction to any other thing; but as a text, it points to the world beyond it and inscribes within itself a theory of its own being that is also a theory of its own method of interpreting the world of those other things. I will discuss these matters through-out the rest of this book.

11. Carroll, *Subject in Question,* 3.
12. Marcel Proust, *Remembrance of Things Past,* trans. C. K. Scott Moncrieff and Terence Kilmartin, and Andreas Mayor (New York, 1981), III, 916.

In chapter 1, "Among Other Things," I show how certain structuralist and poststructuralist principles have challenged traditional definitions of the novel's components. I also discuss the varieties of presence, the complex relationships of matter and consciousness, that too often get simplified in an ontology based in language, and the way in which the novel's presence in our hands as a physical object influences our experience of it as literary text.

Chapter 2, "Narrative Lines and Paradigms," develops an explanation of the kind of narrative structure that is intrinsic to the novel. The basic structuralist model of a narrative is the sentence, in its twofold nature as a syntagmatic line and a vertical paradigm of other possibilities. I argue that every novel's narrative generates a paradigm of possible interpretations that is built into the structure of similarity-and-differences in a novel's characters, who inhabit and enact the plot and sponsor some of its possible meanings. Other elements, such as themes, contribute meaning, but the novel's particular disposition of character is intrinsic to its narrative mode and to its realism.

In chapter 3, "A Character Is Also a Sign," I work out a definition of character by starting with the word's etymology and then examining the ways in which novelists—Austen, Eliot, Conrad, Woolf, and Pynchon, among others—understand character. For all of them, a character is a sign to read and a faculty with which we read another's character. But for all of them, character is also an intimate aspect of the relationship between one's consciousness and one's own body. Character has a necessary material component, and I think it is in this bodily sense of ourselves that we feel most violated by ideas which would reduce everything to language, theory, or textuality.

In this third chapter, I also treat two other related topics: point of view and the narrative style we call free indirect discourse. One very advantageous result of recent interest in narrative theory is that the narrator has become less important. She is, even in George Eliot, just another character; and it is character itself, the power to read and be read, that is the novel's most fundamental form of mediation. Tolstoy, the aspect of himself implicit in his narrator, the narrator separately considered, Anna Karenina, translator Constance Garnett, and you and I as readers can all be construed and comprehended as characters, whether we speak Russian or not. In this context, free indirect discourse becomes very important, not only because it is the most supple form of the novel's and modernism's impersonality, but also because it is the most *written* of the novel's narrative styles. For in free indirect discourse, narrator and character can enact their relationship *only on the page* where style itself links and distinguishes them in the language that they have in common as the only thing that constitutes them both.

In chapter 4, I explain "The Ideal of Realism" that the novel always aspires to. However variously individual novelists may define the real, realism is always, first, an epistemology; under its auspices in the realistic novel, there is a relationship of reciprocal intelligibility between human beings and physical objects. Insofar as they occupy the same ontological plane, the concept of character the novel develops is also always correlative to its theory of things. But realism is also always a distribution of authority among characters who are empowered to interpret their experience and common world. The narrator is only one among these characters. Realism's impersonality marks not only its modernity, but the narrator's limits, too, in a world that has no single meaning, or no meaning that can be fulfilled or exhausted by consensus or summation. The barber's basin that Sancho Panza sees is also the helmet of Mambrino that Don Quixote *reads* it to be.[13] But it is also something else in Cervantes' narrative discourse, and something else again, perhaps, to the reader, who reads the book by opening it to everything she brings to it, herself a text, a character to read and be read in turn.

Chapter 5, *"Flaubert's Parrot* / Postmodernism / *Roland Barthes,"* uses Julian Barnes's novel to recapitulate the argument and apply in some detail the principles developed in the preceding chapters, and then to extend my discussion of the novel's place in the discourses of postmodernism. This leads to a consideration of autobiography, autobiography's relation to the novel, and then a closer reading of *Flaubert's Parrot* against *Roland Barthes by Roland Barthes* in order to educe a description of the postmodernist writing the novel has most deeply influenced. I also try to illustrate in this chapter the pertinence of Valéry's maxim, "There is no theory that is not a fragment, carefully prepared, of some autobiography," as one way of explaining why autobiography has become the signal genre of postmodernist practice.

Then, in a brief, final chapter I call "And Now for Something Completely Similar-and-Different," I discuss six characters from novels by Austen, Forster, Rushdie, and Morrison, to restate my argument's central points that a character is a sign we read and read-with the world; that in the structure of every character there is posited a relationship between consciousness and matter, which makes character not merely a zone of legibility but also a representation of physical presence; and that this structure is repeated in every novel's material delivery of its text. What it feels like to read these characters, however, is not so bloodless as this summary suggests—and this, too, is part of my final statement.

Flaubert's Parrot receives, perhaps, a span of attention disproportionate to

13. See Carlos Fuentes, *Myself with Others: Selected Essays* (New York, 1990), 57. Fuentes says: "But Don Quixote does not *see:* Don Quixote *reads.*" It is a wonderful observation, applicable in some degree to every character in every novel we will discuss.

its importance; but had I used another more or less traditional novel informed with the principles of recent theory—such as Carlos Fuentes's *Distant Relations,* or Don DeLillo's *The Names,* or Nadine Gordimer's *A Sport of Nature*—the whole chapter would have been different to begin with, and nothing else has served my point as well as Flaubert's "original" parrot. And there are other novels and novelists I treat at some length who are more firmly established: I have mentioned Austen, Eliot, Conrad, Woolf, and Pynchon; Cervantes, Dickens, Joyce, Stendhal, Fielding, Balzac, Flaubert, Hemingway, James, Dostoevsky and Tolstoy, Lawrence, Kafka, Faulkner, and Updike also appear. For each novel I discuss, my argument deals with the novel's structures. Characters themselves can be aware of themes and patterns in the plot, ironies and peripeties in the stories they inhabit and tell, originating intentions and putative ends. Structure is a level of organization no character can fully recognize or comprehend, owing to his inability to know he is in fact a character in a novel. Narrators as sophisticated as Marlow and as "naive" as Huck Finn know they are part of the story they are telling and know how their choices shape it, but not even Marlow knows the general narrator's role in the opening chapters of *Lord Jim* and his relation to the framing narrative, which is one of the novel's most important features; and Huck cannot hear in the narrative he speaks the way his own dialect amounts to a different discourse, not merely a different accent. Not even Proust's narrator, or the narrator of any other self-reflexive novel, can know everything the reader does. These arrangements and values, these structural orders, exist for the author and the reader first, and these structures are open and dynamic—not static scaffolding, but processes that are always amenable to a further arrangement, the changes involved in another characterization, the unanticipated authorization of another reading.[14]

It is this sense of structure that, in my mind, links old and new ideas of what the novel is and how it works. In writing this book, I have come to realize that the kind of criticism I have always preferred has been "structural" without necessarily being "structuralist"—an explanation of what the parts are and how they fit together without the themes of linguistics or the extraliterary values involved in themes of any kind. (It is impossible, I know, to be themeless and value-free, but the aspiration, like modernism's aspiration to impersonality, is worthwhile.) So I think that Edwin Muir's *The Structure of the Novel* (1928)— for instance, his reply to Percy Lubbock and E. M. Forster—is still a valuable study of the novel; by organizing his argument in loose categories of space and

14. For a brief survey of the values that the idea of structure has come to represent, see John Carlos Rowe, "Structure," in *Critical Terms for Literary Study,* ed. Frank Lentricchia and Thomas McLaughlin (Chicago, 1990), 23–38.

time, Muir achieves more rigor than there is in Forster's charm and more tolerance than Lubbock allows in his strict construction of Jamesian principles. Similarly, Richard Ellmann's *Ulysses on the Liffey* would be valuable just for his discussion of the differences between the structural schemes Joyce gave to Stuart Gilbert and Carlo Linati; but Ellmann also offers, in his own argument for the triadic structuration of the chapters, an order that exposes many more riches than any delineation of plot could, and one that does not depend solely on Joyce's language or on the obvious big themes.

After I had thought through most of this book's argument, I read Jonathan Culler's *Flaubert: The Uses of Uncertainty.* I admire the book because Culler is so fluent in structuralism's premises, values, and practice that he can spend most of his time actually discussing Flaubert's novels and the method of reading their writing implies. Culler admits his debts to theory, but he never reduces Flaubert to mere exemplification or explains him away: the novelist remains as compelling and rebarbative as ever. On the other hand is Hugh Kenner's *The Stoic Comedians,* a short study of Flaubert, Joyce, and Beckett, which I read some time ago and which has probably influenced my thinking more than most of the other books I cite. Kenner makes several fundamental points: that his three subjects write for the eye rather than for the ear, that print technology and the physical book have affected both language and literature in radical ways, and that the Stoicism he coyly defines is actually, in these writers, an acceptance of the alphabet as a *system* and therefore a set of limitations. In doing so, Kenner acknowledges the structural linguists and their insights (this in 1962), but he dedicates his book to the voice of their loyal opposition, Walter Ong. Yet, despite the polemical cast of these gestures, Kenner writes as though a very close reading of his masters, on their own, can educe *all* the principles theory would systematize, implying that theory is good sport but redundant. Kenner is a brilliant close reader, and I agree with him that literature is more important than anything that explains it, but his ultimate disingenuousness is somehow unseemly. So, somewhere on a line between *The Structure of the Novel* and *The Uses of Uncertainty,* I hope *Among Other Things* finds a place. There, I can think of myself as a reader of novels, and a student of their values, who is always subject to the sometimes immiscible realities they place in our hands.

1

AMONG OTHER THINGS

*They could see that there were things wrong with it—a novel is
a prose narrative of some length that has something wrong with it—
but they felt that, somehow, the things didn't matter.*
—RANDALL JARRELL, *The Third Book of Criticism*

*Let me admit to the hopeful fancy that some book such as I have
imagined—a short novel, approaching the compact, riddling condition of
an object—may serve as the vehicle of a philosophic revolution.*
—JOHN UPDIKE, *Picked-Up Pieces*

DIFFERENCES ARE CRITICAL

IN *THE PERPETUAL ORGY: Flaubert and Madame Bovary,* Mario Vargas
Llosa writes: "Flaubert discovered, around the beginning of 1854, the interac-
tion between the theory and the practice of literature, that is to say, the fact that
every work of creation contains implicitly, whether the author perceives it or
not, a general conception of textual writing and structure and of the relationships
between fiction and reality. After two and a half years of work on *Madame
Bovary,* he wrote to Louise: 'Every oeuvre to be undertaken has its own inherent
poetics, *which must be found.*'"[1] Flaubert's insistence on each work's particularity, each novel's intrinsic rules, is a good point from which to begin again. So
is *The Perpetual Orgy,* which is a combination of autobiography (Flaubert's and
Vargas Llosa's), traditional critical practices, and theories old and new. Flaubert
insists on each novel's "inherent poetics" because he knows the novel itself has
none, ultimately, and *The Perpetual Orgy* mirrors this rulelessness in its own
improvised method. In this chapter, I want to explore some relationships between
theory and practice by answering such questions as: Why exactly does fiction,
as David Carroll claims, have to inscribe its own theory? Does Carroll's answer
accord with Flaubert's? How has the novel's relationship to theory changed
lately, and what have these changes meant to our thinking about realism,

1. Mario Vargas Llosa, *The Perpetual Orgy: Flaubert and Madame Bovary,* trans. Helen Lane
(New York, 1986), 68n.

character, and plot? And finally, since theory has grounded ontology in language, what do we now make of presence as an aesthetic category and of the novel's presence as an object in the reader's hand?

David Carroll's claim that fiction wants to resist all forms of speculation that are merely *about* fiction, rather than within it, seems a little misleading insofar as it suggests that the novel has to protect its virtue, or defend its borders, against the ideas and discourses that it has always incorporated and entertained. Flaubert, on the other hand, begins to suggest something else: not the now-disreputable notion that each work has to realize its own essence, but the possibility that novelistic narrative is so capacious that novels do not have to resist theory so much as each individual novel has to reveal, to explain exactly, what kind of novel it is and what theory or "inherent poetics" it tries to realize. An individual novel's embodied theory is not, therefore, an act of self-defense, but an attempt at singularization. Narrative is so fundamental a mode of human intelligence and culture, so much a part of our history and our making sense of history, that it can never be defined simply and completely. "Storytelling," writes Fredric Jameson, is "the supreme function of the human mind."[2] Yet in the opening lines of *What Stories Are*, Thomas N. Leitch is relieved that "everyone knows what stories are—fortunately. For it is excessively difficult to say just what they are. Despite the recent efflorescence of work in narrative theory, the problem of formulating a rule which shall distinguish things which are stories from things that are not, a rule which would establish what makes a story a story, has remained unresolved."[3]

What seems true of narrative in general seems true of the novel, which developed out of other forms of narrative, high and low, by posing and defining itself both with them and against them. As it was in its beginning, it remains in our midst, as described by Walter L. Reed in *An Exemplary History of the Novel:*

> The novel . . . is a long prose fiction which opposes the forms of everyday life, social and psychological, to the conventional forms of literature, classical or popular, inherited from the past. The novel is a type of literature suspicious of its own literariness; it is inherently antitraditional in its literary code.
> . . . I would rephrase the critical commonplace that the novel deals with the difference between appearance and reality. The novel

2. Fredric Jameson, *The Political Unconscious: Narrative as a Socially Symbolic Act* (Ithaca, 1981), 123.

3. Thomas M. Leitch, *What Stories Are: Narrative Theory and Interpretation* (University Park, Pa., 1986), 3.

explores the difference between the fictions which are enshrined in the institution of literature and the fictions, more truthful historically or merely more familiar, by which we lead our daily lives.

. . . Literary paradigms are not simply modified in the novel, they are confronted by paradigms from other areas of culture.[4]

So if we accept Reed's terms, which are not at all unprecedented, we can also see why it makes sense to say that each individual novel has to produce its own self-justifying definition not only to particularize itself, but also to keep itself open to the contest with other discourses and other kinds of novels, open to change and play. Therefore it makes sense, in England at least, that the novel's first major phase displays such a discrepancy of modes and precedents: Defoe's materialism and use of travelogues, journals, and spiritual autobiographies; the psychology of Richardson's use of letters and conduct manuals; Fielding's typology and traditionalism; and Sterne's intuition that autobiography is so ineluctably eccentric that it needs the apologetics of theory maybe most of all.

Even Jane Austen had to explain herself, although she may seem to be the first English novelist to write at a time when the novel had consolidated and she could feel secure that she shared with her readers their general expectations. In what is usually considered her earliest mature work, *Northanger Abbey*, Austen creates a character who has some difficulty distinguishing between life and literature, between the Abbey itself and *The Castle of Otranto*. It is important, therefore, that the drama of Catherine Morland's education include the scene in which Henry and Eleanor Tilney instruct her in even subtler conventions when they discuss the differences between readers as well as the differences between historical and fictional narratives. Henry, to Catherine's surprise, thinks novels are not only enjoyable, but even important for men to read. Eleanor argues that she, on the other hand, is "fond of history—and am very well contented to take the false with the true." For Eleanor says she can easily distinguish what the author has added—such as the dialogue there could have been no record of—to the real historical case. By implication, Austen is arguing here that the practical reader of a novel can similarly distinguish the "truths" of discourse in a fictional story. All the reader has to know are the conventions, as the spectator of a landscape must know the conventions of "real taste."

The Tilneys were soon engaged. . . . They were viewing the country with the eyes of persons accustomed to drawing, and decided on its

---

4. Walter L. Reed, *An Exemplary History of the Novel: The Quixotic Versus the Picaresque* (Chicago, 1981), 3–4, 5.

capability of being formed into pictures, with all the eagerness of
real taste. Here Catherine was quite lost. She knew nothing of drawing—nothing of taste:—and she listened to them with an attention
which brought her little profit, for they talked in phrases which
conveyed scarcely any idea to her. . . . It seemed as if a good view
were no longer to be taken from the top of an high hill, and that a
clear blue sky was no longer a proof of a fine day. She was heartily
ashamed of her ignorance.[5]

Austen immediately says Catherine's shame is "misplaced" and clearly implies
that artistic conventions are neither natural nor intuitively obvious.

More than fifty years later, Mark Twain seems compelled to make the same
kind of point about novelistic conventions in the "Explanatory" remark he
prefixes to *Adventures of Huckleberry Finn*, where he makes clear that he does
not want the values of tradition or gentility brought to bear against Huck:

> In this book a number of dialects are used, to wit: the Missouri
> negro dialect; the extremest form of the backwoods South-Western
> dialect; the ordinary "Pike-County" dialect; and four modified va-
> rieties of the last. These shadings have not been done in a haphazard
> fashion, or by guess-work; but painstakingly, and with the trustwor-
> thy guidance and support of personal familiarity with these several
> forms of speech.
>
> I make this explanation for the reason that without it many readers
> would suppose that all these characters were trying to talk alike and
> not succeeding.[6]

Although Twain does not say so explicitly, he argues that his story's discourse
and its moral are inseparable and that neither can be anticipated too readily.
For in both, the differences are critical; they are not flaws but values.

Passages such as Austen's and Twain's, Fielding's prefatory chapters and
James's prefaces, the running commentaries of Thackeray and Eliot, Flaubert's
letters, Zola's manifesto, Woolf's diaries, the theories of narrative implicit in
the styles of consciousness and prose in *A Portrait of the Artist* and its concluding
diary, the styles of storytelling in *Absalom, Absalom!*—these and many other
instances of conscious self-definition within novels—have accrued to give the

5. Jane Austen, *Northanger Abbey* (Harmondsworth, 1972), 123, 125.
6. Mark Twain, *Adventures of Huckleberry Finn*, ed. Sculley Bradley, Richard Croom Beatty,
and E. Hudson Long (New York, 1962), 1.

novel a formidable body of internal theory long before this period that Stanley Fish has called "the moment of critical boom." As Michael McKeon has explained in *The Origins of the English Novel, 1600–1740*, the novel has always been involved in the theoretical negotiation of "how to tell the truth in narrative": "The evidence . . . contradicts the general view that the practical origins of the novel were unsupported by any self-conscious critical theory, stylistics, or 'poetics.' In fact, the conceptual bases of naive empiricism and extreme skepticism are explicitly elaborated at the same time they are experimentally put into practice [by the novel]. Theory develops in dialectical relation to genre as a supplementary discourse of detached commentary that is yet inseparable, in its own development, from the corollary process of genre formation."[7] However, the balance of collaboration seems to have changed lately, and the novel, at least in Joyce's hands, has become the senior partner in the firm. Note the testimony of Jacques Derrida: "So, yes (I'm replying to your suggestion), every time I write, and even in the most academic pieces of work, Joyce's ghost is always coming on board. Twenty years ago, in the *Introduction to 'The Origin of Geometry,'* at the very centre of the book, I compared the strategies of Husserl and of Joyce: two great models, two paradigms with respect to thought, but also with respect to a certain 'operation' of the relationship between language and history." Derrida is not trying to prove "by algebra that Hamlet's grandson is Shakespeare's grandfather and that he himself is the ghost of his own father," but is testifying to the enduring effect of Joyce on his thought: "With this admiring resentment, you stay on the edge of reading Joyce—for me this has been going on for twenty-five or thirty years. . . . I have the feeling that I haven't yet begun to read Joyce, and this 'not having begun to read' is sometimes the most singular and active relationship I have with this work."[8] With Derrida specifically in mind, J. Hillis Miller has said of the novel's influence on recent theory, and of Joyce's influence in particular: "Modern theory of narrative, even in those who are in no sense of the word Joyce specialists, has been strongly motivated in those questionings I have named by Joyce himself. There is little that deconstructive theory of narrative knows about the undecidability of words or of story lines which Joyce did not already know."[9]

7. Michael McKeon, *The Origins of the English Novel, 1600–1740* (Baltimore, 1987), 27, 118.

8. Jacques Derrida, "Two Words for Joyce," in *Post-Structuralist Joyce: Essays from the French*, ed. Derek Attridge and Daniel Ferrer (Cambridge, U.K., 1984), 149, 148. See also Jacques Derrida, "Ulysses Gramophone: *Hear say yes in Joyce*," in *James Joyce: The Augmented Ninth*, ed. Bernard Benstock (Syracuse, 1988), 27–75, for another exploration of Joyce's influence on Derrida's theory and practice.

9. J. Hillis Miller, "From Narrative Theory to Joyce, From Joyce to Narrative Theory," in *The Seventh of Joyce*, ed. Bernard Benstock (Bloomington, 1982), 4.

I am pretty sure that neither Joyce nor Derrida could be moved to answer so bright a question as, "Well, just what is the novel?" since both of them have come to stand for the transgression of traditional definitions. But the answers that have been given traditionally are important to review in order for us to see how their assumptions have been affected by recent theory. To this question, then, there have been two kinds of answers: those of the realists and those of what I call the "textualists." The first group is still epitomized by Ian Watt in *The Rise of the Novel*, a landmark book because of its combination of formalist and sociological principles. Watt argues that novelistic realism is a "formal realism," not a naive mimesis, that it is concerned with the identity of ordinary individuals who have proper names and who exist in actual places under the duration of real time, hence it is more rooted in historical experience than in literary history. His sociological theory that the novel grew to serve a new class, which needed expression, instruction, and confirmation, and his epistemological argument that the novel adopted the critical attitude of British empiricism, are as important as his emphasis on the novel's referentiality and susceptibility to translation. So is his alertness to the novel's basic epistemological problem: realism, he says, has "given a peculiar importance to semantics, to the problem of the correspondence between words and reality."[10]

Watt's premises have been developed in a number of ways. In *The Life of the Novel*, for instance, David Goldknopf emphasizes the epistemological character of literary realism, rather than its merely descriptive or referential surfaces, by saying that the novel depended on the development of two complementary sciences, empiricism and psychology: a rigorous method of examining the external physical world and a similar method for examining the operations of the individual mind that makes these examinations.[11] Maurice Z. Shroder realigns Goldknopf's dualism by stressing the novel's intrinsic structure of irony, an irony that opposes any unitary or authoritarian theory of meaning. He calls the novel an "ironic *Bildungsroman*" devoted to the education of the individual who moves out of innocence into the experience of a world no longer sanctioned by a sacred, totalizing myth.[12] The importance of the material contents of this world is confirmed by all the critics who emphasize the value of the novel's social reportage and satire. Two recent, full-scale histories of the novel's origins pay

10. Ian Watt, *The Rise of the Novel: Studies in Defoe, Richardson, and Fielding* (Berkeley, 1964), 12. Daniel R. Schwarz, *The Humanistic Heritage: Critical Theories of the English Novel from James to Hillis Miller* (Philadelphia, 1986), provides a survey of the Anglo-American theoretical tradition in which Watt works.

11. David Goldknopf, *The Life of the Novel* (Chicago, 1972), 1–24.

12. Maurice Z. Shroder, "The Novel as a Genre," in *The Theory of the Novel*, ed. Philip Stevick (New York, 1967), 13–29.

their debt to Watt, whom they also "correct," by expanding on two of his basic concerns. I have already mentioned Michael McKeon's *Origins of the English Novel,* which places the novel in the context of its intellectual history, maps the relationships among idealism, empiricism, and a reactive skepticism, and relates these epistemological modes to differences in class and political orientation. In *Before Novels,* J. Paul Hunter explores (as his subtitle says) the cultural contexts of eighteenth-century English fiction by investigating, among other things, the statistics of literacy, who read what and why, and the appetites and expectations early readers brought to the novels they read because only novels gave them the information and sense of possibility they sought.[13]

The "textualists" are represented here by Northrop Frye, Watt's automatic counterpart, who defines novels by distinguishing them from other forms of extended prose narrative—romance, confession, and anatomy. Frye argues that literature grows out of other literature, not out of life; and the most important argument he makes is that character is not simply the representation of psychological individuality, but a function of the kind of narrative in which it is found. The characters of romance, he maintains, are not so much individuals as they are archetypes—not substances, in other words, but conventions—so they signify the world in a different way from realistic characters.[14] In his essay "An Approach through Genre," Robert Scholes plays in a more open historical field than Frye does, and he defines the novel according to its complex relations to a whole spectrum of other narrative modes: satire, picaresque, comedy, history, sentiment, tragedy, and romance.[15] Walter Reed, whom I have already quoted, has affinities with Frye and Scholes, but because he poses, against the novel's fictions, "worldly" fictions that are not merely literary, he seems to admit more of the world's "content" into the novel's loose and baggy comprehension. This points to a problem of definition.

It has never been easy to draw a firm line between content and form, because the novel has developed, or grown "more" realistic,[16] sometimes simply by addressing a different, often "lower," realm of experience, which had been the

13. J. Paul Hunter, *Before Novels: The Cultural Contexts of Eighteenth Century English Fiction* (New York, 1990). See chapter 3, "Readers Reading," in particular. On p. xx, Hunter also offers a nice tribute to Watt and his inescapable influence.

14. Northrop Frye, *Anatomy of Criticism* (Princeton, 1957), 303–14.

15. Robert Scholes, "An Approach through Genre," in *Towards a Poetics of Fiction,* ed. Mark Spilka (Bloomington, 1977), 41–51.

16. "Realism is a relative matter, but in discussions of the novel, the term has tended to become normative, so that novels tend to be judged qualitatively on the degree or amount of realism to be found in each, as if more is better." This is from Hunter's *Before Novels,* 32; as he indicates, it's hard to know exactly what a standard such as "more realism" means.

material of a different, lower form of "literature." We could say that Dickens's use of melodrama, for instance, is raised into art as the novel lowers its standards, if we believed that the novel ever had standards to begin with. Harry Levin points to this dynamic in the classical formulations he makes in *The Gates of Horn:*

> Fiction approximates truth, not by concealing art, but by exposing artifice. The novelist finds it harder to introduce fresh observations than to adopt the conventions of other novelists, easier to imitate literature than to imitate life. But a true novel imitates critically, not conventionally; hence, it becomes a parody of other novels, an exception to prove the rule that fiction is untrue.
>
> One of Joubert's maxims asserts that illusion is an integral part of reality. In that case, the part is easier to define than the whole. The significance of reality, as Carlyle complained, "is too apt to escape us." The stuff of illusion, to the extent that we recognize it as such, has already been pinned down. It is an artificial world, which may be discredited by comparison with the real world, but which exists concretely enough on paper; whereas our printed record of the real world consists, to a surprising degree, of objections and exceptions to this artificial world. On paper, where romance may seem concrete, realism is elusive; for romance works with a definite repertory of symbols and conventions, which realism—in the name of undefined and unexpressed realities—shows to be inadequate.[17]

Levin's premises here are formalist and aesthetic; he first published this study of nineteenth-century French realism in 1961. By contrast, George Levine's study of nineteenth-century British realism, *The Realistic Imagination,* was published in 1981; and although Levine had read recent French theory, his argument's historical and cultural premises are clear in this epitome: "The impelling energy in the quest for *the world beyond words* is that the world *be there,* and that it be meaningful and good; the persistent fear is that it is merely monstrous and mechanical, beyond the control of human meaning. Realism risks that reality and its powers of disruption."[18] Reality for Harry Levin is not monolithic but plural—it is "realities"—and neither monstrous nor unknowable

17. Harry Levin, *The Gates of Horn: A Study of Five French Realists* (New York, 1966), 51, 50.

18. George Levine, *The Realistic Imagination: English Fiction from Frankenstein to Lady Chatterley* (Chicago, 1981), 22. Italics added.

but "undefined" and "unexpressed." These realities may appear in a novel to come. Levin's formulas are important because they explain how form can change in time, as the novel resists its own historical habits and keeps trying to write what's new and unwritten. The not-yet-written is one definition of *the real*, which is the ideal of realism. The irony is that this ideal can be stipulated in language, but it cannot exist there. The realists know this; the textualists seem not to be bothered by the discrepancy; and this is perhaps the deepest difference between them. It also makes the idealism of realistic practice seem like naïveté. On the other hand, it is the not-yet-written which means that the novel is not yet dead.

Roland Barthes, apparently, dismisses all of the above in *S/Z:* "the realistic author spends his time referring back to books: reality is what has been written."[19] The preemptive quality of Barthes's fragment makes it impossible to determine everything it means. Don Quixote, for instance, could subscribe to it, although Cervantes has made that kind of subscription one of the cardinal points of *Don Quixote*'s realistic irony. And Joyce would also subscribe in part, if he could reserve the right to unwrite or rewrite the texts he refers to. What Barthes excludes from his meaning, however, is easier to define. Mimesis in its traditional sense has no part in his formulation, for there is no acknowledgment of a reality prior to writing. Therefore, there is no textual or dialectical contest between romance and realism, because there is no objective reality to judge them against. There is also no possibility that realism, as I will argue later, is an epistemology, because the interpretive agency of a novel's characters is neither at stake nor in play. And, finally, there is no place for the metaphysical longing we will see in writers such as Dostoevsky and Flaubert to get at realism's ideal—the real thing, the signified outside of discourse, the *ding-in-sich* that is an idealist formation, necessarily misrepresented, they suggest, by any representation at all. For Barthes, in this case, novelistic realism is merely a convention of writing, and all the world's a text, always already there in the black and white ontology of the page.

An important consequence of Barthes's premise can be found in Nancy Armstrong's *Desire and Domestic Fiction: A Political History of the Novel.* Armstrong's Aristotle is Michel Foucault, and the basis of her argument is that language, or discourse, now *produces* the reality that novelistic realism was once thought to imitate. Her study shows, she says, that "the domestic novel antedated—was indeed necessarily antecedent to—the way of life it represented." And: "My reading of *Emma* shows . . . Austen also understood the principle of Bentham's theory of signs—that is, the degree to which words constitute the

19. Roland Barthes, *S/Z*, trans. Richard Miller (New York, 1974), 39.

objects they represent."[20] *Represent* is obviously the key term here and seems to mean something like *present* rather than re-present; but it does not mean to imitate and representation is not mimesis. Imitation is dependent on a prior reality; representation is not dependent on a world of objects, but productive of their meaning and value. Novelistic realism is political, usually urging change and progress, but it pretends its style is transparent, neutral, immediate, impersonal (an important adjective we will see later), and finally styleless. Representation, on the other hand, knows it is political and argues that the gap between signifier and signified is always mediated by social and historical forces that are never disinterested. Realism is in principle inclusive, comprehending, a complete picture; representation is always conscious of what it excludes, of the ways in which a map is neither a landscape nor the land, the senator is never his constituency. "The one genuinely new focus added to the history of representation by contemporary thinkers," say Wesley and Barbara Alverson Morris, "is the displacement of models drawn from the visual arts by those taken from semiotics."[21] This is important because within realism, which is a discourse itself, the model or ground of causality is the impingement of the physical world upon the senses; whereas within representation, the model or ground of causality is the effect of signs, of language, on the mind. Realism, therefore, is an attitude writers take toward the world; representation is an idea readers have of writing. It makes a difference whether we think we are reading writers or their writing, novels or the language they are embedded in as texts. It is possible to do both, of course, to regard the novel as both book and text, print and writing, and to realize in doing so that the practice of realism is never simply the formal or naive relationship of one object to a single subject, but that the meaning of any thing is given in the interpretation of many characters, many subjects who are interpreting one another as well.

"We have begun a chapter on meaning with a consideration of characters and their ways of meaning, because characters are the primary vehicles for meaning in narrative." This is Scholes and Kellogg in *The Nature of Narrative.* "Objects and actions can also have . . . significance. . . . But objects cannot act without becoming characters in a sense, and without characters there can be no action."[22] This has been critical orthodoxy since Henry James declared that

20. Nancy Armstrong, *Desire and Domestic Fiction: A Political History of the Novel* (New York, 1987), 9, 156. See also Helena Michie, *The Flesh Made Word: Female Figures and Women's Bodies* (New York, 1987), especially chapter 4.

21. Wesley Morris with Barbara Alverson Morris, *Reading Faulkner* (Madison, 1989), 4. See also Stephen A. Tyler, *The Unspeakable: Discourse, Dialogue, and Rhetoric in the Postmodern World* (Madison, 1987), especially chapter 5.

22. Robert Scholes and Robert Kellogg, *The Nature of Narrative* (London, 1966), 104.

character is action, action character, and that is all we need to know. What this principle clearly implies is that the realistic novel is more interested in the ways in which characters interpret their actions than in those acts themselves. The novelistic world lacks the kind of action that in epic and religious narrative can often seem meaningful in itself. Novelistic actions are semantically neutral, and novels therefore tend toward plotlessness; what characters make of what they do, of what one another does, is the story.

Jonathan Culler writes in a cardinal passage from *Structuralist Poetics:*

> Character is the major aspect of the novel to which structuralism has paid least attention. . . . Although for many readers character serves as the major totalizing force in fiction—everything in the novel exists in order to illustrate character and its development—a structuralist approach has intended to explain this as an ideological prejudice rather than to study it as a fact of reading.
>
> The reasons are not far to seek. On the one hand, the general ethos of structuralism runs counter to the notions of individuality and rich psychological coherence which are often applied to the novel. Stress on the interpersonal conventional systems which traverse the individual, which make him a space in which forces and events meet rather than an individuated essence, leads to a rejection of a prevalent conception of character in the novel.[23]

In this century characterized by total war, totalitarian governments, and programs of genocide, calling character an "ideological prejudice" seems scandalous. Nonetheless, it makes us notice that we have forgotten character is a convention so totally taken for granted that we no longer realize that one's character is not one's whole being. Character is not defined as a literary convention even in those places where we would expect it to be, such as M. H. Abrams's *Glossary of Literary Terms* or Scholes and Kellogg's *The Nature of Narrative*. If we look again at the sentences I quoted from Scholes and Kellogg and substitute "human beings" for "characters," we can see how imprecisely we understand what we mean by character. The first sentence—"human beings are the primary vehicles for meaning in narrative"—still holds a truth, but the third—"objects cannot act without becoming human beings in a sense"—does not. (Can objects *act* at all? Except in the Circe chapter of *Ulysses?*) This confusion affects even W. J. Harvey's admirable study *Character and the Novel*,

---

23. Jonathan Culler, *Structuralist Poetics: Structuralism, Linguistics, and the Study of Literature* (Ithaca, 1976), 230.

which he wrote in order to defend character from Jean-Paul Sartre, who, like the structuralists, wanted to deny human being a fixed essence; and from the New Critics, especially the British working on Shakespeare, for whom character was already only a linguistic function. As British scholar L. C. Knights wrote, "'Character' . . . is merely an abstraction from the total response in the mind of the reader or spectator, brought into being by written or spoken words."[24]

Culler and Knights show us that the nature of character is best revealed by those critics who do not take it for granted, who want, rather, to reveal the idea of character as *an idea*, a convention.[25] But there are important things to say in qualification of their statements. For Knights, there is no difference at all between a character on the stage, played by an actor, and the same (?) character on the page, represented only in language: no difference, in other words, between presence and absence, between speech and writing, between an actor and print's actuality. And Culler's statement seems incomplete or misleading because he does not quite acknowledge the experiments by which the modernist novel had also begun to question the concept of character received from earlier novels. Virginia Woolf, for instance, wrote in her diary in 1923, "Characters are to be merely views: personality must be avoided at all costs," a statement which denies to character any hint of substantive essence or of psychological individuality.[26] In *The Waves*, Woolf's most radical experiment in both narrative and characterization, Bernard the writer (but not the only character who thinks about problems of perception and representation) says:

> But here and now we are together. . . . We have come together at a particular time, to this particular spot. We are drawn into this communion by some deep, some common emotion. Shall we call it, conveniently, 'love'? Shall we say 'love of Percival' because Percival is going to India?
>
> No, that is too small, too particular a name. We cannot attach the width and spread of our feelings to so small a *mark*. [Italics mine.]

---

24. Quoted in Norman Holland, *The Dynamics of Literary Response* (New York, 1975), 265.

25. One of the best arguments against the conventional meaning of character is in Leo Bersani, *A Future for Astyanax: Character and Desire in Literature* (New York, 1984). A good contrast to Bersani is Martin Price, *Forms of Life: Character and Moral Imagination* (New Haven, 1983), particularly chapter 3. Price does not define character as anything but a fictional version of a psychological individual, although he treats many different kinds of psychology. Closer to my own argument is Thomas Docherty, *Reading (Absent) Character: Towards a Theory of Characterization in Fiction* (Oxford, 1983), but Docherty's emphasis is on the *reader's* reading and his model novel is the *nouveau roman*.

26. Virginia Woolf, *A Writer's Diary*, ed. Leonard Woolf (New York, 1954), 59.

We have come together (from the North, from the South, from Susan's farm, from Louis's house of business) to make one thing, not enduring—for what endures?—but seen by many eyes simultaneously. There is a red carnation in that vase. A single flower as we sat here waiting, but now a seven-sided flower, many-petalled, red, puce, purple-shaded, stiff with silver-tinted leaves—a whole flower to which every eye brings its own contribution.[27]

Bernard speaks, as it were, in writing, but to no one; Percival, who never speaks, is an occasion, an emotion, a name, and a mark, as well as a center constructed from several "views," which are not so much fully individuated characters as they are points of poise in the transpersonal current of her style.

Many of her narrators or "narrative principles" are as disembodied as these "characters" are because Woolf believed in the possibility of a disembodied consciousness. In his study of Woolf's style, James Naremore has preserved the following passage from an early version of *Between the Acts:* "Certainly it is difficult to find a name for that which is in a room, yet the room is empty; for that which perceives . . . knife and fork, also men and women; and describes them; and not only perceives but partakes of [the]m, and has access to the mind in its darkness. And further goes from mind to mind and surface to surface, and from body to body, creating what is not mind or body, not surface or depths, but a common element in which the perishable is preserved, and the separate become one."[28] There is a great deal of Woolf distilled in this passage. We will return to the idea of character as a *mark*, its first and most *physical* definition in the *OED*, in the third chapter, "A Character Is Also a Sign." It is sufficient to say here, I think, that the "common element" Woolf is seeking, which is neither body nor mind, material surface nor immaterial depth, is in effect language itself or a consciousness, disembodied and impersonal, that we can imagine as an operation of language, since it is hard for us to imagine it as anything else. She, however, can. She says in "A Sketch of the Past," to explain the connection between her "moments of being" and her writing:

27. Virginia Woolf, *The Waves* (New York, 1959), 126–27. In *A Writer's Diary* she says: "What I think now (about *The Waves)* is that I can give in a very few strokes the essentials of a person's character. It should be done boldly, almost as caricature" (153). "Almost as caricature" seems more important to Woolf's effects and to contemporary value than the traditional implications of "the essentials of a person's character."

28. Quoted in James Naremore, *The World Without a Self: Virginia Woolf and the Novel* (New Haven, 1973), 75–76.

I feel that I have had a blow; but it is not, as I thought as a child, simply a blow from an enemy hidden behind the cotton wool of daily life; it is or will become a revelation of some order; it is a token of some real thing behind appearances; and I make it real by putting it into words. It is only by putting it into words that I make it whole; this wholeness means that it has lost its power to hurt me; it gives me, perhaps because by doing so I take away the pain, a great delight to put the severed parts together. Perhaps this is the strongest pleasure known to me. It is the rapture I get when in writing I seem to be discovering what belongs to what; making a scene come right; making a character come together. From this I reach what I might call a philosophy; at any rate it is a constant idea of mine; that behind the cotton wool is hidden a pattern; that we—I mean all human beings—are connected with this; that the whole world is a work of art; that we are parts of the work of art. *Hamlet* or a Beethoven quartet is the truth about this vast mass that we call the world. But there is no Shakespeare, there is no Beethoven; certainly and emphatically there is no God; we are the words; we are the music; we are the thing itself. And I see this when I have a shock.[29]

One of her ultimate values here is a kind of mystical formalism (a Beethoven quartet without Beethoven), but another one is the rapture she feels in writing, in writing as a state of being: "we are the words." This is not exactly language-as-ontology. It is actually more like Mrs. Ramsay's experience of herself as the wedge of darkness—and Mrs. Ramsay is one of Woolf's most important attempts to define character in wholly nontraditional ways, to provide a reality deeper than the merely psychological, and to examine another relationship of consciousness to matter and the body. Mrs. Ramsay, whom we will look at later, is reified without being dehumanized: "We are the thing itself." This "we" may be still "the primary vehicle for meaning in narrative," in Scholes and Kellogg's phrase, or "the major totalizing force," in Culler's, but it is not a state to which we are either quite accustomed or reduced. Woolf's formulations point to the fact that character in the novel has always been related to writing. Recent theory has helped to explain the full meaning of this relation, but it has not created its fact. And Woolf's most valuable insight is that, as different as language and the body are, for the novelist they cannot be thought of apart from each other.

In *Reading for the Plot*, Peter Brooks says: "Plot is so basic to our experience

29. Virginia Woolf, "A Sketch of the Past," in *Moments of Being*, ed. Jeanne Schulkind (2nd ed.; San Diego, 1985), 72.

of reading, and indeed to our very articulation in general, that criticism has often passed over it in silence, as too obvious to bear discussion."[30] One reason for this neglect, perhaps, is that the plots of so many traditional novels have been, more or less, the chronological story of a life. In these novels, the pace of personal change gives a rhythm and value to time because it also organizes the order of causality we conventionally call education or progress. The common plot's "shape" or "structure" is manifest, then, when some transformation— success or failure, self-knowledge or disillusionment, death or marriage—is clear or complete. At this point, nonetheless, it is usually the fate of the character that is still of paramount importance to us, not the nature of the plot for its own sake, because all of us do fail or succeed, marry or not, and die. Another reason for this neglect, however, is that the plot for its own sake simply doesn't exist, or doesn't exist in a novel as plot.

> Let us define a plot. We have defined a story as a narrative of events arranged in their time-sequence. A plot is also a narrative of events, the emphasis falling on causality. "The king died and then the queen died" is a story. "The king died, and then the queen died of grief" is a plot. The time sequence is preserved, but the sense of causality overshadows it.[31]

In this famous passage from *Aspects of the Novel,* E. M. Forster does distinguish between time and causality. He does not, however, make any explicit distinction between historical narrative and fiction, nor does he develop all the factors that go into this simple construction of a cause. Fictional events do not preexist their telling as historical events do: in fiction, the statement "The king died" creates that king and his life in the same breath that it takes them away. At its simplest, as in Forster's example, fiction presents what it is supposedly imitating. More-over, "and then the queen died of grief" is not a simple mechanical reaction, but a representation of character and a theory of psychology that the reader has to accept in order to accept this sequence of events as a causal order. "Of grief" is also an interpretation that an unacknowledged narrator makes. We would still call Forster's "story" a story, but his "plot" we would now call "discourse"— the whole of everything about a narrative that is not simply the event we can

---

30. Peter Brooks, *Reading for the Plot: Design and Intention in Narrative* (New York, 1984), xi. Brooks's phrase, *"the anticipation of retrospection,"* quoted below, occurs on page 23.

31. E. M. Forster, *Aspects of the Novel* (New York, 1955), 86.

remove from the telling by logical inference.[32] And the most crucial aspect of its discourse is the ambiguity of the narrator's status.

Narratives need narrators. Narrative discourse creates the narrator to develop a meaning through its origin in an intentional, performing source: the privileged, omniscient narrator knows that the queen dies of grief. Sentences, on the other hand, do not need narrators. They are structures of relationship, with subjects and objects that are not necessarily characters of any kind. Sentences are written to be read in ways different from the ways narratives are ordered to be received or stories are to be heard. But as Forster inadvertently suggests, novels are both narratives and sentence structures. We can read them for the narrator's character, the characters' identities, and the unfolding plot. But when we know how they end, we can reread them for discursive and structural relationships that may not involve causality (or the narrator's account of it) or the characters' fates. There are, for instance, more important things about *A Passage to India* than the final mistake Dr. Aziz makes about Fielding's marriage.

The subtitle of Peter Brooks's *Reading for Plot: Design and Intention in Narrative* indicates his interest in narrators and their agency as well as in the structural relations. "Design" entails the relationships between beginnings and ends and what we do as we read, in his wonderful phrase, with the *"anticipation of retrospection."* It seems disingenuous, therefore, for him to complain that plot has been left undiscussed, when what he means by plot is not the line of events, but the structural and discursive principles of novelistic order that have been treated elsewhere under other names. One of the most important of these names is point of view. From Henry James and Percy Lubbock to Wayne Booth and Hugh Kenner in *Joyce's Voices,* point of view has been a special province of American criticism. James gave the topic great prestige, and this tradition has produced one of the best books on the novel that we have, Wayne Booth's *The Rhetoric of Fiction.* Point of view is undoubtedly important to the meaning of any narrative. It is important because it feeds into our democratic ethos— everyone has a point of view—and is the formal aspect of narrative easiest to explore in the classroom. Point of view can also be an aspect of character: in *The Sound and the Fury, Jealousy,* and *Jazz,* for instance, narrative consciousness is not just another character's way of looking at things, but another mode of characterization itself. But most important for my discussion of plot, point of view governs narrative order. For anyone who realizes that narrative is not simply

---

32. See Seymour Chatman, *Story and Discourse: Narrative Structure in Fiction and Film* (Ithaca, 1980), for a discussion of the derivation of the distinction between story and discourse. See Culler, *Structuralist Poetics* (192–202) for a discussion of the origins of these terms in Emile Benveniste.

a linking of events, but a structure of relationships, the relationship of the narrator to the order of telling and to the other characters is crucial.

Since design and intention in narrative determine the value of the narrative's end, plot has been studied by critics interested in closure, as a formal and historical problem. Robert M. Adams's *Strains of Discord* (1958), Alan Friedman's *The Turn of the Novel* (1970), and Walter J. Slatoff's *The Quest for Failure* (1960) are important books on open-ended fictions. Adams's is the most general; Friedman deals with Hardy, Conrad, Forster, and Lawrence; Slatoff's book is about Faulkner. All of them deal with the meaning of narrative structure—not with acts that are meaningful in themselves, but with narrative relationships that finally resist closure and admit that the end is not the all. The most influential book of this kind has been Frank Kermode's *The Sense of an Ending*, which is a kind of climax to officially pre-structuralist thinking. In the Prologue to *The Art of Telling*, Kermode offers this short narrative of his own fate:

> [M]y purpose is to recall the importance in those days of Barthes, the invigorating effect of his fertile and surprising mind. As the years went by he became not less exciting but less didactic, and I am certainly not alone in my conviction that much of his finest work came after *S/Z*; but his major impact on students of narrative was felt between, say, 1967 and 1974. My own way of thinking about narrative (as in *The Sense of an Ending)* had nothing, or very little, in common with what was going on in *Communications* or *Tel Quel,* and I remember feeling rather dismally that quite a lot of work had gone into a book which became antediluvian almost on publication.[33]

The Sense of an Ending was published in 1967; its principles are psychological and cultural: the connection between tick and tock is charged with meaning that the interval between tock and tick does not have, and within our culture every Genesis sets up the expectations of an Apocalypse or Revelation. Barthes's "Introduction to the Structural Analysis of Narratives" was published in France in 1966; its principles are linguistic, so narratives can be analyzed according to the syntax of sentences without regard for character. Barthes writes: "Structural analysis, much concerned not to define characters in terms of psychological essences, has so far striven, using various hypotheses, to define a character not as a 'being' but as a 'participant.'"[34]

33. Frank Kermode, *The Art of Telling* (Cambridge, Mass., 1985), 3.
34. Roland Barthes, "Introduction to the Structural Analysis of Narratives," *Image / Music / Text*, trans. Stephen Heath (New York, 1977), 106.

However, as Barthes points out in "Introduction" and in *S/Z*, it is hard to dismiss the whole humanistic tradition of character. The new critical principles we have been examining have not simply supplanted or obviated the old. Theories of representation do not replace mimetic practices so much as they reveal the premises and boundaries of mimesis as one style of representation. Cyclops and Circe, therefore, do not cancel the mimetic value of the interior monologues in Proteus and Lestrygonians; the play of *all* the styles of representation in *Ulysses*, as I will argue in chapter 4, constitutes the basis of the realism that keeps it open to limitless interpretive possibilities. Similarly, the different ideas of character in Oxen and Penelope do not cancel each other out, but illustrate the ways in which Joyce, like Woolf, had begun to question the notion of character itself. In questioning character as an autonomous, substantive entity, writers such as Woolf and Joyce also call into question the authority attached to the narrator and the simple linear development of meaning as it issues from the narrator's control. When this form of authority and order is abandoned, structure is allowed in as a principle of meaning and so, therefore, is the possibility of many meanings developing from the play of relationships any structure holds.

This development seems truly new. Realism has a history, and it has national and historical styles that keep it from being monolithic. At least since Flaubert, novelists had begun to deconstruct character before all of us were aware that character was a construct to begin with. But to write a narrative as a sentence, to organize a story according to a solely linguistic ordination, is not something any novelist I know of has tried to do.[35] The sentence as narrative model sponsors a new way to read, rather than to write, a new way to think about narrative in any period; and this is what makes it important.

Barthes's "Introduction" enlarged my mind as much as *The Rhetoric of Fiction* once did, and it prepared me to find answers for questions I was barely beginning to formulate while reading Tzvetan Todorov's *The Poetics of Prose*. Although Todorov's collection and Barthes's essay have not been as generally influential as *S/Z*, *Of Grammatology*, and Genette's *Narrative Discourse*, and although the five of them do not share a method, the principles of language that inform them

35. However, an idea such as this seems to be somewhere in Italo Calvino's mind when he writes *If on a winter's night a traveler*, in which alternate chapters are titled with the phrases that compose this sentence: If on a winter's night a traveler / Outside the town of Malbourk / Leaning from the steep slope / Without fear of wind or vertigo / Looks down in the gathering shadow / In a network of lines that enlace / In a network of lines that intersect / On the carpet of leaves illuminated by the moon / Around an empty grave / What story down there awaits its end?" See also Calvino's essay, "Levels of Reality in Literature," in *The Uses of Literature*, trans. Patrick Creagh (San Diego, 1986), 101–21.

all have changed the way we read and think about writing. It is these principles that have determined the theories I consider throughout this book and my responses to them.

The first of these principles is the arbitrary relationship of the signifier to the signified in the structure of the sign. For the novel, this means that there can be no imitation of the world, simply defined—which has never been the real case anyhow. "Language signifies without imitating," Genette says. "Unless, of course, the object signified (narrated) be itself language."[36] Or some form language has taken. "Novels, a distinctly post-Gutenberg genre," Barbara Herrnstein Smith points out, "have typically been representations of chronicles, journals, letters, biographies, and memoirs."[37] Genette and Herrnstein Smith confirm the arguments of Frye and Barthes we considered earlier, and they seem once again to preclude any kind of traditional realism based on ideas of mimesis and psychological character. Novels that imitate other books confront the kinds of discourse embedded in those books and interpret them and their utility. It is possible, therefore, to define a realism that is interpretive rather than referential and to keep it consistent with the concept of a sign that is never finally stable, a signified that can never be exhausted. This definition of realism is the center of chapter 4.

Second, but actually more basic than the arbitrary relationship within the sign, is the principle of difference, or of similarity-and-difference, that is so important to Saussure's system. The stark differentiation between self and other (whatever the other is), which has been a basic theme of psychological life, political organization, and therefore novelistic practice, has now been supplanted by the ideal of the constant play of similarity-and-difference. Self-and-other implies substantive entities. The infant's first cognitive act of any significance is probably to distinguish self from other. Beyond this point, however, even as the infant learns its place in the first triangle with its parents, and then within the other geometries of the whole family, the unending play of similarity-and-difference seems a more normative experience. No one from a large family needs to learn this from Lacan. And if happiness is a univocal or unitary state, as Tolstoy deems it to be in the opening sentence of *Anna Karenina,* it is the unhappiness of difference that makes for the more interesting families and novels.

Proust's is a pertinent example here. For the young Marcel, the opposition of

36. Gerard Genette, *Narrative Discourse: An Essay in Method,* trans. Jane E. Lewin (Ithaca, 1980), 164.

37. Barbara Herrnstein Smith, *On the Margins of Discourse: The Relation of Literature to Language* (Chicago, 1978), 8.

self and other is paramount. He is a child who must possess the other absolutely in his imagination, who must virtually engulf it in order not to be engulfed himself; so he often finds it impossible to simply *see* another thing unless he has first imagined it totally. But for the older Marcel, the social critic and anatomist of great families, the play of similarity-and-difference is constant. Elstir and Vinteuil are not merely other than himself, but different from each other, too, in very important ways, as the Baron de Charlus is significantly different from Swann. One purely linguistic sign of this great shift in psychology and narrative focus is, as Genette points out, Proust's less and less frequent use of the iterative.[38] Childhood Saturdays were always the same: one was the other. But for the adult writer who discovers his true nature on the residuary ground of his involuntary memory, difference across time is the important counter to those moments of transcendence or essentialization; and those differences need a different kind of verb.

However, the way in which similarity-and-difference plays itself out in most other novels is related to the third principle that has shaped this description of the novel. We can now think of narratives as sentences, as a structure governed not by the author's intentions, the narrator's rhetoric, and the characters' themes, but by a syntax that governs functional relationships. I am not interested in all the transformations that can be generated from a Chomskian grammar, nor in the elaborate schemata that Seymour Chatman develops in *Story and Discourse*, nor even in all the applications inherent in Barthes's "Introduction." The fact that a sentence's syntagmatic line generates a paradigm of possible alternatives is enough. For this means that a novel's narrative embodies alternative possibilities of meaning in the story's different characters, each of whom has, at least potentially, a different interpretation of the novel's other characters, action, and the world. As Todorov says, "a character is a potential story that is the story of his life. Every new character signifies a new plot."[39] This principle not only undercuts the singular or summary authority of the narrator, and the formalist dream of meaning's oneness, it also makes narrative closure formally impossible. There is always another version of any story that contains another character, who does not have to be a psychological entity, but simply another principle of interpretive organization, another signifier pointing to the world it signifies. These issues we will take up in greater detail in the next chapter, when we discuss narrative lines and their paradigms and the structure of embedding.

Before we do, however, it is necessary to consider the matter of presence. The nature of the sign; what this idea of language has meant to naive mimesis

---

38. Genette, *Narrative Discourse*, 113–23.
39. Tzvetan Todorov, *The Poetics of Prose*, trans. Richard Howard (Ithaca, 1977), 70.

and the prospect of referentiality; the denial of substance in a linguistic ontology; the play, therefore, of similarity-and-difference—all of these are related to the idea of presence that Derrida, in particular, has held under scrutiny. In an ontology grounded in language, presence is going to be *the* key issue, and the way the novel points to the limits of this idea is very important.

PRESENCE AND THE NOVEL

The physical being of the novel, the fact that it is not merely a text but also necessarily a book, is fundamental to both its history and its meaning in a number of ways we have not yet discussed. First among these is that the book's feel, its weight and texture in the reader's hand, is a form of presence its text can neither fully represent nor comprehend. A novel has to be a book. Poems can be composed and carried in the memory, plays spontaneously performed as mime or dance, but a novel cannot be either unwritten or unprinted, which makes the act of reading both a delicate manual labor and a visual experience before it is an act of interpretation. A novel's physical being also points, therefore, to the bodily being of both its author and its reader and to the concept of its characters' individuality as it is based in physical circumstance and material individuality. That assumption of empiricism is reinforced by the fact so many early novels are named eponymously: *The Princess of Cleves, Moll Flanders, Tristram Shandy.* The book's physical integrity, which is a new development itself, also points to the new identity and agency of its author, who puts his or her name on the title page to signify authority and its mode of defining property. This signed author is not a scribe or an amanuensis (there are no theories that Cervantes was a committee, as his own narrators are, as some have argued Homer and Shakespeare, and now Rembrandt, were), and the novel is one of the first books to underwrite this new role for the author.[40] The book in the reader's hand signals a new aspect of her role, too: the autonomy of her reading experience and the ground of her interpretive authority as a materially differentiated individual such as the author. Novels are no longer experienced, usually, in common, as drama and movies and concerts are. They are read in the condition that Walter L. Reed calls "mass privacy."[41] They are read, too, in a world that assumes the literacy of the general populace and the formative effect literacy has had on our sense of the nature of individuality, and in which print has had an effect on the idea of writing and what Derrida now calls *écriture*. So

---

40. See Michel Foucault, "What Is an Author," in *Language, Counter-Memory, Practice: Selected Essays and Interviews*, ed. Donald F. Bouchard, trans. Donald F. Bouchard and Sherry Simon (Ithaca, 1980), 113–38.

41. Reed, *Exemplary History*, 264.

the novel's being in our hands indicates not only its modernity, but modernity's problems with a definition of presence, which has been an important topic throughout twentieth-century aesthetics before it became the more pervasive problematic Derrida has made it in taking Saussure's concept of the sign to its logical conclusion in metaphysics. Signs always signify what is absent; presence is itself a condition of the signified. But printed signs have to the eye a necessary presence, too, in the world, where presence has too many modes to be exhausted only as a category of consciousness or language.

It is still always amazing, I think, to look again at Derrida's *Speech and Phenomena* and to realize that presence, as he describes it in this particular critique, has nothing to do with *physical* being, that matter is absence: "The first advantage of this reduction to the interior monologue is that the physical event of language there seems absent. Insofar as the unity of the word . . . is not to be confused with the multiple sensible events of its employment or taken to depend on them, is ideal. . . . Its being an expression owes nothing to any worldly or empirical existence, etc.; it needs no empirical body but only the ideal and identical form of this body insofar as this is animated by a meaning."[42] This is language-as-ontology in one of its purest expressions. While Derrida reveals the fallacy of assuming the purity of self-presence, he does not return to a nonlinguistic world to ground his new science. As he restates this principle in the opening pages of *Of Grammatology,* Derrida begins with "the presence of the thing to sight as *eidos,*" which idea is the basis of both empirical science and literary realism. But he lists other forms of presence which have nothing to do with matter: "We already have a foreboding that phonocentrism merges with the historical determination of the meaning of being in general as *presence,* with all the subdeterminations which depend on this general form and which organize within it their system and their historical sequence (presence of the thing to sight as *eidos,* presence as substance/essence/existence [*ousia*], temporal presence as point [*stigmé*] of the now or of the moment [*nun*], the self-presence of the cogito, consciousness, subjectivity, the co-presence of the other and of the self, intersubjectivity as the intentional phenomenon of the ego, and so forth)."[43]

Literature has dealt with many of these forms of presence, although not perhaps in the same way that philosophy has, and certainly not with metaphysics' indifference to the physical. In fact, to imagine even the philosophically impossible presence of an object to itself (something like Sartre's *en-soi*), the self-consciousness of a state that by definition is impossible of consciousness and therefore of its own "language," has not been an unthinkable undertaking: in

42. Jacques Derrida, *Speech and Phenomena,* trans. David B. Allison (Evanston, 1973), 41.
43. Jacques Derrida, *Of Grammatology,* trans. Gayatri Chakravorty Spivak (Baltimore, 1976), 12.

Wordsworth's apostrophes to Nature, Keats's empathic address to the Grecian Urn, and Stevens's exposition of the phenomenology of the Snow Man, modern literature has sought in *things* a purer authenticity than the subject can have in *thought.* The most powerful expression of this longing is probably Rilke's "Archaic Torso of Apollo," in which the headless torso is suffused with an apparently self-knowing illumination. The poem and the torso are both complicated entities because they lend themselves to so many different constructions. Both, for instance, are in Pound's sense an image, although the putatively preexistent statue is not the language of Rilke's poem. It is possible to construe the statue as a kind of character (in the way I will define character later) as much as the poem's speaker is. The torso is also a fragment and therefore a kind of metonymy for its once-fuller state, a metaphor for classical art in general, and a version of the idealized form of presence that Hegelian critics say distinguishes the epic world from the fallen world of modernity. The "Archaic Torso of Apollo" stands, in other words, for a whole complex of aesthetic ideas about presence which cannot be resolved into one thing merely because the statue and the poem display matter's relation to consciousness in many different ways. As we look more closely at these varieties of presence in a number of other contexts, we can begin to see how ideas of presence ramify throughout the novel's history. Issues of presence are at stake in realistic description, characters' knowledge of one another, points of view, the confusions within our expectations of metonymy, what we have come to call voice, and some differences between orality and literacy. We will also see the effect the physical technology of print has had upon our ideas of language. Many of these issues are epitomized in the novel's disparate being as a box of words. But, first, let us turn to Pound's very influential desire for immediacy.

Pound says: "An Image is that which presents an intellectual and emotional complex in an instant of time. . . . It is the presentation of such a 'complex' instantaneously which gives that sense of sudden liberation; that sense of freedom from time limits and space limits; that sense of sudden growth, which we experience in the presence of the greatest works of art." It is important to remark that Pound uses the word "presents." The image is not an imitation; it does not re-present something else in the other ontological mode of language; nor is it, in our current sense, a representation. Pound's Image is *itself,* and by it, according to Herbert Schneidau, Pound and his followers meant "something like a 'manifestation of essence,' or an 'epiphany.'"[44] This idea of the Image is not the analogue of Eliot's objective correlative so much as it is the correlative of

---

44. The Pound quotations come from Herbert N. Schneidau, *Ezra Pound: The Image and the Real* (Baton Rouge, 1969), 21, 27.

Hemingway's "real thing—the sequence of motion and fact which made the emotion and which would be as valid in a year or in ten years or, with luck and if you stated it purely enough, always."[45] This "real thing" is a timeless essence, and in Hemingway's phrasing there is implicit a fundamental problem.

The image, the real thing, the narrative description presented realistically; all of these imply that getting it once gets it, literally, for all: that the object rendered without mediation, rhetorical interference, or interpretive warp is simply *there* for the reader, for every reader, in exactly the same way. The object perfectly presented not only resolves any discrepancy between its essence and its empirical accidents, it resolves into "objectivity" the viewer, too, denying the individuality of the perceiving subject that is also always assumed to be a condition of the novel's realistic epistemology. Impersonality is the name given to the convention, in science and literature both, that attempts to discipline or erase the subjectivity of all empirical experience, and to give the object, therefore, the full force of *its* kind of presence by pretending the subject is absent from the act of representation. Not only is impersonality a stylistic goal, it is also an important moral strategy for authors and narrators who attempt to bestow on their characters the equivalent of physical freedom. Against Don Quixote's expressive insistence that windmills are giants, for instance, Cervantes poses Sancho's belief that they are just windmills; so in no way does his *Don Quixote* share the limits of the Don's intensely personal vision or the ascesis of his authoritarianism.

Moreover, more than the poetic image and the novelistic detail are entailed in this particular dilemma of empiricism. The ambiguities of presence and the goal of impersonality "to let things speak for themselves" are as obvious and problematic in the aesthetic situation of the photograph. Walter Pater maintained at the end of the nineteenth century that all art aspires to the condition of music—contentless, *symboliste* formality. A lot of subsequent poetry, however, has seemed to aspire to the condition of the snapshot, which is obviously an image, the sign of something absent, but which is also a thing itself: it is a picture and a piece of paper in the way a novel is both a text and a book. Susan Sontag has argued that this ontological "confusion" gives the aesthetics of photography its special character. Is the secret of its art to be seen or read in the carefully wrought, fully *intended* images of Edward Weston and Ansel Adams? Or is it in the more accidental images of Robert Frank or of Garry Winogrand, who says, "I photograph to find out what something will look like

---

45. Ernest Hemingway, *Death in the Afternoon* (New York, 1953), 2. The definition of the objective correlative can be found in T. S. Eliot, "Hamlet," in *Selected Essays* (New ed.; New York, 1964), 124–25.

photographed"?[46] Photographs seem more like objects than communicative acts, yet we expect them to communicate something. Usually we want them to tell us not only what they are, but why they are being produced or "expressed." And when they don't, they seem as enigmatic as the image of Stevens's Snow Man, Pound's subway station, or Williams's wheelbarrow—all presence and no message. The "Archaic Torso of Apollo" is finally not such an image; for however mysterious the torso itself may be, its ontological imperative is clear: "You must change your life."

The Archaic Torso, however, does not belong to the Snow Man's fallen modern world, but to the epic world of full and simple presence that Georg Lukács depicts in *The Theory of the Novel:*

> Hence the mind's attitude within such a home [the Homeric world] is a passively visionary acceptance of the ready-made, ever-present meaning. The world of meaning can be grasped, it can be taken in at a glance; all that is necessary is to find the *locus* that has been predestined for each individual. . . .
>
> . . . The novel is the epic of an age in which the extensive totality of life is no longer directly given, in which the immanence of meaning in life has become a problem, yet which still thinks in terms of totality. . . .
>
> The epic gives form to a totality of life that is rounded from within; the novel seeks, by giving form, to uncover and construct the concealed totality of life.[47]

This third paragraph describes the effort of a novelist such as George Eliot, whose intricate structure in *Middlemarch* attempts to recover a form of immanence that reveals stability and order in the changing world. But Lukács's remarks about the epic, grounded in the principles of Hegel, could be applied to the work of Hegel's contemporary, Jane Austen. Not everyone in Austen's

---

46. Quoted in Susan Sontag, *On Photography* (New York, 1977), 197. See also Richard Schiff, *Cézanne and the End of Impressionism: A Study of the Theory, Technique, and Critical Evaluation of Modern Art* (Chicago, 1986), for a relevant discussion of the theory and history of "the subject/ object distinction" in early modernist painting. Hugh Kenner's important take on empiricism's impersonality is in *The Counterfeiters: An Historical Comedy* (Garden City, N.Y., 1973). See especially chapter 3.

47. Georg Lukács, *The Theory of the Novel*, trans. Anna Bostock (Cambridge, Mass., 1973), 32, 56, 60. The best counter to Lukács's nostalgia, before Robbe-Grillet, is M. M. Bakhtin's essay, "Epic and Novel," in *The Dialogic Imagination*, ed. Michael Holquist, trans. Caryl Emerson and Michael Holquist (Austin, 1981), 3–40.

works can take in the world's ready-made meaning at a glance, but when we examine Elizabeth Bennet's attempts to read Darcy's character in his face, we will see that she thinks she can. Mr. Knightley in *Emma* can, in fact, do so because he knows exactly the locus he and Emma have in their world, which assumes a very stable relationship between matter and consciousness. It is not, however, a world so *simple* that it obviates all interpretation or guarantees every character is always in agreement with every other one. But it is a world Arnold Kettle believes is entirely materialistic in its premises. Austen's "complete lack of idealism," he argues, never implies a transcendental realm that is absent from the eye.[48]

By the end of the nineteenth century, by the time we get to Conrad, Austen's confident poise before the world of matter is no longer quite possible. As Ian Watt argues in *Conrad in the Nineteenth Century*, Conrad's style is the result of his attempt to respond to a physical world in which visual attentiveness and empirical disinterest no longer suffice:

> For Conrad, the world of the senses is not a picture but a presence, a presence so intense, unconditional, and unanswerable that it loses the fugitive, hypothetical, subjective, and primarily aesthetic qualities which it usually has in the impressionist tradition. Ramon Fernandez . . . remarks that [Conrad's] way of describing the physical world is the exact opposite of traditional narrative description such as Balzac's: Conrad's art, he writes, "does not trace the reality before the man, but the man before the reality; it evokes experiences in their subjective entirety because the impression is the equivalent of the entire perception, and because the whole man experiences it with all the powers of his being."[49]

Here, from *Heart of Darkness*, is an example of Watt's point from Marlow's mouth:

> Trees, trees, millions of trees, massive, immense, running up high; and at their foot, hugging the bank against the stream, crept the little begrimed steamboat, like a sluggish beetle crawling on the floor of a lofty portico. It made you feel very small, very lost, and yet it was not altogether depressing, that feeling. After all, if you were small, the grimy beetle crawled on—which was just what you wanted it to

48. Arnold Kettle, *An Introduction to the English Novel* (New York, 1960), I, 93.
49. Ian Watt, *Conrad in the Nineteenth Century* (Berkeley, 1981), 179.

do. Where the pilgrims imagined it crawled to I don't know. To some place where they expected to get something, I bet! For me it crawled towards Kurtz—exclusively; but when the steam-pipes started leaking we crawled very slow. The reaches opened before us and closed behind, as if the forest had stepped leisurely across the water to bar the way for our return. We penetrated deeper and deeper into the heart of darkness. It was very quiet there. At night sometimes the roll of drums behind the curtain of trees would run up the river and remain sustained faintly, as if hovering in the air high over our heads, till the first break of day. Whether it meant war, peace, or prayer we could not tell. The dawns were heralded by the descent of a chill stillness; the wood-cutters slept, their fires burned low; the snapping of a twig would make you start. We were wanderers on prehistoric earth, on an earth that wore the aspect of an unknown planet.[50]

There is very little straight description here, for this is a world being swallowed into consciousness, into the attenuation Erich Auerbach laments in the final chapter of *Mimesis,* where *To the Lighthouse* is his example of all that is wrong with modern fiction, in which there is no longer the reality before the characters, but only the characters before the reality: a state, in other words, where consciousness has greater presence than matter.[51] Conrad himself is not unaware of this shift from emphasis on the world to emphasis on consciousness, and he is eager to resist it. In the preface to *The Nigger of the "Narcissus,"* he says he wants to "render the highest kind of justice to the visible universe," which suggests his commitment to retinal experience; but he completes the sentence with the statement that this is done "by bringing to light the truth, manifold and one, underlying its every aspect." He says his "task" is "before all, to make you see. That—and no more, and it is everything"; but he also says that written words "must strenuously aspire to the plasticity of sculpture, to the colour of painting, and to the magic suggestiveness of music."[52] This is a far cry from any aesthetic implicit in Austen's two-inch square of ivory or even the sculptural ideal of Pound's Hugh Selwyn Mauberley, but Conrad's insistence on the synecdoche of seeing, on the priority of physical presence and passive observation to any act of the mind, is telling.

50. Joseph Conrad, *Heart of Darkness* (Harmondsworth, 1973), 50–51.

51. Erich Auerbach, *Mimesis: The Representation of Reality in Western Literature,* trans. Willard R. Trask (Princeton, 1953), 535–41.

52. Joseph Conrad, *The Nigger of the "Narcissus," Typhoon, and Other Stories* (Harmondsworth, 1963), 11, 13, 12.

It is a value often easier to maintain with points of view that are not first person, as illustrated by James in a great moment from *The Ambassadors* when Strether has lunch with Madame de Vionnet:

> Strether was to feel that he had touched bottom. He was to feel many things on this occasion, and one of the first of them was that he had travelled far since that evening in London, before the theatre, when his dinner with Maria Gostrey, between the pink-shaded candles, had struck him as requiring so many explanations—he had stored them up; but it was at present as if he had either soared above or sunk below them—he couldn't tell which; he could somehow think of none that didn't seem to leave the appearance of collapse and cynicism easier for him than lucidity. How could he wish it to be lucid for others, for anyone, that he, for the hour, saw reasons enough in the mere way the bright clean ordered water-side life came in at the open window?—the mere way Madame de Vionnet, opposite him over their intensely white table-linen, their "omelette aux tomates," their bottle of straw-coloured Chablis, thanked him for everything almost with the smile of a child, while her grey eyes moved in and out of their talk, back to the quarter of the warm spring air, in which early summer had already begun to throb, and then back again to his face and their human questions.[53]

Strether's experience at this moment evokes Randall Jarrell's paraphrase of "Goethe's beautiful saying that it is nicer to think than to do, to feel than to think, but nicest of all merely to look."[54] For there is in this passage all the modern tension between the need to make meaning and the desire to find peace in the simply physical. Moreover, to transpose the elements of this scene into the ontology of language, to make the water-side view and the bottle of Chablis merely signs of something else, metonyms of Paris or of Strether's anxiety, is not to imbue them with meaning so much as it is to void them completely of the being they have for Strether as pleasure. At this point, James's narrator is closer to Austen's than to Conrad's Marlow, but from this point on, sheer presence such as James's becomes increasingly difficult to render. Hemingway can do it in some of his landscapes, but the price he pays for the depthless world is the depthless character for whom sensory experience is the mind's prophylaxis: Nick Adams, for instance, making coffee on the Big Two-Hearted River. Kafka's

53. Henry James, *The Ambassadors* (Harmondsworth, 1973), 192.
54. Randall Jarrell, *Selected Poems of William Carlos Williams* (New York, 1968), x.

depthlessness, which in Robbe-Grillet's eyes is his great strength as a "visionary of presence," is so hard for many readers to accept that Kafka's narratives are immediately accorded the height of allegory as compensation.[55]

A more typical and more complicated—and therefore more truly novelistic—treatment of the various modes of presence than occurs in Hemingway or Kafka occurs in *To the Lighthouse*. The end of the linear plot, the plot of action, is the arrival of James, Cam, and Mr. Ramsay at the lighthouse, but the end of the plot of consciousness is the gesture by which Lily finishes her painting. As a physical entity, the lighthouse is present to the senses of the characters in the novel. It is also present to them socially as a landmark, a utility, and an institution, and it is present psychologically as an end, as the destination of a boat trip that has acquired more than literal significance. Lily's painting is also a sensible physical object, which she has shown to Mr. Bankes, and it is an institutional object insofar as its subject is a traditional motif in painting, the Madonna and child, and its style falls within long-established modern practice, Impressionism verging on abstraction. It also represents Lily's insight that only relationships are knowable, that bodies such as Mrs. Ramsay's do not have within them an essence to read, as she had once hoped: "Sitting on the floor with her arms round Mrs. Ramsay's knees, close as she could get, smiling to think that Mrs. Ramsay would never know the reason of that pressure, she imagined how in the chambers of the mind and heart of the woman who was, physically, touching her, were stood, like the treasures in the tombs of kings, tablets bearing sacred inscriptions, which if one could spell them out, would teach one everything, but they would never be offered openly, never made public. What art was there, known to love or cunning, by which one pressed through into those secret chambers?"[56]

In Proust, the narrator Marcel's relation to physical objects and the mystery of furniture is even more self-conscious and self-critical because his need for identification and integrity is more extreme. Lily may need Mrs. Ramsay's love desperately, but her anxiety never sinks to the ontological level reported in this passage from the "Overture" to *Swann's Way:*

> But for me it was enough if, in my own bed, my sleep was so heavy as completely to relax my consciousness; for then I lost all sense of

---

55. Alain Robbe-Grillet. *For a New Novel: Essays on Fiction,* trans. Richard Howard (New York, 1965), 164–65. In *Enlarging the Temple: New Directions in American Poetry During the 1960s* (Lewisburg, 1979), Charles Altieri also develops an idea of presence without depth or Derridean metaphysics in his treatment of Frank O'Hara. See 108–27. Michael Bell, *D. H. Lawrence: Language and Being* (Cambridge, U.K., 1992), argues that Lawrence's treatment of presence has more in common with Heidegger than with Derrida. See 1–12, 51–96.

56. Virginia Woolf, *To the Lighthouse* (San Diego, 1955), 78–79.

the place in which I had gone to sleep, and when I awoke in the middle of the night, not knowing where I was, I could not even be sure at first who I was; I had only the most rudimentary sense of existence, such as may lurk and flicker in the depths of an animal's consciousness; I was more destitute than the cave-dweller; but then the memory—not yet of the place in which I was, but of various other places where I had lived and might now very possibly be—would come like a rope let down from heaven to draw me up out of the abyss of not-being, from which I could never have escaped by myself: in a flash I would traverse centuries of civilisation, and out of a blurred glimpse of oil-lamps, then of shirts with turned-down collars, would gradually piece together the original components of my ego.

Perhaps the immobility of the things that surround us is forced upon them by our conviction that they are themselves and not anything else, by the immobility of our conception of them.[57]

This first person account succeeds, I think, because these objects are not given the magnifying symbolism that Marlow's jungle has: that it's Africa isn't enough, it has to be the heart of darkness, too. Marlow realizes that there "was surface-truth enough in these things to save a wiser man," but he is more interested in the drama of his deep anxiety and elevated rhetoric. Marcel, like Strether, wants to cling to simple things as anchors or buoys, and what gives this passage from *Swann's Way* its value is the utter clarity with which Proust recognizes that essences are idealist projections which we need in order to secure matter, against our own intermittence, so that it can secure us. Marlow is ultimately interested in systems of belief and their moral discipline; Marcel is interested in the ontological system of subject-and-object in which objects, whatever else they are, are *limits* to consciousness, things that save us from consciousness alone.

Had he lived to read Robbe-Grillet, Proust might have agreed with the spirit of his argument. The theorist whom Robbe-Grillet immediately opposes in his polemic is Sartre, and the historical irony of this argument is that the kind of philosophy Sartre turned to in the 1930s, when he was anguished by the inability of language to "touch things themselves," was the phenomenology of Husserl that Derrida came to critique, not for its materialism, but for the transcenden-

---

57. Marcel Proust, *Remembrance of Things Past*, trans. C. K. Scott Moncrieff and Terence Kilmartin (New York, 1981), I, 5–6. Another version of Proust's feelings on these matters can be seen in his essay, "Chardin: The Essence of Things," in *Writers On Artists*, ed. Daniel Halperin (San Francisco, 1988).

talism of phonocentric presence. Here is Simone de Beauvoir's anecdote of Sartre's introduction to Husserl:

> Raymond Aron was spending a year at the French Institute in Berlin, and studying Husserl simultaneously with preparing an historic thesis. When he came to Paris he spoke of Husserl to Sartre. We spent an evening together at the Bec de Gaz in rue Montparnasse. We ordered the speciality of the house, apricot cocktails. Aron said, pointing to his glass: "You see, my dear fellow, if you were a phenomenologist, you could talk about this cocktail glass and make a philosophy out of it." Sartre turned pale with emotion at this. Here was just the thing he had been longing to achieve for years—to describe objects just as he saw and touched them, and extract philosophy from the process.[58]

Extracting philosophy is exactly what Robbe-Grillet objects to and what he wants the new novel to oppose. I have quoted some of this before, but it bears repeating:

> Instead of this universe of "signification" (psychological, social, functional), we must try, then, to construct a world both more solid and more immediate. Let it be first of all by their *presence* that objects and gestures establish themselves, and let this presence continue to prevail over whatever explanatory theory that may try to enclose them in a system of references, whether emotional, sociological, Freudian, or metaphysical.
>
> In this future universe of the novel, gestures and objects will be *there* before being *something;* and they will still be there afterwards, hard, unalterable, eternally present, mocking their own "meaning," that meaning which vainly tries to reduce them to the role of precarious tools.[59]

This passage has always confirmed my belief that things *do* mock their meanings, and it measures exactly the amount of hubris we spend on an ontology of language alone. I know, of course, that Robbe-Grillet is too simple, that his longing alone doesn't refute Derrida, and that this passage is a losing last-ditch defense against the vanguard of theory that now dominates so much of our thought about writing.

58. Quoted in Arthur C. Danto, *Jean-Paul Sartre* (New York, 1975), 16, 15.
59. Robbe-Grillet, *For a New Novel*, 21.

But at least the world of objects he proposes does not have the nostalgia for the Homeric world that Auerbach, a Hegelian such as Lukács, describes in the opening chapter of *Mimesis* to set up his censure of Woolf. This lack of radiance in Robbe-Grillet has two important consequences. The world without the depth of a hidden immanence is also a world without a superior realm of transcendence, because immanence and transcendence are isomorphic. And, secondly, without this depth, neither metaphor nor metonymy works for Robbe-Grillet as a legitimate operation of language.[60] He points, therefore, to a nice confusion in metonymy, which is a rhetorical figure that we sometimes assume performs a physical operation. This, in turn, points to how complex the matter of presence is in the novel's use and representation of it.

Metaphor is always the context for any discussion of metonymy, and metaphor, Jonathan Culler argues, always presupposes some kind of traffic in essences, as the metaphor either discovers an otherwise hidden essential similarity or transforms one term into the other by creating their identity.[61] Metonymy, by contrast, deals not in essences but accidents, so metaphor is the governing figure of the poetic, metonymy of realistic prose. Within the model of the sentence, metaphor is a mode of substitution along the vertical axis of the paradigm, metonymy a relation of contiguity along the horizontal line of the syntagm. One term of a metaphor can take the place, the slot, of another, but a metonym can only approach, get closer to, as it were, its other term. Along the syntagmatic line of a novel's narrative, therefore, things in contiguity with each other suggest, without *becoming*, each other's properties. Characters are represented by their dress, houses, and furniture, by their "natural" neighborhood or locale, and like these objects, these characters are subject to social forces of determination, other systems of meaning. Roman Jakobson has tried to root metaphor and metonymy in different kinds of aphasia, in natural if not quite healthy motions of the neurological brain.[62] No neurologist now understands aphasia as Jakobson presents it, but his effort to ground these basic tropes in something other than language, in the matter and mechanics of perception itself, which ultimately has to involve some concretely causal agency, is not incomprehensible or unworthy. Hayden White has recently tried to do the same thing by tying the tropes

60. See Roland Barthes, *Critical Essays*, trans. Richard Howard (Evanston, Ill., 1972), 14–15.

61. Jonathan Culler, *The Pursuit of Signs: Semiotics, Literature, Deconstruction* (Ithaca, 1981), chapter 10. For other readings of metaphor's relation to metonymy, see Jane Gallop, *Reading Lacan* (Ithaca, 1985), chapter 5, and Paul de Man, *Allegories of Reading: Figural Language in Rousseau, Nietzsche, Rilke, and Proust* (New Haven, 1979), chapter 3.

62. Roman Jakobson, "Two Aspects of Language and Two Types of Aphasine Disturbance," in *Selected Writings II, Word and Language* (The Hague, 1971), 239–59.

to the developmental psychology of Jean Piaget.[63] Novelists as different as Austen and Balzac (who seriously believed in the organic sign systems he understood as physiognomy and phrenology) have written as though faces can be *read* for characterological significance, as though the sacred writing Lily Briscoe believes is hidden within the chambers of Mrs. Ramsay's inner being were manifest as facial features.

Yet Woolf's metaphor for Lily, so deliberately articulated and disproportionate, not only reveals the whole premise of this kind of reading as slightly ridiculous, it also reveals Woolf's having her cake and eating it, too. Woolf constructs a figure for what's valuable to Lily beyond Mrs. Ramsay's surface beauty in a way that allows her reader to accept Lily's judgment and yearning without exactly sharing her naïveté. And Woolf's style obviates the difficult questions that can arise in a more traditional description, such as Stendhal's description of the face of Julien Sorel:

> His cheeks were flushed, his eyes downcast. He was a short lad, about eighteen or nineteen years of age, with irregular, but delicately cut features and an aquiline nose. His large black eyes, which in calmer moments revealed a thoughtful, fiery spirit, were at that moment alive with the most savage hate. His dark auburn hair, growing down over his forehead, made it seem low, and gave him, in moments of anger, a rather forbidding, ill-natured air. Of all the innumerable varieties of the human countenance none perhaps has been distinguished by such striking individuality. His trim, slender figure gave more promise of agility than of strength. The thoughtful expression and the extreme pallor of his face had from his early childhood made his father think he had not long to live, or would live only to be a burden to his family.[64]

We can accept without question the expressiveness of Julien's eyes. We can accept, too, the narrator's interpretation, his opinion, of the "striking individuality" of Julien's whole face. But what force cuts the "irregular" features so "delicately," giving the face its oxymoronic interest and his nose the appropriately noble aquilinity? This facial conformation is supposed to tell us a lot about Julien's superiority and alienation, but have these attitudes in him actually produced the shape of his nose, which is offered to us not as the narrator's

---

63. Hayden White, *Tropics of Discourse: Essays in Cultural Criticism* (Baltimore, 1978), 1–25.

64. Stendhal, *Scarlet and Black*, trans. Margaret R. B. Shaw (New York, 1953), 37.

interpretation but as physical fact? Is Julien's nose a metaphor for his nobly Roman soul? Or is it a metonymy because it is simply closer, more contiguous, to the "thoughtful, fiery spirit" behind his eyes? Funny questions, until we place them within the field of Baudelaire's quintessentially nineteenth-century belief that "the perpetual correlation between what is called the 'soul' and what is called the 'body' explains quite clearly how everything that is 'material,' or in other words an emanation of the 'spiritual,' mirrors, and will always mirror, the spiritual reality from which it derives."[65] *Matter that derives from spirit* makes matter a lesser form of presence. And noble noses that emanate from fiery souls seem to indicate that metonymy operates as some kind of osmotic pressure at the molecular level, or that ontology is actually a mode of physics. Although we do not finally believe in the emanation of matter from spirit, especially when the concept is stated so baldly, something like that principle is latent in every novelistic description of a face, a house, the weather, or the land that is supposed to signify something more than the merely material surface. And we do believe in something like this principle's converse: that, if spirit does not actually derive from matter, spirit is affected by matter, as Stendhal's description of Verrières's relation to its setting suggests:

> *Bringing in money*—that is the magic phrase determining everything in Verrières; by itself alone it represents the usual subject for thought of more than three-quarters of its population. *Bringing in money* is the decisive reason for everything in this little town you thought so pretty. A stranger to it, on his first arrival there, enchanted by the cool, deep valleys that surround it, imagines its inhabitants are sensitive to beauty. They speak all too frequently of the beauty of the town and its environment; nobody can deny that they set a high value on it; but that is only because this beauty attracts visitors, whose money makes the innkeepers rich, while they, in their turn, by paying tax on commodities from outside, increase the revenue of the town.[66]

Romantic sensitivity to nature's beauty, its immanent spirituality, and the virtue inherent in that exchange, is a *materialism* the narrator counts on the reader to

---

65. Charles Baudelaire, "The Painter of Modern Life," in *The Painter of Modern Life and Other Essays*, trans. Jonathan Mayne (New York, 1964), 14. A more recent, and more embarrassing, version of this argument appears in the section of Thomas Mann's *The Magic Mountain* entitled "Research," in chapter 5.

66. Stendhal, *Scarlet and Black*, 28.

share so that they both may condescend to the natives' susceptibility to another, more modern materialism: the matter of manufacture and commerce, which harbors no spiritual component, which pinches the soul and demeans it. The spirit that derives from matter is a principle intrinsic to all forms of naturalism, all systems of material causality; and although putting it like this and preserving the hierarchy of spirit and matter rings false, it reveals quite clearly, I think, how resistant physical presence is to any simplification into categories of consciousness or language and how constantly the novel reminds us that this representational dilemma is also to our advantage.

A more satisfying explanation of metonymy than Jakobson's is Kenneth Burke's. In a relatively brief, deceptively nonchalant discussion in his essay "Four Master Tropes," Burke says:

> The basic "strategy" in metonymy is this: to convey some incorporeal or intangible state in terms of the corporeal or tangible. E.g., to speak of "the heart" rather than "the emotions." If you trail language back far enough, of course, you will find that all our terms for "spiritual" states were metonymic in origin. We think of "the emotions," for instance, as applying solely to the realm of consciousness, yet obviously the term is rooted in the most "materialistic" term of all, motion (a key strategy in Western materialism has been the reduction of "consciousness" to motion). . . .
>
> Language develops by metaphorical extension, in borrowing words from the realm of the corporeal, visible, tangible and applying them by analogy to the realm of the incorporeal, invisible, intangible; then in the course of time, the original corporeal reference is forgotten, and only the incorporeal, metaphorical extension survives (often because the very conditions of living that reminded one of the corporeal reference have so altered that the cross reference no longer exists with near the same degree of apparentness in the "objective situation" itself); and finally, poets regain the original relation, in reverse, by a "metaphorical extension" back from the intangible into a tangible equivalent; . . . and this "archaicizing" device we call "metonymy."[67]

The advantage of Burke's explanation is that it recognizes matter's primacy, but does not make it a causal principle or *the* causal principle in a deterministic system; so, the mind's play back and forth between matter and spirit, the

67. Kenneth Burke, *A Grammar of Motives* (Berkeley, 1969), 506.

metonymic relation the two in fact have to each other, and their interpenetration, are fully recognized. And the "weakness" of metonymy, its softness at the edges of things, its implication of the *effect* one object can have on the other along the line of Jakobson's axis of contiguity, is correlative to Burke's idea of the reduction of consciousness to motion. Plots, we can say in this context, are a motion of consciousness through space and especially time; and *as motion*, they resist too much investment of meaning in originary beginnings, consummatory ends, and governing centers. Metonymies, like plots, keep things diffused but not inchoate, different but similar enough, and ultimately blur unanswerable questions of causality such as that involved in the shape of Julien Sorel's nose.

If we seem to have come some way from the difference between phenomenological self-presence and the presence of things in Robbe-Grillet, presence as significance itself and presence that refuses signification, we have, but haven't. The idea of presence has many ramifications, and these have their intrinsic structural conflicts. The presence we construct as self-presence, express as intention, and then extrude into expressive form, is an idea that has to do with our sense of the nature and authority of narrators. The presence of objects to the senses, and whatever form this then takes as presence to the mind, entails the world that the narrator occupies and, in some way, has to represent to the reader, through the language on the page, which is present itself as both object and idea, print and writing.

Another, but very different, point of convergence for the varieties of presence in the novel is what we have come to call "voice." In Philip Roth's *The Ghost Writer,* Lonov defines voice for his protégé Zuckerman: "I don't mean style. . . . I mean voice: something that begins at around the back of the knees and reaches well above the head."[68] Voice, in this description, might be called the phonocentrism of the body: its sound to itself when expression is without influence or obstruction, a sensation Zuckerman has to have to believe in his personal truth. It is a distinction we apply to the prose we value, precisely because it is a quality that prose cannot have, a quality writing dissolves: an audible bodiliness, the absolute pitch of the particular that is always a quality of the material. Voice, as we perceive it in the famous opening sentences below, reveals one of the most curious aspects of our reading: our ability to *hear* the silent page.

68. Philip Roth, *The Ghost Writer* (New York, 1979), 93. See also novelist John Hawkes, "The Voice Project: An Idea for Innovation in the Teaching of Writing," in *Writers as Teachers / Teachers as Writers,* ed. Jonathan Baumbach (New York, 1970), 89–144. Voice "in writing . . . may be taken to mean the whole presence of the writer-as-writer rather than the writer-as-man" (91). Obviously, Roth and Hawkes mean something much more physical than Genette does in *Narrative Discourse.*

It is a truth universally acknowledged that a single man in possession of a good fortune must be in want of a wife.

All happy families are alike but an unhappy family is unhappy after its own fashion.

Whether I shall turn out to be the hero of my own life, or whether that station will be held by any body else, these pages must show.

I am a sick man . . . I am a nasty man. A truly unattractive man. I think there's something wrong with my liver.

You don't know about me, without you have read a book by the name of "The Adventures of Tom Sawyer," but that ain't no matter.

On my naming day when I come 12 I gone front spear and kilt a wyld boar he parbly ben the las wyld pig on the Bundel Downs any how there hadnt been none for a long time befor him nor I aint looking to see none agen.

Austen's irony in the first quotation is easy to oppose to Tolstoy's imperial self-assurance in the second, although they agree that the family is the novel's great topic. David Copperfield's modesty is equally easy to oppose to the Underground Man's aggression. Huck Finn and Riddley Walker, however, have more in common: each speaks not only in a singular voice, which is not so easy, perhaps, to translate as those of Tolstoy and Dostoevsky, but also in a dialect; and what gives each dialect its particular flavor or pitch is not only the "faulty" grammar of their statements but their orthography as well. Their "voices" sound different because they look different.

Reading is always a visual experience before it is an interpretive act.[69] We are used to thinking that the referentiality of prose and the justified right-hand margin make prose transparent. We look *at* a poem, which looks *like* a poem because its lines are not justified—they stop before the margin. The end of the line refers back to, and is explained by, the form the poem itself takes rather than by the size of the page. Prose runs on, however, and we seem to look through it because we have always taken its conventions so much for granted. Yet

69. For a full discussion, see Terrence Doody, "Reading Is a Visual Experience," *New Orleans Review*, VIII (1981), 273–77, and the first and last chapters of John Hollander, *Vision and Resonance* (New York, 1975).

indentations and capitals signify beginnings; periods and widows define ends. Quotation marks usually distinguish thought from speech, or the narrator from a character, yet they seem too casual (Joyce after all does without them) to be making such fundamental ontological distinctions. Still, quotation marks also engage us in deciding those differences between speech and writing, although on the page neither the speaker nor the writer is *there*. Exclamation points can give this absence emotion. Italics can make any thing, even *me*, vivid.

It is instructive to read Derrida on the book, which for him is the "idea of the book," and then to read Walter J. Ong on the printed object and its differences from a written manuscript. Derrida writes: "The idea of the book is the idea of a totality, finite or infinite, of the signifier; this totality of the signifier cannot be a totality, unless a totality constituted by the signified preexists it, supervises its inscriptions and its signs, and is independent of it in its ideality. The idea of the book, which always refers to a natural totality, is profoundly alien to the sense of writing."[70] Realistic writing depends on a world that can be realized in some writer's language, but between these new terms, signifier and signified, there is *not* assumed an agent to arrange the connection. Like Forster describing narrative without a narrator, Derrida wants to describe writing without a writer because he is defining here the system of language-as-ontology that alters completely the act of arranging signifiers in lines along a page. The new and inescapable signified by which Derrida's argument is supervised, by which he operates only as a signifier, obviates *him*. This sense of writing, profoundly alien to the idea of the book, is also profoundly alien to the writer. Narratives are sentences, in this construction, not narrations.

Ong's emphasis and implications are quite different:

> Print encourages a sense of closure, a sense that what is found in a text has been finalized, has reached a state of completion. This sense affects literary creations and it affects philosophical or scientific work. . . . By contrast, manuscripts, with their glosses or marginal comments (which often got worked into the text in subsequent copies) were in dialogue with the world outside their own borders. They remained closer to the give-and-take of oral expression. The readers of manuscripts are less closed off from the author, less absent, than are the readers of those writing for print. The sense of closure or completeness enforced by print is at times grossly physical. A newspaper's pages are normally all filled—certain kinds of material are called 'fillers'—just as its lines of type are normally all justified.

70. Derrida, *Of Grammatology*, 18.

. . . Print is curiously intolerant of physical incompleteness. It can convey the impression, unintentionally and subtly, but very really, that the material the text deals with is similarly complete or self-consistent.[71]

The invention of print technology has been a revolution as important as any other in man's history. In historical terms, its advent is relatively recent, but for most of us print has always been there. Certainly anyone reading this book is an example of the new phenomenological subject that Marshall McLuhan calls "typographic man." He is not merely different because he is literate; he is different because literacy and print have altered human consciousness and our sense of place in the world. For a person in an oral culture stands at the center of a circle, a "lifeworld" that surrounds everyone with sound. Harmony is one of the highest values; the world is concrete and tactile; language is an *event* rather than the sign it is for the literate subject, and the oral person's life is profoundly conservative, more "religious" than "scientific." Oral narratives tend to be not only copious and repetitious, they are also a performance before an engaged, participating audience.

Amos Tutuola's *The Palm-Wine Drinkard* is better than any modern translation of Homer for illustrating these points. It comes in printed form from Faber and Faber but is narrated in the oral style native to Tutuola's Yoruba origins. Although its publication in 1952 was overseen by T. S. Eliot, and the book was praised by no less a bard than Dylan Thomas as a "thronged, grisly, and bewitching story," after its opening archetypal pages in which the narrator introduces himself and defines his quest, it does not seem like a novel. Its narrator calls it a "storybook," and he himself seems to be more conduit than character. He is suffused and overwhelmed by the magical or surrealistic movement of the world, and he offers nothing like the interpretation of his experience we expect from novelistic characters, especially those who narrate their lives. Consequently, to the literate, habitual reader of novels, his narrative seems haphazard, a lot of consecution with very little consequence, and very resistant to succinct, illuminating quotation, because transformation is a more fundamental experience and a greater value than is any interpretation of it.

It is instructive to contrast Tutuola's novel with George Eliot's reflecting on the problems of knowledge and representation involved in the different ontologies of the human face and language, as she describes Mr. Grandcourt in *Daniel Deronda*: "Attempts at description are stupid: who can all at once describe a

---

71. Walter J. Ong, *Orality and Literacy: The Technologizing of the Word* (London, 1982), 132–33.

human being? even when he is presented to us we only begin that knowledge of his appearance which must be completed by innumerable impressions under differing circumstances. We recognize the alphabet; we are not sure of the language."[72]

Now let's look at three passages from Tutuola:

> Now as I took the lady as my wife and after I had spent the period of six months with the parents of my wife, then I remembered my palm-wine tapster who had died in my town long ago, then I asked the father of my wife to fulfil his promise or to tell me where my tapster was, but he told me to wait for some time. Because he knew that if he told me the place by that time, I would leave his town and take his daughter away from him and he did not like to part with his daughter.
>
> I spent three years with him in that town, but during that time, I was tapping palm-wine for myself, of course I could not tap it to the quantity that I required to drink; my wife was also helping me to carry it from the farm to the town. When I completed three and a half years in that town, I noticed that the left hand thumb of my wife was swelling out as if it was a buoy, but it did not pain her. One day, she followed me to the farm in which I was tapping the palm-wine, and to my surprise when the thumb that swelled out touched a palm-tree thorn, the thumb bust out suddenly and there we saw a male child came out of it and at the same time that the child came out from the thumb, he began to talk to us as if he was ten years of age. . . .

"On the Way to an Unknown Place"

> The same day that the father of my wife told me the place that my tapster was, I told my wife to pack all our belongings and she did so, then we woke up early in the morning and started to travel to an unknown place, but when we had travelled about two miles away to that town which we left, my wife said that she forgot her gold trinket inside the house which I had burnt into ashes, she said that she had forgotten to take it away before the house was burnt into ashes. She said that she would go back and take it, but I told her that it would

---

72. George Eliot, *Daniel Deronda* (Harmondsworth, 1967), 145–46.

burn into ashes together with the house. She said that it was a metal and it could not burn into ashes and she said that she was going back to take it, and I begged her not to go back, but she refused totally, so when I saw her going back to take it, then I followed her. When we reached there, she picked a stick and began to scratch the ashes with it, and there I saw that the middle of the ashes rose up suddenly and at the same time there appeared a half-bodied baby, he was talking with a lower voice like a telephone. . . .

"To Travel by Air"

Then I told my wife to jump on my back with our loads, at the same time, I commanded my juju which was given me by "Water Spirit woman" in the "Bush of the Ghosts" (the full story of the "Spirit woman" appeared in the story book of the Wild Hunter in the Bush of the Ghosts). So I became a big bird like an aeroplane and flew away with my wife, I flew for 5 hours before I came down, after I had left the dangerous area, although it was 4 o'clock before I came down, then we began to trek the remaining journey by land or foot. By 8 o'clock p.m. of that day, then we reached the town in which the father of my wife told me that my palm-wine tapster was.[73]

Despite the headlines which are as clearly and mysteriously *written* as the headlines in the Aeolus episode of *Ulysses*, the organization of this narrative is oral. There is no increment to the repetitions to suggest the narrator's attempt to control his own rhetoric or his audience's reaction. He does not dwell on the problems of representation, as Eliot does, although Tutuola has to know what is real to his narrator is not even realistic to his Western reader. For the transformations his narrator undergoes and reports are not metaphors, not literary events, but real; and the rapid insubstantiality of this world is the necessary condition of his perfect narrative fluency.

For the literate individual, as distinct from the oral person, the world has no such polymorphous permeability. The literate individual is not the center of a mobile surround, but a point on a line of sight, from which the viewer takes a

73. Amos Tutuola, *The Palm-Wine Drinkard* (London, 1961), 31, 34–35, 40. An interesting contrast to Tutuola's style can be found in Mario Vargas Llosa's *The Storyteller*, trans. Helen Lane (New York, 1990), which sets his imitation of an oral style into a realistic novel. See especially 37–69.

point of view and then proceeds to construct a world, and the novel, as a solid geometry or architecture in which even narratives have "lines." Visual experience is more important to typographic man than oral experience is; thick things have been given a greater credence than airy rhetoric; and metonymy, therefore, is a more realistic figure of the mind's limits than metaphor is, which acknowledges no physical boundaries. Visual experience promotes separation and individuality and also a greater sense of abstraction and analysis than orality does, which fosters the tactile more than the ideational, the redundant, conservative, harmonizing performance rather than reductive mental discriminations. Abstraction and analysis, in turn, foster the values of clarity and distinctness. Originality has come to mean not a return to the source, but the location of that source, that origin, in the individual, for whom the opportunity for self-analysis is not only new but imperative.[74] There seem to be no traditional oral autobiographies. There are oral epics and lyrics, there are plays that have been improvised without a script, perhaps with a singer-narrator such as Brecht uses in *The Caucasian Chalk-Circle*. A novel, however, must always be in print; and in order to be marketed in another way, popular movies are now "novelized" for sale in drug stores and supermarkets.

Print is the first technology of replaceable uniform parts, whether that part is the type itself or the book it produces in mass quantities. Among the many ways in which print has affected our new sense of human individuality is Elizabeth Eisenstein's argument that individuality is grounded exactly in the play of similarity-and-difference that print promoted before structural linguistics did:

> Concepts pertaining to uniformity and diversity—to the typical and the unique—are interdependent, they represent two sides of the same coin. In this regard one might consider the emergence of a new sense of individualism as a by-product of the new forms of standardization. The more standardized the type, indeed, the more compelling the sense of an idiosyncratic self.
>
> It should be noted that a new alertness to both the individual and the typical was likely to come first to circles frequented by those printers and engravers who were responsible for turning out the new costume manuals, style books, commemorations of royal entries and regional guides. . . . It seems likely that a new alertness to place and period and more concern about assigning the proper trappings to

---

74. These distinctions between the oral and literate worlds are summarized from Ong's argument throughout *Orality and Literacy*.

each was fostered by the very act of putting together illustrated guidebooks and costume manuals.[75]

The similarity-and-difference entailed in *writing,* in the ontology that denies the privilege given to substance as it has been projected onto and then modeled after physical objects, is a "higher" version, perhaps, of the similarity-and-difference that arises from print. But the connection between the two is not accidental, for as print changed the nature of the book, it also changed our sense of ourselves, as individuals, as authors, and as readers.

Eisenstein explains that before print took over "it was customary to register many texts bound with one set of covers as but one book, so that the actual number of texts in a given manuscript collection is not easily ascertained. That objects counted as one book often contained a varying combination of many provides yet another example of the difficulty of quantifying data provided in the age of scribes."[76] Books were copied in noisy scriptoria such as that described by Umberto Eco in *The Name of the Rose,* and the scribes both were and were not authors in our sense of the word. They were, of course, copyists, a medium of transmission, with no original "authority" at all. Yet each of them wrote—not always, perhaps, but often—an "original" text that was produced by the silent redactions of inattention and error. So not only was every book more often an anthology, such as the Bible, rather than a unit, such as the Koran, but all copying was a kind of interpretation. It seems easier to accept the recent and notorious "death of the author" when we realize he wasn't always with us to begin with, for the term *author,* like the term *character,* is not coterminous with person. An author is a human function, the name of a behavior, and authors have always been mediated by language, the medium in which they behave. For those of us who had read Wayne Booth before we read Barthes and Foucault, we can see the author starting to "die" in *The Rhetoric of Fiction,* where he or she is also a behavior or function, someone of whom knowledge can only be implied, a fiction.[77]

In the meantime, one of the things that makes the novel at least relatively new is that a single author got to put a name on the title page. That name, Henry

75. Elizabeth L. Eisenstein, *The Printing Press as an Agent of Change: Communication and Cultural Transformation in Early-Modern Europe,* I and II (Cambridge, 1980), 84, 85. Another aspect of the changes effected by printing is explored in Alvin Kernan, *Printing Technology, Letters, and Samuel Johnson* (Princeton, 1985).

76. Eisenstein, *Printing Press,* 45.

77. See Roland Barthes, "The Death of the Author" and "From Work to Text," in *Image / Music / Text.* Eisenstein's remarks in *Printing Press* are relevant here, 121; and so are Marshall McLuhan's in *The Gutenberg Galaxy* (New York, 1969), 160.

Fielding, referred to a real historical person who alone claimed authority for the other name on the title page, Tom Jones, a fictional character, for whom Fielding never claims the kind of independent existence Cervantes ascribes to Don Quixote or Defoe wants to claim for Moll Flanders. What Fielding does instead, or what the narrator who implies him does, is enact all the difference this new relation makes, all the freedom and power, all the possible fun. What this means for the reader is a similar kind of authority, a correlative freedom, and maybe some fun, too. "Reader, I think proper, before we proceed any farther together, to acquaint thee, that I intend to digress, through this whole history, as often as I see occasion: of which I am myself a better judge than any pitiful critic whatever. And here I must desire all those critics to mind their own business, and not to intermeddle with affairs, or works, which no ways concern them: for, till they produce the authority by which they are constituted judges, I shall plead to their jurisdiction."[78] The reader who does not align herself with the "pitiful critic," which is an almost unthinkable act of self-denial as Fielding means it, accepts the authority the narrator bestows, as she also agrees to have their relationship mediated by a fictional character. This acceptance aligns her with that fiction, makes her a character in the same way the narrator is, triangulates (at least) the play of similarity-and-difference among them, and affirms her own autonomy in the same gesture that enacts her individuality as a *relationship*. The point at which this reader ceases to be a function, the name of a behavior, is the point at which her hand touches the page to turn it at her own rate of expectation and consent. The book in her hand is part of her place in the physical world, and the time the reader spends in this realm is both isolating and liberating, highly individualistic and also impersonal in the way print contributes to both: "mass privacy," as Walter Reed says. Whether this private power sponsors and confirms alienation, or contributes to the general sense of community, is still debatable. Community and privacy are a mode of similarity-and-difference written in another way; they also seem to be a basic fact of psychological life and a determining factor of social and economic life as well. When any one of us finishes a novel and wants to know more about this kind of experience, or about the novel itself, we almost never reread what we have just read, but read another novel. And even if we want to know more about a particular novel, say *Rabbit Is Rich,* we might read not only *Rabbit Run* and *Rabbit Redux* but *Phineas Finn* and *Phineas Redux,* too. As novels, they dramatize for us how novels work and the way we live now. And although they may seem like "replaceable uniform parts," like typeface, they are not. They are, as we are, separate, highly individuated objects that help us refine and extend the indi-

78. Henry Fielding, *Tom Jones* (Harmondsworth, 1966), 54–55.

viduality we ground in the material differentiation of our bodies. And some of us keep acquiring them from the same necessity that Madame Bovary keeps acquiring beautiful things for herself.

Northrop Frye says: "A book, like a keyboard, is a mechanical device for bringing an entire artistic structure under the interpretive control of a single person."[79] But it doesn't feel like that: reading a book does not feel like playing a piano, nor does a book feel like a machine. "In view of its three-dimensionality, the copy of the novel we hold in our hands could be conceived of as a sculpture, where the sculptor has not satisfied himself in representing the gross physical and visual qualities of a book, but has sought to represent the very text of one."[80] This proposition from Barbara Herrnstein Smith is more satisfying because it is as emphatically physical and still more mysterious. Her description suggests to me why the book is the quintessential object: opaque and mute, but with an immanent "essence" which is legible, literally, to the light of the eye, as Lily Briscoe once wanted Mrs. Ramsay to be. A novel's weight in our hands is a form of presence that is always impossible for its text to render, although its presence to our eye as print has fostered an idea of writing that disembodies meaning by extending it into limitless textuality. So, as a book and a text, a novel makes several ontological claims, some of them opposed to the others. And the novel, more than any other kind of book, seems the perfect instrument at hand for realizing again and again these conflicting truths, as it keeps us entertained with rehearsals of our endless human predicament, which resists reduction into language merely, into theory, or into anything else.

79. Frye, *Anatomy of Criticism*, 248.
80. Smith, *On the Margins of Discourse*, 31.

2

NARRATIVE LINES
AND PARADIGMS

*What I want you to see in it is this. Here is a character, imposing itself
on another person. Here is Mrs. Brown making someone begin almost
automatically to write a novel about her. I believe all novels begin with an
old lady in the corner opposite. I believe that all novels, that is to say, deal
with character, and that it is to express character—not to preach doctrines,
sing songs, or celebrate the glories of the British Empire, that the form of
the novel, so clumsy, verbose, and undramatic, so rich, elastic and alive,
has been evolved. To express character, I have said; but you will at once
reflect that the very widest interpretation can be put on those words.*
    —VIRGINIA WOOLF, "Mr. Bennet and Mrs. Brown"

"I look, you look, he looks; we look, ye look, they look."
    —HERMAN MELVILLE, *Moby-Dick*

*Deeds, therefore, are nothing in themselves:
they exist entirely in the ideas other people have about them.*
    —HONORÉ DE BALZAC, *Lost Illusions*

NARRATIVE IS NOT exclusive to the novel; it is not even exclusive to
literature. Dreams and gossip, histories and newspapers, the still pictures on
Native American blankets and robes and the moving pictures of television—all
are narrative forms. To discuss narrative in the novel as I want to in this chapter,
it is not necessary to discuss all of narrative, or to define it; but it will be helpful
to begin by stating some general principles and then, by developing the way
they apply to the novel, to illustrate what the novel does to these in practice.
Therefore, after discussing a narrative's narrator, the nature of his interpretation
or discourse, and the problems of defining a beginning, middle, and end, I want
to propose that in its realistic narrative mode, the novel makes meaning as a
sentence does: that is, in the constant play of the syntagmatic line of the story
against the paradigmatic possibilities of its interpretation by the characters in

it. By paradigm, I mean simply a scheme of the simultaneous similarity-and-difference that exists between, and among, a novel's characters. Every realistic character, even minor ones who are not just named cartoons, is capable, at least potentially, of offering an authoritative interpretation of the world she or he inhabits; so the meaning of any realistic novel grows from the interpretive possibilities its characters embody and provide. In other words, each character operates as a different discourse, a different mode of interpretation deliberately integrated with and played against all the other characters, who also constitute entirely different discourses. This principle will become clearer in all its implications as we consider the nature of discourse itself and give to the paradigmatic sets of characters, in the novels we examine, visual embodiment. But first, some general principles of narrative that the novel and its history suggest.

The first principle of narrative is this: a narrative must have a beginning, a middle, and an end . . . and something else. The French film-director Jean-Luc Godard once told an interviewer that his movies did have a beginning, middle, and end, but not necessarily in that order—which suggests that these very basic terms are hard to define clearly because they are sometimes indistinguishable. In his "Introduction to the Structural Analysis of Literature," Roland Barthes suggests that the same kind of confusion exists in our notions of linear sequence, chronological order, and causality, by calling "the mainspring of narrative . . . the confusion of consecution and consequence." *Post hoc, ergo propter hoc* is a "good motto for Destiny," he says, but it is not always a principle applicable to narrative.[1] This remark seems especially useful in regard to discontinuous narratives such as *Bouvard and Pécuchet*, but it is also illuminating of more traditional, more "inevitable" narratives such as *The Death of Ivan Ilych*. So a narrative needs something else, an ulterior principle of some kind by which the three points along the metaphorical line become part of a significant whole—raised, integrated, or transformed into phases of initiation, complication or transition, and then closure, in a larger unity that is *not* intrinsic to the narrated events themselves.[2]

This brings us to the second principle of narrative: narrative must have a

1. Roland Barthes, "Introduction to the Structural Analysis of Narrative," in *Image/Music/Text*, trans. Stephen Heath (New York, 1977), 94.

2. The clearest discussion of the need for an ulterior principle comes in Hayden White, "The Value of Narrativity in the Representation of Reality," in *On Narrative*, ed. W. J. T. Mitchell (Chicago, 1981), 1–24. In the same volume, White is challenged explicitly by Martha Robinson Waldman in "'The Otherwise Unnoteworthy Year 711': A Reply to Hayden White," 240–48; and less successfully by Louis O. Mink, "Everyman His or Her Own Annalist," 233–39. For someone who agrees with White, see Frank Kermode, *The Genesis of Secrecy* (Cambridge, Mass., 1979), chapter 5.

narrator, who must have an audience. Like the first, this principle seems obvious, but its polemical implications have been controversial and profound. It means, first of all, a narrative is an *act* rather than an order of relationships that in some way is self-substantial, regardless of its embodiment. A narrative version of *Don Quixote*, for instance, informs Cervantes's novel, several imitations of that novel, a Broadway musical, a movie version of that play, and ballets by both Petipa and Balanchine. Where, therefore, the pure form of *Don Quixote* exists in itself, is a question many narrative theorists ask and want to answer. Seymour Chatman, for instance, says: "This transposability of the story is the strongest reason for arguing that narratives are indeed structures independent of any medium. . . . Clearly a narrative is a whole because it is constituted of elements—events and existents—that differ from what they constitute. Events and existents are single and discrete, but the narrative is a sequential composite."[3] Chatman's argument seems plausible if we avoid asking who determines what constitutes a whole. What origin or end determines the sequential composite's full presence? It also seems plausible that a narrative may be essentially intact in a "deep structure" outside or beneath any particular version when the evidence investigated is the kind of traditional material Vladimir Propp studied or the three hundred forty-five versions of the Cinderella tale discovered by a British anthropologist.[4] But the position that a narrative can exist in a "versionless version" has ontological implications impossible to accept outside of Plato's world or the world of the fabulist fictions invented by Jorge Luis Borges or John Barth. The novel is not such a pure form. The unmistakable presence of a narrator, who need not be a character in the story, but who is the character telling it, assumes by his very role an audience, even if it is only another aspect of himself rereading his own manuscript, such as John Dowell in *The Good Soldier*. Sometimes the narrator's act is depicted as speaking, as telling a story; in others, such as Dowell's and Nick Carraway's, it is a written act; but in any case it is intercourse between two parties.

Roland Barthes wants to name this narrative intercourse an "exchange" and to place it in a materialist economy.[5] John Barth wants to make the exchange erotic, and he dramatizes it as love-play in his own short version of Schehera-

---

3. Seymour Chatman, *Story and Discourse: Narrative Structure in Fiction and Film* (Ithaca, 1980), 20, 21.

4. See Barbara Herrnstein Smith, "Narrative Versions, Narrative Theories," in Mitchell, *On Narrative*, 212–13. Robert Scholes, *Structuralism in Literature* (New Haven, 1974), discusses the "origin" of the idea of the "versionless version" in Lévi-Strauss. See 60–61.

5. Roland Barthes, *S/Z*, trans. Richard Miller (New York, 1974), 88–89. See also Barthes, *Image/Music/Text*, 109.

zade.[6] Yet, regardless of how it is couched, this second principle has three corollaries to develop on our way back to discussing the beginning, middle, and end of the novel. The first of these corollaries is that because narrative has a narrator, what he offers us is an interpretation. Meaning is not inherent in the events he narrates, it is created in the way he narrates them. Even if there were a time when a primitive storyteller such as Tutuola's palm-wine drinkard thought he was simply retailing the versionless version, we now read him, in whatever redactive form he has taken, as we read Conrad's storyteller Marlow. So, because the narrator is an interpreter himself, he is open to his audience's further interpretation. One contingency naturally begets another, not some absolute, so narrative remains essentially open-ended insofar as it can only be brought to an end that exists in some way, according to some principle, not intrinsic to the events in the story itself. In *The Poetics of Prose*, Tzvetan Todorov argues that this endlessness is an aspect of even the most primitive narrative. In *The Genesis of Secrecy*, Frank Kermode makes it a principle of the complementary, contradictory, overlapping narratives in the four canonical Gospels. And John Barth illustrates at least Todorov's argument with the Moebius strip that is the frame tale of *Lost in the Funhouse*. This Moebius strip assumes a three-dimensional configuration of the supine figure-8 mathematicians use to signify infinity, so the literally endless surface of Barth's figure reads: "Once upon a time there was a story that began once upon a time there was a story that began . . . " and so on, but never back to another origin or forward to an end.[7]

The second corollary is this: the narrator's interpretation, what he offers to the audience, is a form of discourse. *Discourse* is not *the story*, in Chatman's useful adaptation of the terminology that says *le récit* is not *l'histoire*, *fabula* not *sjužet*. Although the content of a realistic novel is obviously important, it is not the matters by themselves, but the manner of their presentation and development that constitutes their meaning. And there is nothing necessary about the shape this process takes, no ineluctable modality of the narratable. The freedom inherent in discourse is easier to see, perhaps, in the case of historical narratives because historical events—although not their meaning—do exist before or beyond their telling, in a way the events of a novel do not. There are many different "factual" accounts and interpretations of World War II, but the events of *The Naked and the Dead* exist only in that novel. And while the novel does not by definition deny or exclude history—it is, of all modern narrative fictions,

6. John Barth, *Chimera* (Greenwich, Conn., 1973), 11–64.

7. John Barth, *Lost in the Funhouse* (Toronto, 1981), 1, 2. See also John Barth, *The Friday Book: Essays and Other Nonfiction* (New York, 1984), in which Barth talks at every turn about narrative endlessness and embedding.

in fact the most historical—the greatest novels have never really denied their own artifice either. Therefore, what keeps one of these values from canceling the other is the novelistic discourse that remains aesthetically self-conscious of the *version* it is creating. Another account of World War II is another account of World War II, but another version of *The Naked and the Dead* would be logically impossible, another novel altogether. And it is exactly this difference or its possibility that a novel is always ultimately proposing of itself. Defining discourse, Hayden White says:

> If, as Harold Bloom has suggested, a trope can be seen as the linguistic equivalent of a psychological mechanism of defense (a defense against literal meaning in discourse, in the way that repression, regression, projection, and so forth are defenses against the apprehension of death in the psyche), it is always not only a deviation *from* one possible, proper meaning, but also a deviation *towards* another meaning, conception, or ideal of what is right, and proper *and true* "in reality." Thus considered, troping is both a movement *from* one notion of the way things are related *to* another notion, and a connection between things so that they can be expressed in a language that takes account of the possibility of their being expressed otherwise. *Discourse is the genre in which the effort to earn this right of expression, with full credit to the possibility that things might be expressed otherwise, is preeminent.*[8]

It is probably not useful at this point to begin calling discourse a genre, just as it would not be useful yet to rename literary character a trope. To call discourse the language of any telling that takes account of the possibility its tale can be told otherwise, for our purposes at least, seems compelling enough. And to realize that another character's narration *is* another discourse, seems more powerfully accurate than calling the act of characterization a troping. This use of the term discourse, though, does remind us that within an ontology of language, interpretation, not mimesis, is the fundamentally realistic act.

   This brings us to the third corollary of the principle that narrative must have a narrator, and he must have an audience. The corollary is this: narrative does not exist outside a community, in which narrator and audience share the principles, values, assumptions, or culture that gives their language meaning, that provides a semantic dimension to the syntax of the story. This is one way of

---

8. Hayden White, *Tropics of Discourse: Essays in Cultural Criticism* (Baltimore, 1978), 2. Final italics added.

suggesting the nature of the "something else" that must be attached to a beginning, middle, and end to make them significant. Barthes says in his "Introduction": "Narration can only receive its meaning from the world which makes use of it: beyond the narrational level begins the world, other systems (social, economic, ideological) whose terms are no longer simply narratives but elements of a different substance (historical facts, determinations, behaviors, etc.). Just as linguistics stops at the sentence, so narrative analysis stops at discourse—from there it is necessary to shift to another semiotics."[9] Walter Benjamin makes the same point in "The Storyteller," when he characterizes the teller as the sailor returned home to the community with which he shares the values that will make his stories significant, interesting, and useful.[10] And it is exactly for this reason, that beyond the narrational level the world and other semiotic systems begin to take over, that critics such as Walter Reed argue a full *poetics* of the novel can never be developed.[11]

So: what the world does with narrative to make it meaningful can often be explained in terms of what it makes of a narrative's beginning, middle, or end. These are not innocent terms; at a sufficient level of abstraction, which is not very high, they signify transcendental values and, thereby, become terms convertible with each other. It is helpful to remember at this point that Aristotelian thought distinguishes several causes—efficient, material, instrumental, formal, and final, among them—in order to clarify this problem. The efficient cause is an agent, the final cause is the action's purpose; but when a final cause is construed as an intention, it becomes a beginning, an origin, in the agent himself. In mythic or religious discourse, beginning, middle, and end can be a genesis, incarnation, and apocalypse. As metaphysical discourse, they can be an origin, center, and telos. In political theory, they might be something like natural law, history, and progress. In any case, all of these are ultimate terms of value, not just points along a line. And even in literary discourse, where ultimacy can be displaced by the terminology of technique, critics such as Northrop Frye and René Girard want to begin narrative in desire and move it through a course of mediations to transformation and fulfillment. Edward Said does not want so much; yet when he says the beginning of a novel may simply be the intention to write a novel, which he calls the novel's enabling act, sponsored by the genre

9. Barthes, *Image/Music/Text*, 115–16.

10. Walter Benjamin, *Illuminations*, ed. Hannah Arendt, trans. Harry Zohn (New York, 1969), 84–85.

11. See Walter L. Reed, "The Problem with a Poetics of the Novel," in *Toward a Poetics of Fiction*, ed. Mark Spilka (Bloomington, 1977), 62–74. This is an earlier version of the argument Reed makes at the beginning of *An Exemplary History of the Novel*.

and designed, as it were, for the genre's own conservation, he, too, begins to collapse distinctions: for fulfilling the novel's original end entails realizing the novelistic conventions we could say are distributed throughout the middle.[12] In this sense, a novel that has as its origin the end of becoming a novel, is also its own center. In both theory and practice, the beginning, middle, and end are hard to distinguish, for they interpenetrate one another.

Nonetheless, we can see the three terms with greater clarity if we keep in mind Roman Jakobson's diagram of the six different components of a speech event—sender, message, receiver; context, contact, code—and how these apply to beginning, middle, and end of a narrative;[13] and then reflect on the kind of criticism that focuses on each of the terms. Criticism interested in the *beginning* of the novel, for instance, can focus on the author or sender in any of several ways—his or her psychology, the phenomenology of consciousness, the broader autobiographical aspects of the writer's work, the influences that make the writing allusive or anxious; it can also focus on the origin of a novel from its relation to the genre itself or from its place in cultural history; and, finally, it may even focus on the manuscript and its authentic or corrupted editions. Perhaps only a naive reader would now construe meaning as wholly constituted by the author's intention, but sophisticated versions of this interest persist in the expressive, psychoanalytic, or phenomenological theories implied in the options above; and they persist especially in the various theories of point of view that have, as we have seen, descended to us from Henry James.

Yet criticism interested in a novel's end has a bias to overcome that may be even more persistent than the one that expects all meaning to issue from intention. It is this: the expectation that meaning resides at the end: at the end of the story, in the climax of the action, in the final score, on the bottom line. Of course, this presumes the conclusion of an action which is itself intrinsically meaningful. And as Frank Kermode has argued, this sense of an ending is a very fundamental one, both in biological experience and in cultural and religious belief. If it can be displaced in modern thought and narrative to a sense of perpetual crisis, immanent in the middle, it cannot be wholly forgotten or abandoned.[14] That the end is now everywhere (and, therefore, of course, nowhere as well) also implies what a reader interested in the end has as her options: to transfer the end to a point, a source of value and meaning, "outside" the text, or to relocate the end back in the middle. In *Reading for the Plot*, Peter Brooks finds the "end" of all

12. Edward W. Said, *Beginnings: Intention and Method* (Baltimore, 1975), 82–83.

13. See Scholes, *Structuralism in Literature*, 24–25.

14. Frank Kermode, *The Sense of an Ending: Studies in the Theory of Fiction* (London, 1979), 25–26.

narrative plotting in the master plot of Freud's *Beyond the Pleasure Principle;* but his argument obviously depends on the non-novelistic value of Freudian theory and responds more to questions about why we narrate stories rather than to what a novel's narrative is.[15] In *The Form of Victorian Fiction,* J. Hillis Miller follows a similar strategy; his outside value is a phenomenological conscious- ness, a kind of disembodied universal mind, that hovers above the text's middle, mediates the author, the characters, and the readers, and becomes a transcen- dent center.[16] And Alan Friedman, like Frank Kermode but without his cultural or theological perspective, relocates the novel's final values back in the middle, in aesthetic terms that define the open-endedness of novels by Hardy, Conrad, and Lawrence. In Friedman's scheme of things, the end of the novel, in every sense, becomes experience itself, and more experience, in a world without end, in narratives that resist any kind of closure supposedly common in the nineteenth century. Consequently, formal openness, like social alienation, has become as much a feature of modern novels as closure and comic incorporation seemed to be of earlier novels.[17]

On the other hand, criticism that moves the end to another point outside the text (Jakobson's receiver or the reader herself) can do so in several ways: it can emphasize the moral or didactic utility of the work, as Augustan, Victorian, and Marxist theorists have; or it can emphasize the affective quality of the work and its narrow relation to the reader personally—as a species of Romantic sincerity in reverse;[18] or it can emphasize the broader rhetorical aspects of the work and its relation to all reading—a strategy that is a feature now of postmodernism. This last move can become very complex, as we have seen it demonstrated in *S/Z;* but making the reader responsible for the meaning of the work does not put the end of the narrative entirely outside itself. For this strategy also seems to relocate the reader, then, back into the middle with the codes and contexts, devices and locutions of the work that is a text like herself. The meaning the reader makes arises from her participation *here,* not from her autonomous fiat.

15. Peter Brooks, *Reading For the Plot: Design and Intention in Narrative* (New York, 1984), chapter 4.

16. J. Hillis Miller, *The Form of Victorian Fiction* (Notre Dame, 1968). Miller's *Ariadne's Thread: Story Lines* (New Haven, 1992) offers a completely different theory of narrative (decon- structive rather than phenomenological) and a measure of how things have changed.

17. Alan Friedman, *The Turn of the Novel: The Transition to Modern Fiction* (London, 1966), chapter 2. See for contrast D. A. Miller, *Narrative and Its Discontents: Problems of Closure in the Traditional Novel* (Princeton, 1981). Miller's category of "narratability," as opposed to Friedman's "experience," grounds his argument in completely different theoretical principles of language but works toward the same effect; it also measures how things have changed.

18. See Lionel Trilling, *Beyond Culture* (New York, 1965), 3–27, for his view of how his students put modernist literature into their own lives.

Novelists themselves have always recognized hcw problematic endings can be. Part I of *Don Quixote* stops in haste and uncertainty; *Tristram Shandy* seems to end accidentally, short of the number of volumes Sterne had projected, with a joke, of course, against itself; and even if Knightley's move to Hartfield is Oedipally appropriate and agreeably kind, Austen knows, as do we, that it is preposterous. George Eliot once wrote: "Conclusions are the weak point of most authors, but some of the fault lies in the very nature of a conclusion, which is at best a negation."[19] And E. M. Forster says in *Aspects of the Novel:* "If it was not for death and marriage I do not know how the average novelist would conclude. Death and marriage are almost his only connection between his characters and his plot, and the reader is more ready to meet him here, and take a bookish view of them, provided they occur later in the book."[20] Stronger even than Eliot's implication that narrative is endless, and conclusion no part of it, is Forster's that character and plot have nothing to do with each other, except in those acts that close a novel conventionally. Action that seems meaningful in itself, like the action of a game or a musical performance, is not hard to end; but in novelistic narrative no action is meaningful in itself, so it is very hard to end a novel because interpretation, like Jamesian relationships, can exfoliate forever.[21]

But another way of construing this is: The action essential to novelistic narrative is the act of interpretation, embodied in a character, so a novel can "end" when a character's interpretation, which is not all interpretation, is "complete." For instance, *Pride and Prejudice* may "end" at the point at which Elizabeth Bennet discovers her identity, which she does *before* she marries Darcy. We have known from very early on that she will marry him. The question has been, how will she discover that she wants to; and although her marriage seems like a reward for her self-knowledge, even in *Pride and Prejudice,* marriage isn't always so. For Charlotte Lucas discovers who she is in her decision to marry Mr. Collins. There are also novels that can end as the hero discovers his vocation, as Stephen Dedalus does; his "reward" seems to be his new status as an author, for the diary he writes becomes the final pages of the novel Joyce himself had begun. Still, Stephen's fictional fate leaves a great deal about him unsaid and the expectations of the undistanced reader unfulfilled. Many have

19. George Eliot, quoted in A. S. Byatt's introduction to *The Mill on the Floss* (Harmondsworth, 1979), 36.

20. E. M. Forster, *Aspects of the Novel* (New York, 1955), 95.

21. Henry James, *The Art of the Novel,* ed. R. P. Blackmur (New York, 1962), 5: "Really, universally, relations stop nowhere, and the exquisite problem of the artist is eternally but to draw, by a geometry of his own, the circle within which they shall happily *appear* to do so."

assumed that Stephen grows up to be Joyce, but what really happens to him is that another version of his life is developed in another novel. For all its finish as an artifact, as a life *A Portrait* is still incomplete, and its incompleteness is worth remarking for at least three reasons. One, novels, by generic definition, resist generic prescriptions, such as when and how to end. Two, one of the reasons they resist formalist prescriptions is that they are committed to dealing with human experience in time, which means dealing with change, which has no end. And, three, language is always open to still another interpretation. Moreover, Joyce was not unaware of the novelists before him who projected or translated a character from one novel to another. They include, among others, Cervantes, James Fenimore Cooper, Balzac, Trollope, Zola, Arthur Conan Doyle, and Conrad. Since then, Galsworthy, Lawrence, Proust, Woolf, Faulkner, John Barth, Philip Roth, John Updike, Larry McMurtry, Raymond Chandler, and Thomas Pynchon have all done it, too. The centrality of this list to the novel's tradition suggests that the novel favors the middle: not the concentration of authority in a narrator, nor the distillation of a meaning in the finality of an end, but what lies in the middle and is the field on which the beginning's efficacy is tested, the end's aptness measured, and their relationship to each other negotiated, questioned, and kept open.

> We must begin *wherever we are* and the thought of the trace, which cannot take the scent into account, has already taught us that it was impossible to justify a point of departure absolutely. *Wherever we are:* in a text where we already believe ourselves to be.
> —Jacques Derrida, *Of Grammatology*

Middles do not usually have the salience of beginnings and ends. They can, however, become centers—principles of meaning, points around which structures rise and stand, like tent poles. Since we will be talking about middles from now on, it is perhaps best to begin by illustrating a few of the ways middles can become centers and dominate, determine, burden, or even "distort" a novel's narrative. Themes are of the middle, and themes can come to dominate both action and character when they take on a value or interest in themselves. This can happen in formulaic novels, in novels with a great deal of "extraliterary" action, in books that offer specialized information. We know that Sherlock Holmes and Hercule Poirot will solve their cases without learning much more about themselves; the centers of their novels are not the education of self-knowledge but the theme of detection. We also know that Henry Miller is likely

to leaven his treatises on cosmic freedom with a lot of fornication, so we bring
to him a different appetite than we bring to Nietzsche's works on freedom. We
may also read the novels of James Michener because we are more interested in
Hawaii or Texas than we are in novels. But there is always Balzac, and his *Lost
Illusions* is to the point.

If we set *Lost Illusions* (1837–1843) between Stendhal's *Scarlet and Black*
(1830) and Flaubert's *Sentimental Education* (1869), we see it clearly as a novel
of the young man from the provinces, with all of the type's obligatory elements:
sexual enthrallment with an older woman; the intimate connection between sex
and ambition; the attack ambition mounts against the reactionary bourgeoisie;
the hero's subsequent need for a father surrogate; his disillusion and, usually,
his failure. Lucien Chardon's failure to become a poet receives this telling
epitaph: "He's not a poet," says the lawyer Petit-Claud, "he's a serial novel."
Not transformed, in other words, just To Be Continued. And throughout the
middle of Lucien's serial ordeals is Balzac's lengthy exposition of the journalism
trade and printing industry he himself failed at before he became a novelist.
Four of the chapters in Part II explicitly anatomize the five varieties of publisher
Balzac has distinguished; and at one tender point in their early relationship,
Lucien's sister Eve Chardon and his best friend David Sechard are interrupted
by Balzac with this passage:

> At a question from Eve, who had no idea what pulp was, David
> gave her some information about paper-making which will not be out
> of place in a work which owes its very existence as much to paper
> as to the printing press: but no doubt this long digression between
> the two lovers will be better for being summarized.

At this point, you can almost hear Balzac draw a deep breath.

> Paper, which is no less wonderful a product than printing, of
> which it is the basis, had long been in existence in China when it
> penetrated through underground channels of commerce to Asia Mi-
> nor where, about 750 A.D., . . .

And so on, until he ventures this theory of language, which is his version of the
relationship between print and writing: "This rapid glance amply demonstrates
that all the great advances due to man's ingenuity and intelligence were only
achieved exceedingly slowly and by means of imperceptible accretions, just as
Nature proceeds. In order to reach perfection, writing and perhaps language

itself passed through the same groping stages as typography and paper-making."[22]

The novel has always recognized a generic obligation to record social history, and an emphasis on this responsibility feeds right into its naturally critical bias, its utility throughout the nineteenth century as a reformer's platform, the development of an eventually more sophisticated naturalism, and then muckraking novels about meat-packing plants. Moreover, the discrepancy between the economic motives of journalism and the higher aspirations of poetry is an easy mark for the romantic novel; it may not be as interesting as the theme potentially there in the opposition between printing and writing which haunted Mark Twain after the failure of the Paige typesetting machine bankrupted him, but it is not as untoward in itself as the bulk of its development in *Lost Illusions* suggests. The bildungsroman of Lucien Chardon, who would like to transform himself into Lucien de Rubempré, could be told, however, without all the facts Balzac accrues that Stendhal and Flaubert found unnecessary. They, of course, have their own subsidiary thematic interests: Napoleon's legacy and grand opera, in Stendhal's case; the culture and politics of the generation of 1840, in Flaubert's.

Without facts and interests like Balzac's, the middle of a novel can also become a center by establishing in itself some kind of aesthetic value. Repetition and symmetry, reversal and concordance are aspects of interpretation, not properties of fictional raw material. Therefore, when the middle of *Tom Jones* becomes too well-done by the overheated events at Upton, the novel moves away from realistic plotting, which favors shapelessness, toward farce and romance. Fielding's virtuosity in these episodes points directly to the bias he has toward his characters, which makes *Tom Jones* seem not quite a modern novel in the way that Richardson's novels are. For it is nothing Fielding's characters *do* that establishes their virtue; it is what they *are* in Fielding's godlike disposition of them to begin with. The characters are a part of nature, rather than of history, so they remain immutable in their essences. It is as impossible for Tom to do something irredeemable as it is for Blifil to be selfless.

In the melodramatic romance plot of *An American Dream,* Norman Mailer displays the same kind of disposition toward his own characters as Fielding has toward his, although Mailer seems to make at least his hero Rojack part of a super-nature. Rojack's successive conquests of his wife Deborah, Ruta the spying maid, and Cherry the Mafia singer, as well as his triumph over Shago Martin, which delivers him the talismanic umbrella, turn out to match the conquests of Deborah's incestuous father, the politically powerful Barney Os-

22. Honoré de Balzac, *Lost Illusions*, trans. Herbert J. Hunt (Harmondsworth, 1971), 665, 107–109.

wald Kelly. In fulfilling this unanticipated pattern and in winning the test he undertakes as he walks a penthouse parapet, Rojack acquires power himself, by which he is able to resist Kelly, elude the Mafia, and get away with murder. When he lights out for the Central American territory and wins enough money in Las Vegas to stake him for a long time, he stops at a desert phone booth and calls Cherry and Marilyn Monroe in heaven. From the earlier phone calls Rojack has made to his television producer and department head, it is clear that Mailer has perfect pitch for certain kinds of realism and dialogue. But *An American Dream*, as its central correspondences suggest, is not intended to be a completely realistic novel.

It is not, however, an anomaly. Its title links it to Dreiser's naturalistic masterpiece *An American Tragedy;* its allusion in the first paragraph to Fitzgerald's "A Diamond as Big as the Ritz" puts it in the tradition of self-conscious American romance; and Mailer explores the formal tensions between these two narrative modes. *An American Dream* is a characteristic contemporary novel because it exacerbates realistic equilibrium and pushes its top and bottom boundaries up toward romance and down toward naturalism. More important, there are no other characters in the book who have an interpretation of its world that can compete with Rojack's. So he becomes superior both to the novel's other figures and to the world it defines, and his romantic self-conception becomes his resistance to that world's naturalistic occlusion and hostility.

The fact that he is the narrator of *An American Dream* gives Rojack another advantage. Tom Jones cannot be aware of the symmetry of the events at Upton. This symmetry becomes a center and establishes a value—Augustan harmony and counterpoint—that has no psychological relation to Tom's character, no agency in his motivation. The symmetry Fielding creates is a part of *Tom Jones*'s structure, which we have defined broadly as those related aspects of a novel's organization that its characters cannot be aware of. Most obvious is the fact that they are in a novel, so their relationships exist within a closure, or under a focus, much sharper and more exclusive than the world's. Because Rojack is aware of the occult symmetries that surround him, he is romantically privileged (although sometimes afraid he's a paranoid lunatic—like Oedipa Maas in *The Crying of Lot 49*). And his narrative perspective also means that the center of *An American Dream* need not be the melodramatic coincidences of the plot, but is Rojack's consciousness, which has been primed by his professional interest as an existential psychologist in dread, death, and magic. An emphasis on Rojack's consciousness makes Mailer's novel somewhat more conventional, for it places it in the mainstream of modernist fiction with the books of Joyce, Woolf, Lawrence, Proust, and Faulkner that are centered both in consciousness and in the nature of internalized time.

About time, in his *Lectures on Russian Literature*, Vladimir Nabokov says of Tolstoy: "What really seduces the average reader is the gift Tolstoy had of endowing his fiction with such time values as correspond exactly to our sense of time. . . . This time balance, absolutely peculiar to Tolstoy alone, is what gives the gentle reader that sense of average reality which he is apt to ascribe to Tolstoy's keen vision. Tolstoy's prose keeps pace with our pulses, his characters seem to move with the same swing as the people passing under our window while we sit reading his book."[23] Nabokov then discusses Joyce and Proust, comparing them unfavorably to Tolstoy, but he is never entirely convincing. Tolstoy's prose may keep pace with Nabokov's pulse, but it is the prose of the Lestrygonians chapter in *Ulysses* that keeps pace with mine—except on warmer days when it is the prose of the first chapter of *Light in August*. And I am sure there are those whose hearts beat at Mrs. Dalloway's pace as she steps out to shop for her party. There are even readers, I'm sure, who move at Rojack's fevered speed, and when they do, they locate in this theme of time still another center of *An American Dream*, with the patterned plot, the test of realism, Rojack's point of view and rhetoric, the power theme, the incest theme, the paranoia theme.

The middle of a novel may become a center of value and meaning by any of these means: a narrative shape, a certain theme, a specific strategy, a special interest; and centers, as we have seen, can be as difficult to pin down as beginnings and ends because they can be as fluid and mutable, as finally indeterminate. But all three of them provide an access of meaning to any narrative, give a narrative its plurality of meanings, and remain interpenetrating. None we have mentioned so far, however, is specific to the novel. A beginning, middle, and end is common to all narrative. What sets the novel's narrative apart, what distinguishes it as the novel, is the presence of several characters throughout the narrative's course who are themselves free to interpret their world in an authoritative way, who are in fact principles of interpretation themselves. The nature of the realistic character as interpreter we will examine at length in the next chapter; the nature of the realistic world as interpretable, in the chapter after that. What we have left to explore here is how the narrative of the novel deploys its characters so that they can make their interpretations, how it keeps the middle open and free of any central or *final* element that would end interpretation by taking it away from the characters themselves.

23. Vladimir Nabokov, *Lectures on Russian Literature* (New York, 1981), 141–42.

A novel makes meaning, I have argued, as a sentence does, by the constant play of the syntagmatic narrative line against the paradigmatic structures that the narrative develops; in other words, the line of action plays against the internal possibilities of its interpretation. As Barthes says in his "Introduction to the Structural Analysis of Narrative":

> From the outset, linguistics furnishes the structural analysis of narrative with a concept which is decisive in that, making explicit immediately what is essential in every system of meaning, namely its organization, it allows us to show how a narrative is not a simple sum of propositions and to classify the enormous mass of elements which go to make up a narrative. This concept is that of *level of description.* . . .
>
> . . . No level on its own can produce meaning. A unit belonging to a particular level only takes on meaning if it can be integrated in a higher level; a phoneme, though perfectly describable, means nothing in itself: it participates in meaning only when integrated in a word, and the word itself must in turn be integrated in a sentence. The theory of levels (as set out by Benveniste) gives us two types of relations: distributional (if the relations are situated on the same level) and integrational (if they are grasped from one level to the next); consequently, distributional relations alone are not sufficient to account for meaning. In order to conduct a structural analysis, it is thus first of all necessary to distinguish several levels or instances of description and to place these instances within a hierarchical (integrational) perspective. . . .
>
> . . . But however many levels are proposed and whatever definitions they are given, there can be no doubt that narrative is a hierarchy of instances. To understand a narrative is not merely to follow the unfolding of a story, it is also to recognize construction in "storeys," to project the horizontal concatenations of the narrative "thread" on to an implicitly vertical axis; to read (to listen to) a narrative is not merely to move from one word to the next, it is also to move from one level to the next.[24]

I want to adapt to Barthes's formulation a different concept of the basic unit of a novel's narrative. This unit is not the sentence; it is not an action, or a change

---

24. Barthes, *Image/Text/Music*, 85, 86, 87. See also Tzvetan Todorov, *The Poetics of Prose*, trans. Richard Howard (Ithaca, 1977), 24.

in a state of equilibrium; it is not a formalized actant or existent. The basic unit of the novel is *the character*. As we have also seen already, classical structuralist theorists of narrative at first tried to demote character to the level of a function in the narrative action, but these theorists tended to work with traditional materials rather than with the novel. Their formalism also tended toward the correlative belief in narrative's "versionless version," which exists in itself and constitutes, in effect, its own interpretation, and needs no characters to interpret it from within. By the time Barthes wrote *S/Z*, his commitment to "the infinite paradigm of difference" and the *"scriptible"* text allowed character to make a comeback, staged on the code of the "symbolic," as another site of semic intersection and, therefore, of interpretation, too.[25] Consequently, if we consider each individual character a potentially authoritative interpreter of its whole fictional world, we can say, as Barthes himself does, that each character constitutes a *level of description*[26]—or in Hayden White's terms, another level of *discourse*—and integrating that character into another level means bringing that one character into relationship with another character and eventually, in fact, with *all* the other characters in a novel. As a character acts itself out through space and time, in the specified locale that is its metonymic extension, and in the process of change that is its historical life; as it moves forward along the line of narrative action, it must also move through the network of relationships with other characters that most novels (but not all) set up. When these relationships are then integrated, when they are placed, that is, within an arrangement dependent on the values that each novel itself privileges and defines, they then constitute what I think of as the novel's always open middle—the paradigm of its characters, with all their similarity-and-difference, who are each another separate discourse.

Let me step ahead of myself here and make some preliminary remarks about the nature of character, which I will explore at greater length in the next chapter. In the ontology of language, a character is a sign—a sign to read, and to read other signs with. It need not be construed only as a psychological entity, substantialized to stand self-contained and independent. For "character," like "individual," is a term of *relation;* and characters, like letters of the alphabet, have significance only in combination with other signs, letters, characters. A novelistic character, therefore, is also legible as a kind of *discourse* because character stands not simply for its own interpretive ability but also for the possibility, in fact the need, of other, complementary interpretations, too: the

25. Barthes, *S/Z*, 3, 4, 67–68.
26. Barthes, *Image/Music/Text*, 105.

whole cast of characters necessary to spell out the world and have it realistically open to other phrasing, another "characterization."

To illustrate some of these points, I want to take another look at *Pride and Prejudice.* Its theme of marriage novelists have acknowledged as almost universal because it so obviously involves society's own structures and values, the participation of happy and unhappy families, the play of each individual's psychology, and comic plots that allow Austen to give her fairly simple stories a structure that is usually complex and often, in her mature novels, seemingly exhaustive. A paradigm of the meaning of the marriage theme in *Pride and Prejudice* might look like this:

Elizabeth	Darcy
Jane	Bingley
The Gardiners	
Charlotte	Collins
The Bennets	
Lydia	Wickham

Elizabeth and Darcy eventually make the best marriage in the book, for great intelligence allows each of them to correct pride and prejudice in the other, which assures us that they will then conduct their public life as responsibly as they do their private relationship. Their status, intelligence, and force of character distinguish them from Jane and Bingley, who are both handsome and nice, and in love at first sight, but who do not have the strength and wit Elizabeth and Darcy have. The worst marriage seems to be the one between Lydia and Wickham. He is dishonest and opportunistic, she is stupid and romantic. Their relationship represents the disaster of joining heedless ambition to appetite. The Bennets' marriage probably began in something like this same heedlessness, and in his want of a son. Their five handsome daughters suggest that Mrs. Bennet's physical gifts at one time persuaded her husband that beauty was more important than compatibility, and what Austen calls Mr. Bennet's reserve and caprice suggest that his wife's "mean understanding" and nerves have not been the only cause of their estrangement.

The middle level of this paradigm is more interesting because of the different questions involved in ranking the couples or in integrating them in the novel's scheme of values. The Gardiners, for instance, play an important role as surrogate parents and mediators, and theirs is a good marriage. But the Gardiners do not belong to the aristocracy as Darcy does, and they are not members of the country gentry, as Elizabeth is. Gardiner is in business in London. This paradigm, therefore, does not simply reflect a rigid social hierarchy; if it did, Darcy's most compatible partner would have to be Lady Catherine. What it does reflect is a social order in transition: Elizabeth does not consider Lady Catherine's rank an absolute moral privilege; Austen does not disqualify the Gardiners simply because he works for a living. In fact, this paradigm calls our attention to Austen's belief that a woman like Elizabeth can transcend the accident of her birth, so it also calls our attention to the situation of Charlotte Lucas. She makes the best marriage she thinks she can. She is not a romantic fool like Lydia, nor as attractive and lucky as Jane; she obviously does not think she has as much time left as Kitty and Mary do; and she knows that Collins is a fool. Is Charlotte, therefore, to be commended for her prudence, or pitied for her bad luck, or scolded for her haste? And depending on the answer we give, her marriage may well be inferior to the Bennets', as the Gardiners' may well be superior to Bingley and Jane's. In any case, the *meaning* of marriage in *Pride and Prejudice* is not simple because Austen is so thorough, within what seems like narrow bounds, that the points of view she makes possible in her characters are quite distinct. The paradigm represents many different possible interpretations of the state of marriage that all the characters would otherwise agree is socially useful, personally desirable, and for the women economically necessary.

A paradigm, as I have said, is a scheme or diagram that represents the simultaneous similarity-and-difference among the members of a set, the characters of a novel; and it can often be hierarchical in the sense that it organizes individuals into relationships according to the themes and values that the particular novel develops. But not every paradigm will look the same because not every novel develops the same values, and even the same values may have a different relationship to each other in a different novel. In *Wuthering Heights*, which is also about country marriages, the heroic central relationship between Cathy and Heathcliff looks more like the romance between Lydia and Wickham than the relationship of Elizabeth to Darcy, which structurally resembles the marriage Cathy makes with Linton. And even in Austen's own *Emma*, the values of *Pride and Prejudice* are altered somewhat by the presence of different kinds of characters.

Emma's central paradigm can best be diagrammed with the couples along a continuum, rather than up and down a ladder:

| Miss Bates | Harriet | Emma | Jane | Augusta Hawkins |
| Mr. Woodhouse | Robert Martin | Knightley | Churchill | Mr. Elton |

Miss Bates is an aged spinster and Augusta Hawkins the book's *femme fatale;* but they are both foils of Emma and essentially flat characters. Miss Bates is ineffectual and seems silly; Augusta is pompous and self-important; Emma patronizes Miss Bates and is patronized herself by Augusta. But Emma does not see, at least at first, her real relation to either. Emma could have become something like a Miss Bates if she had remained satisfied with her own relationship to Miss Bates's structural counterpart, Mr. Woodhouse—who is silly but, fortunately for him, male and rich. And the social power Augusta Hawkins assumes she has by virtue of her marriage to Elton is the same power Emma always assumes she herself has, which is the power Elton seeks in proposing to her first. Harriet and Jane are fuller characters, closer to Emma in every way. They are alike because they are both disestablished—Harriet is a bastard, Jane an orphan, and both are economically vulnerable. Whereas Harriet is Emma's protégée and clear inferior, Jane is Emma's real rival and not personally inferior at all. She seems, in fact, more intelligent and mature, as does even Harriet when she falls in love with Mr. Knightley after Emma has thwarted her love for Robert Martin and driven Elton off. Emma cannot imagine Harriet in love with Knightley, just as she cannot imagine Frank Churchill *not* in love with her. Emma deceives herself about both Harriet's simplicity and Jane's sophistication. But because Knightley has never been deceived about Emma's potential, everyone is paired off happily at the end. Knightley is surer of Martin's virtue than he is of Frank's, which helps the reader, and only Austen herself indicates the pairing of Miss Bates and Mr. Woodhouse. They are an appropriate couple in another way, however, for through them Austen makes another important point: in a rational world where so much is staked on conversation, both of them talk constantly without ever listening to anyone else, so neither can change, or grow into another interpretation. In this world where status is also important, Austen makes a similar point against the Eltons, who will never succeed because they have no idea of the real place they start from. And as she did with the Gardiners in *Pride and Prejudice,* so does Austen here with the marriages of Mr. and Mrs. Weston, Mr. and Mrs. Churchill, the other Knightleys, and the Campbells. These couples give *Emma* its particular sense of fullness, for their relationships play variations on the themes more completely developed in the other characters and couples; and they could be brought into the play of another broader paradigm that examined the varieties of good and bad fathers, or uxorious husbands, or the selfishness *Emma* makes into an intellectual as well as a moral problem.

The purpose of articulating the paradigms as I have so far is not to close these novels into a diagram. It is to illustrate that the intrinsic narrative structure of the realistic novel is built upon the similarity-and-difference among several separate characters who are each capable of interpreting the particular novel's world. They are not simply actants or functions in an action meaningful in itself. Each of them represents a different possible version of the novel's narrative line that generates their interrelationships; each is potentially a different mode of discourse, a way of telling the story that of itself acknowledges there are also other ways; each represents the possibility in the novel of constructing a different beginning, middle, and end; a different meaning, in other words, that constitutes a different novel. Tzvetan Todorov says in "Narrative-Men":

> Character is not always, as James claims, the determination of incident, nor does every narrative consist of "the illustration of character." Then what *is* character? The *Arabian Nights* gives us a very clear answer, which is repeated and confirmed by *The Saragossa Manuscript:* a character is a potential story that is the story of his life. Every new character signifies a new plot. We are in the realm of narrative-men.
>
> This phenomenon profoundly affects the structure of narrative.

"Every new character signifies a new plot" is Todorov's way of saying what I try to in proposing that every character is another discourse.

Todorov himself, however, goes on to discuss the implications of his position in terms of the syntactical figure of subordination that linguists call *embedding*. This is a principle not unrelated to the principles Barthes explains as distribution and integration. An embedded narrative is one that comes within the middle of another larger one that encloses it; one of Todorov's examples is the "story of Oedipus: at the beginning a prediction, at the end its fulfillment, between the two the attempts to evade it." In "Narrative-Men" he continues:

> But what is the internal significance of embedding, why are all these means assembled to give it so much emphasis? The structure of narrative provides the answer: embedding is an articulation of the most essential property of all narrative. For the embedding narrative is the *narrative of a narrative*. By telling the story of another narrative, the first narrative achieves its fundamental theme and at the same time is reflected in this image of itself. . . . To be the narrative of a

narrative is the fate of all narrative which realizes itself through embedding.[27]

Although traditional novels do not usually embed other narratives in themselves as boldly as the *Arabian Nights* and *Don Quixote* do, novels do embed narratives in more than merely the potentiality of another character's interpretation. Marlow's account of Lord Jim is embedded in the anonymous narrator's story of Jim's youth, accident, and encounter with Marlow; so is Marlow's account of Kurtz, which depends on the embedding frame narrator to serve as audience, too; and as these two novels suggest, the modern novels that do self-consciously embed one narrative in another are often those most self-conscious of the narrative perspectives that dissolve the authority of its single, traditional narrator to distribute consciousness through many characters. The novels that eschew embedding seem to be those given to the isolation or narcissism of the central character, who is very often the narrator, with only himself to explore. And while this is an equally modernist mark, these are not the only routes embedding takes, for some of the most interesting experiments are those which make it difficult to distinguish between figure and ground, the embedded and embedding. Most of *Light in August,* for instance, seems to be enclosed in the saga of Lena Grove, seen first and last on the road, although her story is much shorter than the stories of Joe Christmas and Gail Hightower. And in *Absalom, Absalom!* is Sutpen's story embedded in Quentin's, or is it the other way around? Is there any embedding at all in *As I Lay Dying*? Or is Addie the narrator who embeds everything? The same questions arise from *The Alexandria Quartet.* Yet as soon as we start to question more traditional novels, we see easily the force of Todorov's claim that embedding is "an articulation of the essential property of all narrative." It is so in Twain's stories of Tom Sawyer and Huck Finn as well as throughout Proust's stories of Swann and Charlus; in the story of Magwitch embedded in Pip's and the story of Zossima embedded in the Karamazovs'; in Vautrin's story, which is embedded in both *Père Goriot* and *Lost Illusions;* in the Man of the Hill's story in *Tom Jones;* in "my uncle Toby's" story in *Tristram Shandy,* where the narrator himself plays with the notion of embedding as a *regressus ad absurdam* (see, for instance, the end of chapter 10 in volume I).

In even this quick survey, we can see that traditional novels lie naturally open to extension through another point of view, another character's discourse. And this leads to interesting questions. What, for instance, would Emma's story

---

27. Todorov, *Poetics of Prose,* 70, 72, 21, 72–73. See also Kermode, *Genesis of Secrecy,* chapter 4, for a clear, elegant confirmation of Todorov's argument.

be if the novel she inhabits were named, more appropriately perhaps, *Jane* and told through Austen's namesake, who is handsome, clever, and poor? *Jane Eyre?* And what would happen in *Anna Karenina* if it had been written by a woman, or to Tertius Lydgate if *Middlemarch* had been written by a man and Dorothea's story embedded in his? No doubt the ever-magisterial Tolstoy would have found a way to be as compassionate of Lydgate as he is of Levin; and Eliot, who often sounds as though she is *inventing* compassion, could have invented a way to save Anna's life as she saves Dorothea's. These are not really trivial questions, or exercises for a literary parlor game; for if they do nothing else, they expose our almost overwhelming investment in the idea and authority of the narrator's point of view, and the comforting sense of unity or formal integrity which comes from its control and which seems to assure a novel's *inevitability*. Yet as soon as we accept the principle that the meaning of realistic narrative arises essentially from the play of the narrative line through the perspectives of the characters in the paradigm, then we also have to give up the great privilege we have accorded the narrator, who is formally necessary nonetheless. For this narrator, even if it is "Tolstoy" himself, is simply another character attached to the story, another point of view, another discourse that contains ample evidence that there are possibilities besides itself, that nothing is *inevitable* in narrative.

In *Friday's Footprint,* Wesley Morris formulates what he calls "the first law of plot structure: *that no narrative can be allowed to undercut the immediacy and independence of the incidents that comprise the narrative as a coherent whole.*" He goes on to explain this principle by saying: "The parts are always more than the whole in the sense that the presence of an individual incident implies that there is more than what is being presented."[28] I would amend this only by deleting "incident," to make it read: "the presence of an individual [that is, a character] implies that there is more than what is being presented." And it is the presence of other characters, who are not the narrator or protagonist, that can keep the middle of a novel from becoming a center—a center that is closed and exhaustive as a principle of value or meaning. The paradigms I am proposing as the distinguishing feature of realistic narrative in the novel constantly display the similarity-and-difference of these characters, and these paradigms translate into narrative terms the most important principle Saussure has given us: meaning does not arise from concepts of substance and individual identity; meaning arises out of difference itself, out of the constant, arbitrary, never-stabilizing differentiation of one thing from another. Derrida's explicit

28. Wesley Morris, *Friday's Footprint: Structuralism and the Articulated Text* (Columbus, 1979), 60.

transformation of this linguistic principle into a principle of ontology is of similar importance. When presence is no longer taken for granted and no longer guaranteed, origins, centers, and ends become certainly problematic and probably impossible to define absolutely.

The novel, as Lowry Nelson explains it, begins to articulate its own notion of irreconcilable difference the moment Sancho Panza joins Don Quixote and brings his demystification into play against the Don's idealizations, for Sancho the servant is always his master's equal under the sign of irony.[29] Moreover, Sancho's presence and authority also indicate how Cervantes himself is collusive in "the death of the author"—a fact we will examine more thoroughly in chapter 4, when we look at all his attempts to write himself out of the story of the Don, to distribute his authority among other narrators, extrapersonal sources, and narrative strategies. To claim now that Cervantes and his novel have anticipated some of the features of poststructuralist thought is not to obviate Barthes and Derrida as redundant, but simply to claim again that the novel has been a restless and prophetic mode of modern consciousness since its inception. And the open possibility of interpretation that the novel allows us, we understand to be implicit in the novel's characters and the play of their relationships. These paradigms of simultaneous similarity-and-difference are structurally intrinsic to the novel; we can even argue that they are its "natural" mode of organization. And with this in mind, I think, it is easier to understand the full impact of George Levine's claim: "Realistic plotting begins to break down the simple distinction between self and other at the same time as it thematically asserts, in the form of disenchantment, the necessity to understand the difference between the self and other."[30] As Derrida says: writing, of all kinds, fosters "a prodigious expansion of the power of difference."[31]

The five-term paradigm of linguistic codes that Barthes uses in *S/Z* is the most recently famous heuristic laid on the novel; and Barthes's codes operate in an appropriate syntagmatic-paradigmatic fashion, with the proairetic and hermeneutic codes forming along the line of sequence, and the reversible semantic,

29. Lowry Nelson Jr., "Introduction," in *Cervantes: A Collection of Critical Essays,* ed. Lowry Nelson Jr. (Englewood Cliffs, N.J., 1969), 4.

30. George Levine, *The Realistic Imagination: English Fiction from Frankenstein to Lady Chatterley* (Chicago, 1981), 147.

31. Jacques Derrida, *Of Grammatology,* trans. Gayatri Chakravorty Spivak (Baltimore, 1976), 131.

cultural, and symbolic codes up the axis of substitution.[32] But Barthes's particular paradigm is not the first, the only, or the most useful structural paradigm the novel has encouraged. In *The Structure of the Novel*, Edwin Muir uses space and time to distinguish between novels that fill the canvas with a large number of relatively shallow characters—like *Vanity Fair*—and novels that explore far fewer characters in much greater depth as they change in time—like *Pride and Prejudice*. From these types he then develops a definition of the "chronicle" novel, like *War and Peace*, that is set against a sense of time, an absolute fatality, that we would now attach to the mythic. And he finally poses the chronicle against the much more limited "period novel," which he knows already in 1928 is dying out and being replaced by new and hard-to-define novels like *Ulysses* and *Mrs. Dalloway* that are studies of character set in very detailed circumstances, but nothing at all like the Clayhanger trilogy.

Another kind of paradigm, less impersonal than Barthes's or Muir's and more laden with metaphysical values, is the triangular shape of mediated desire René Girard develops in *Deceit, Desire, and the Novel*. Whereas in theory Barthes's codes should work equally well on any novel, precisely because they are language based, Girard's paradigm works best on highly Romantic novels; and of the five writers he treats—Cervantes, Stendhal, Flaubert, Proust, and Dostoevsky—it is clearly Dostoevsky whom he best serves. In *Ulysses on the Liffey*, Richard Ellmann argues that Joyce's myth can be sorted into a fourfold, neo-medieval scheme of the literal, the ethical, the aesthetic, and finally the anagogic levels. And as I have mentioned, in an appendix he also compares and contrasts the very different schemes of the eighteen chapters Joyce provided in 1920 to Carlo Linati and then later to Stuart Gilbert. But the most fruitful paradigm Ellmann works through the text is his own scheme of triads, for it allows him to organize the chapters in groups of three as a kind of thesis, antithesis, and synthesis; and to balance the first triad against the last, and both of them together against the four triads in the much longer middle. This allows him to propose, in three sets of three propositions each, his own version of what *Ulysses* means.[33]

In *The Political Unconscious*, which he subtitles *Narrative as a Socially Symbolic Act*, Fredric Jameson alludes to the same kind of fourfold medieval scheme as he argues that all interpretation is essentially an allegorical translation of a text into the terms of a "master code," implied in the culture's reigning modes of production. His own three-tiered approach of *symbolic act, ideologeme,*

---

32. See Frank Kermode, *The Art of Telling* (Cambridge, Mass., 1985), 66.
33. Richard Ellmann, *Ulysses on the Liffey* (New York, 1972), xii–xiii, 1–2, 60–61, 124, 184–85.

and *ideology of form* he argues for by saying: "The idea is . . . that if interpretation in terms of expressive causality or of allegorical master narratives remains a constant temptation, this is because such master narratives have inscribed themselves in the texts as well as in our thinking about them; such allegorical narrative signifieds are a persistent dimension of literary and cultural texts precisely because they reflect a fundamental dimension of our collective thinking and our collective fantasies about history and reality."[34] As we have seen already, there is also Robert Scholes's schematic explanation of the historical evolution of genres that contributed to the rise of the novel, which came, he says, from the way in which satire and romance, picaresque and tragedy, and comedy and sentiment fused and informed the conception and writing of history. Scholes's useful, structural scheme is probably too formalist and not sufficiently historical for Jameson, but Scholes presents it by arguing that it is a lot more historical than what had been dominant paradigms at the time he was writing in 1974: the categories Northrop Frye develops in *Anatomy of Criticism*. Apropos of the novel in particular, Scholes wants to argue that Frye's five modes—myth, romance, high mimetic, low mimetic, and irony—are not complete, and neither are his continuous generic forms—novel, romance, confession, and anatomy.[35]

Most of these structural paradigms, which seem natural to the novel, seem more natural to some than to others. Mine, I hope, are like Barthes's: generally applicable to novels of all kinds, but especially to those that implicitly promote character as the novel's primary vehicle of meaning and mediation. It would perhaps be not of much advantage to develop such a paradigm for a novel like *The Trial*, which focuses so intensely on the protagonist's isolation and the unknowability of his fate, or for a novel like *Malone*. Beckett's basic unit, it seems, is not the character or circumstance even, but the shapely sentence that unwrites itself and the narrative. Still, it is possible to organize by similarity-and-difference novels as tight as *A Portrait of the Artist* when they are as concerned with character as Joyce is—rather than with situation, as Kafka seems to be. Joyce's novel, in fact, offers at least two very different, but fundamental paradigms of its interpretive organization. One illustrates the historical and cultural themes at stake in Stephen's attempt to discover who he is, which means in his case discovering what his unlikely names signify.

34. Fredric Jameson, *The Political Unconscious: Narrative as a Socially Symbolic Act* (Ithaca, 1981), 33, 76, 34.

35. See Scholes, *Structuralism in Literature*, 132–38; and Northrop Frye, *Anatomy of Criticism* (Princeton, 1957), 33–35, 303–14.

Stephen	*Dedalus*
Christian	pagan
Roman	Greek
priest	artist
son	father
martyr	hero
history	myth
death	flight

Paradigms like this work only across each line of binary pairs; they do not simply add up, or down, into a sum, but form a synchronic picture of some of a novel's themes or tensions. Therefore, they can reveal the "contradiction" that aligns "priest," which usually signifies a father or authority figure, with the subordinate son, who is opposed to the artist-father-hero. Signifiers like these can be attached to many different signifieds because their relationship is cultural rather than natural, and in the realistic novel it is not necessary that all oppositions be reconciled. Middles that are not allowed to become centers keep narratives open, tentative rather than conclusive, renewable instead of merely original. Stephen's portrait is not definitive, therefore, but open to the possibility of another version in *Ulysses.*

Binary oppositions like this are not hard to generate in any case,[36] but they seem more appropriate in novels where the central figure is obviously a partner in a pair of characters who are not to be reconciled in marriage. Gatsby and Nick, for instance, by the very separation of their roles into hero and narrator, dramatize *The Great Gatsby*'s fundamental exploration of the difference between action and its interpretation; for there are, even in this short novel, many other characters who would not call Gatsby great.[37] And even in novels where the central pair is sexually united, binary pairs can still illustrate important matters of differentiation. In *Jude the Obscure,* Jude and Sue represent the different

36. See Jameson, *Political Unconscious,* 114; and also Vincent B. Leitch, *Deconstructive Criticism: An Advanced Introduction* (New York, 1983), 262, who neatly satirizes this deconstructive ploy.

37. For further discussion of this point see Terrence Doody, *Confession and Community in the Novel* (Baton Rouge, 1980), 126. I also discuss the similar narrative situations in *Lord Jim* and *Absalom, Absalom!*

problems of ambition a culture can make specific to gender. In *As I Lay Dying*, Anse and Addie Bundren represent between themselves the oppositions between comedy and tragedy, the unconscious and consciousness, life and death, and two very different concepts of language. Anse's is primitive, fatalistic, metaphoric; it gives him to believe that God intended vertical things like a tree and a man to stay in place, away from the horizontal temptations to mobility that are found along a road. Addie's sense is that words have no "natural" reference, that they are arbitrarily assigned to what they can hardly "mean," and that this attachment is made by those who have had no real experience. She believes that words rise into meaninglessness and that the realities of suffering, passion, and blood remain horizontal along the roiling earth, as she does, as she lies dying. Yet her quick explanation of how and why she has had her five children is as schematic, as paradigmatic, as exposition ever gets.[38]

The champions of this kind of differentiation, however, may be the two narrators of Dickens's *Bleak House*. A paradigm of some of their differences looks like this:

General Narrator	*Esther Summerson*
male	female
third-person	first-person
centrifugal	centripetal
public	domestic
rhetorical outrage	intuitive sympathy
satire	sentiment
present tense	past tense
stasis	change
history	autobiography
impotent	efficacious

These two figures are more discrepant than, say, Rosa Coldfield and Mr. Compson in *Absalom, Absalom!* for a number of reasons: there is no third character, like Quentin, to mediate them; and they are not simply two different points of view, they are two different kinds of character. He is a construct of

38. William Faulkner, *As I Lay Dying* (New York, 1964), 34–35, 161–68.

language, a narrative function as the narrator the narration needs, the subject of the big sentence, and a bodiless voice. She, of course, is most of these things, too; but she is proposed by the novel as a character who exists outside or prior to the narrator's account, a physically imaginable figure, who writes her way in. And the *disproportion* between them is great. This disproportion, which is indicated at first by his loud outrage and her hush, sets up Dickens's test of the ratio between their modes of being, which is instructive. For although Esther has none of Jane Eyre's self-confidence that she can alter the rules of auto-biography to suit herself (which is the raison d'être of literary autobiography), she is efficacious in the *Bleak House* world in a way the general narrator can never be: he can survey the whole and lament Jo's fate, as we will see in chapter 4, but she can comfort Jo, rescue Caddy, solace Ada, assist Bucket, protect her children from a childhood like her own, and *write*.

She writes herself into being, or into being a writer (the general narrator has no such autonomy); and the status she acquires, her character as an interpreter, is quite unanticipated. If the death of the author has given new life to the reader's role, the diminution of the narrator's authority, in narratives construed as sentences, gives new importance to the characters' interpretations. Esther seems like a character wholly independent of the narrator whose novel she is in; and if she isn't exactly talking back—the novel fails to tell us who requested Esther to write, to whom she's addressed her "letters"—she is speaking out. There is no other narrative arrangement quite like this.

Another paradigm of *A Portrait of the Artist* issues from the symmetrical resolutions of its plot. Hugh Kenner calls the plot's shape chiasmatic,[39] but I would amend that slightly and call it a deep V shape, which describes Stephen's fall and subsequent rise into self-possession and flight.

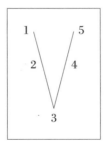

At the nadir of his story, the bottom of the V, is the end of chapter 3 when he returns out of guilt and fear to the communion and self-denying discipline of

39. Hugh Kenner, *Ulysses* (London, 1980), 69.

the Church. We can see how this descent has begun at the end of chapter 2, when he swoons, passive and fearful, into the arms of the prostitute. She represents some solution to the loneliness Stephen experiences at the end of chapter 1. But the end of chapter 2 is more importantly related to the end of chapter 4, in which he transforms the girl on the beach (in whose arms he does nothing) into a sign of his heritage and artistic vocation, as he discovers in the secular imagination the kind of power that he used to think was reserved to sacramental rite. Out of what had been a sin he makes a symbol. The end of the final chapter, therefore, finds him alone again as he was at the end of the first and third. But where he did not know how to celebrate his defiance of the school's tradition in chapter 1, or how to resist the Church's power in chapter 3, here he knows what to do with himself. His solitude here has become a deliberate strategy, and as he takes over the writing of *A Portrait* in the pages of his diary, he begins to embed at the end of this novel the beginning of another book—not *Ulysses* but his own autobiography.

As I have said already, because realistic plotting tends to be more shapeless than shapely, the middle of *Tom Jones* and the symmetrical chapters of *A Portrait* are more exceptional than not; but the difference between them is still clear, for the climactic moments of *A Portrait* are essentially related to Stephen's growth and self-knowledge, even if he is not aware of their perfect V shape. And the growth of characters in time is always one of the novel's first stories. The process of change, moreover, usually involves changing relationships, so the paradigms that can display this change as well seem to be the most satisfying and successful illustrations of a novel and its motives. Two very different novels which lend themselves to illustrating this are *The Portrait of a Lady* and *Wuthering Heights*, and they are interesting together because one seems so open at the end and the other so thoroughly closed.

One paradigm of *The Portrait of a Lady* looks like this:

Warburton		Warburton
Ralph Touchett		Ned Rosier
Mr. Touchett	Osmond	Osmond
ISABEL →		PANSY
Mrs. Touchett	Madame Merle	Isabel
Henrietta Stackpole		Princess Gemini
Goodwood		Goodwood

When Isabel arrives at Gardencourt, she is surrounded by various people interested in her future. Mr. and Mrs. Touchett are important because they illustrate how a bad marriage can be managed civilly. James seems to favor Mr. Touchett over his wife, however, because of Mr. Touchett's closeness to Ralph, who is the novel's exemplar of *appreciation*. He is as unselfishly interested in Isabel's future as Henrietta is, but he is not ridiculous. For although Henrietta is important as an American girl herself, and as a woman of independence, she is the kind of healthy animal toward whom James often commends our condescension. The men, with their British interests and refinement, promote the suit of Lord Warburton, a slightly less healthy animal than Caspar Goodwood, the American whose cause the women espouse.

Isabel rejects all of them and begins to choose her own future as she moves into the orbit of Madame Merle, apparently a woman of independence herself, and an American, and also the partner in another well-managed bad "marriage." Although she might be said to resemble for these reasons both Mrs. Touchett and Henrietta, Merle is pitched in a finer tone. She is also a successful matchmaker. Yet Isabel's marriage to Osmond does not fulfill the paradigm and bring the story to some kind of closure, as it would have in an Austen comedy. In the novel's second half, Pansy replaces Isabel in the role of the ingenue whose uncertain future is at stake. The roles of Warburton and Goodwood do not essentially change: they remain unsuccessful suitors. But Isabel's relation to Pansy casts her in something like the role formerly played by Mrs. Touchett, and we find in the Princess Gemini as apt and unexpected a correlative as Henrietta has been. Osmond acquires something like the position Mr. Touchett once had, and Ned Rosier is now the young man full of appreciation that Ralph had been. The way this paradigm can be seen to dramatize the changes the major characters have undergone also suggests that in James's major novels the future can never be entirely anticipated. Everything is inscribed under the signs of time and change, and even elegantly symmetrical structures remain open to endless interpretation. This is no more clearly apparent than in the very different meanings that can be attributed to Isabel's return to Osmond. He will see it in a different light than Pansy will; Gemini will probably not find Goodwood's hopes plausible; and Rosier will perhaps have more reason to hope at this point than Warburton has.

There is no such openness and difference at the end of *Wuthering Heights,* for what its central paradigm reveals is an order to time and change that can only be attributed to Brontë's theme of incest and the unity to which incest tends to reduce difference. *Wuthering Heights* is a romance, in Frye's terms, as much as it is a novel in the broader terms of the general nineteenth-century syllabus; but it is clearly more committed to the symmetries of romance and its values than it is to the novel's more "shapeless" realism. One of its paradigms looks like this, but it is not a scheme of characters who are free to interpret their lives and the lives of others who are part of them.[40]

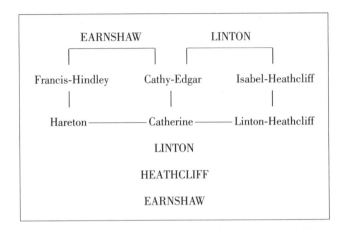

The center of the story is not in the plot's rigid temporal ordination,[41] nor is it fully located in the play of meaning across the differences between Nellie Dean's point of view and Lockwood's, as the story unfolds. Brontë makes relatively little of the possibilities inherent in a completely unsympathetic narrator's acquisition of the story from another who has been a part of it all her life. Lockwood, in other words, is not Shreve McCannon, and the contribution of Zillah the maid is almost unnoticeable.[42] By the end of the novel, when more people have died than usually do in novels three times its length, Catherine Linton, the daughter of Edgar and Cathy Earnshaw Linton, has been married both to her cousin Linton Heathcliff and to her other cousin Hareton Earnshaw. Since she begins as a Linton, she can marry a Heathcliff without committing the "incest" her mother would have committed in marrying Heathcliff herself. Then she can marry Hareton Earnshaw and return to the point at which her mother began, closing the circle, and reducing all the family possibilities to herself: Catherine

40. For the contrasting paradigms of *Wuthering Heights*, see Jameson, *Political Unconscious*, 127; and Dorothy Van Ghent, *The English Novel: Form and Function* (New York, 1961), 156. (Critics with different values and intentions, obviously, create different paradigms from the same material.)

41. See Charles Percy Sanger, "The Structure of *Wuthering Heights*," in Emily Brontë, *Wuthering Heights*, ed. William M. Sale Jr. (2nd ed.; New York, 1972), 286–98.

42. For the best account of why Brontë does not exploit these potential characterological perspectives, see Jay Clayton, *Romantic Vision and the Novel* (Cambridge, U.K., 1987), chapter 4.

Linton Heathcliff Earnshaw. As Q. D. Leavis argues, *Wuthering Heights* bears many traces of Brontë's indecision about who Heathcliff is and how to use him,[43] but it is unmistakably a book committed to the values of unity and therefore closure rather than to those of openness and interpretation, separation or distinction, which would give Heathcliff a less determined identity.

Incest as a structural motivation does not always produce such complete reduction. Moreover, it is also possible for a paradigm of a large, very complex novel to be in some way simple. *Ulysses* provides an example of this and can be diagrammed in the following way:

MOLLY	desires	LOVER	and	FREEDOM
BLOOM	desires	SON	and	MOLLY

These seem like wholly incompatible desires until Bloom adopts Stephen and brings him home with, at least, the thought in mind of offering him to Molly as a lover, a motive she is aware of and agreeable to. They already have Milly, who has been sent away for the summer to give her mother more room and no Oedipal competition. And Molly has Boylan, who is introduced into the story by the letter he sends at the same time Milly is introduced by her letter. Boylan, it turns out, is neither the child nor the lover who will replace Rudy and return Molly and Bloom to parity. And the fact Stephen refuses and leaves 7 Eccles Street amounts to his acknowledgment that the Oedipal prohibition, which Bloom and Molly seem willing to overthrow, still stands. His departure, in effect, acknowledges Bloom's priority as the father just before Molly, in Penelope, admits to his superiority over Boylan as a lover and a mate.[44]

However central this paradigm is to *Ulysses,* it does not, of course, explain the whole book; it does not even try to. No single paradigm does, or can, even when it is *clearly* put in place by the author, in the way he arranges his characters according to the differences in their discourse. In the first five chapters of *The Brothers Karamazov,* for instance, Dostoevsky lays out the novel's central scheme. Chapter 1 is entitled "Fyodor Pavlovich Karamazov": his character is sketched in, as are those of his two wives. Chapter 2 is given to the eldest son Dmitri, chapter 3 to Ivan, and chapter 4 to Alyosha. Chapter 5 is called "Elders"

43. Q. D. Leavis, "A Fresh Approach to *Wuthering Heights,*" in *Wuthering Heights,* 306–21.

44. For a full discussion of these aspects of *Ulysses,* see Terrence Doody and Wesley Morris, "Language and Value, Freedom and the Family in *Ulysses*" in *Novel: A Forum on Fiction,* XV (1982), 224–39.

and deals with religious figures such as Alyosha's mentor Zossima. In the five chapters that make up Book One, Dostoevsky has already done a great deal to establish the differences between Dmitri's sensuality, Ivan's intellectual estrangement, and Alyosha's redemptive love. He has also explained that each of these boys has been raised by the servant Grigory and that each has also had still another surrogate father. By dividing their interests and vocations, he sets them up as heart, mind, and soul; the military, university, and monastery; even as different aesthetic types and preferences.[45] All these differences he deploys between the two poles of conflicting authority—the natural father against the spiritual, biology against religion, history as opposed to idea. But what is most interesting about his opening paradigm is what is missing, and among all that is not there the most crucial missing element seems to be the bastard son and eventual murderer, Smerdyakov. His absence suggests that patricide is not as important to the novel as the differences between the brothers, Smerdyakov included, which are not even close to being resolved when the novel stops; for relationships of difference are more basic to the novel than plots are, and relationship does not close.

Again: no single diagram, no scheme by itself, no one paradigm gives us the whole novel. What the paradigms I have developed here illustrate is how a novel works in the play between its linear, sequential, syntactical plot and its vertical, complementary, paradigmatic characters and the different interpretations, the different discourse each embodies. Every novel will have some kind of internal paradigm, just as every sentence will generate some kind of paradigmatic possibility, too, even if it is only that minimal substitution which insists the meaning of the sentence "John loves Mary" is that John does *not* love Larry, at least in that sentence's version of the story. And this brings us to our final point. While every character paradigm we have drawn so far looks different for each different novel, it is also possible to draw radically different paradigms from the same novel. Here, for instance, is a paradigm of some of the active interpreters from *Light in August,* who all stake a great deal on what they think is their special insight, their particular purchase on meaning:

HIGHTOWER	vs.	GRIMM
HINES	vs.	STEVENS
McEACHERN	vs.	THE FURNITURE MAN

45. See Victor Terras, "The Art of Fiction as a Theme in *The Brothers Karamazov,*" in *Dostoevsky: New Perspectives,* ed. Robert Louis Jackson (Englewood Cliffs, N.J., 1984), 193–205.

What Grimm and Hightower think of the meaning of history is hardly compatible, although both seem to feel that they have been born too late. What Stevens and Hines think of race is probably incommunicable to the other and as alien as the attitudes of McEachern and the furniture dealer toward the humor in sexual desire. Jefferson's society has no real communion, except the kind Faulkner achieves and criticizes in dramatizing the narrative principle of the novel as wholly anonymous, distributed, and unselfknowing.

A completely different paradigm illustrates, in the relations of the major characters, the kind of force that keeps them morally separated and the society divided against itself:

LENA		HIGHTOWER
	BYRON	
JOANNA		JOE

Joe and Lena, tragic victim and comic victrix, never meet; neither, as far as we know, do Joanna and Hightower, who are both prisoners of the past and social and sexual outcasts because of it. The novel seems to be straining away from any kind of social or narrative center, which may hold only Byron. In his funny way, he is an agent of union. He brings Lena to Joanna's place to have her baby in the cabin Lucas Burch shared with Christmas, and he eventually helps Christmas seek sanctuary in Hightower's house, where Hightower, pulled by Byron back into life, even tries to defend Joe against his killers. Byron leaves with Lena then, in thrall to her and his fate, as though to effect a comic closure in the future of their marriage—a closure displaced and embedded into the narrative the furniture man recounts to his wife in their bed, which begins another narrative movement without quite ending the one that precedes it.

However, Byron's role as an interpretive principle, a character to read and read-with, is more interesting than his role as an agent in the plot, and its complexity is deceptive and unsettling because Faulkner's narrator is so evenly implacable, at some points limited to an intense, flat visual account of the scene, at others fluent in an indirect discourse that is subtle and boundless. In the fourth chapter, for instance, the distinction between Byron and the narrator is hard to stabilize not only because Faulkner uses two different kinds of indirect discourse, but also because it is difficult to specify how Byron knows what he knows. What is his place in the community intelligence and in the narrative that begins, "They say"? How is his passivity related to his moments of active interpretation ("I reckon"), and how is that interpretive act related to the familiar silence in which he and Hightower can "understand" each other, even as Byron tries to explain the unprecedented experience of his intuition about Lena? It is very difficult here to tell figure from ground, any narrator's identity in the whole narration (even who and where "Faulkner" is), or one story's end against another's beginning.[46] The permeability of character within Faulkner's narrative method resembles Virginia Woolf, who resembles Pynchon and García Márquez, who was influenced by her and by Faulkner in finding the narrative style for *The Autumn of the Patriarch*. They all remind us that character operates in language, which does not establish difference as material bodies do. And although we do not quite expect Byron to represent Faulkner's *writing*, there is nothing else his characterization can be through stretches like those in the fourth chapter. The characters who think they know, know little and are minor; so what *Light in August* means is very hard to say. Faulkner's novel is much harder to diagram satisfactorily than *Pride and Prejudice*, first, because Faulkner does not offer us, in his account of country marriages, the stable clarity of Austen's narrator and, second, because the nature of writing has changed in the time between them. These are matters we will address more fully in the next chapter, "A Character Is Also a Sign."

All narrative needs a beginning, a middle, and an end—and something else to keep these metaphysical principles in line. All narrative must also have a narrator and an audience with whom he or she shares the story. This narrator does not tell an absolute version of the events he narrates but presents these events in a *discourse* that establishes one of their possible meanings. The novel's essential discourse, the aspect of its telling that can distinguish it from other narrative, is that it does *not* rely solely on the narrator's authority, nor solely on the end of the story he tells, such as the protagonist's success or failure, marriage or death, vocation or new identity. Operating as a sentence does, the novel's narrative syntax also generates a paradigmatic order of characters who are all potentially "authoritative" interpreters of the story they inhabit; and because of them the novel's discourse is that aspect of its telling which acknowledges, or even promotes, other versions, different points of view. The paradigms a novel builds, moreover, are a middle that tries not to become a center, that tries to remain open rather than closed, tentative rather than final, and that thereby

---

46. William Faulkner, *Light in August* (New York, 1987), 86 and 88, 106, 90. For a very different account of this kind of narration in Faulkner, see Wayne C. Booth, *The Rhetoric of Fiction* (Chicago, 1963), 184. Booth does not want to grant so much independence to the characters or their consciousness; he contains this play under the term "conjecture."

allows the reader, who is also a character (as we will see in the next chapter), into the discourse, too, into the whole endless process of interpretation; for every realistic character is a different discourse, an *other* take on the world, a version of the story she or he acts out in the company of those who have their own versions, too, but a version that is commensurate with his or her whole fictional life. And no version can be final: nothing contingent can produce the necessary.

This is one reason, as I have said already, that we have an appetite for novel after novel: rather than rereading the same sacred account, the one Bible or theory, of individual experience, we keep reading different accounts of the "same" experience of individuality. And the heart of these accounts is not their novelty, or their originality, but their finally equal status in the "infinite paradigm of difference." So the novel cannot end until the idea of human character which has been reigning since the Renaissance ends before it. And although a human being understood as a separate *substance* may no longer have our literary culture's fullest credence, as a site of differentiation the human character is still a focal point in its own system of interpretation; that condition seems as inescapable as language itself. Until then, the novel, as Woolf says, "so clumsy, verbose, and undramatic, so rich, elastic, and alive," will work fine, built as it is on this discourse of similarity-and-difference.

3

A CHARACTER IS
ALSO A SIGN

"I have read that a good countenance is a letter of recommendation."
—HENRY FIELDING, *Tom Jones*

*And thus his jealousy did even more than the happy, sensual feeling he had
originally experienced for Odette had done to alter Swann's character,
completely changing, in the eyes of the world, even the outward signs
by which that character had been intelligible.*
—MARCEL PROUST, *Swann's Way*

The signifier is what represents the subject for another signifier.
—JACQUES LACAN, *Ecrits*

OF THE MANY narrative styles Thomas Pynchon uses in *Gravity's Rainbow*—
some of them conventional, some not—none is more important than the style of
a passage that comes from the end of the novel's first phase, "Beyond the Zero":

> You go from dream to dream inside me. You have passage to my last
> shabby corner, and there, among the debris, you've found life. I'm
> no longer sure which of all the words, images, dreams or ghosts are
> "yours" and which are "mine." It's past sorting out. We're both being
> someone new now, someone incredible.[1]

Le style indirect libre or free indirect discourse is what we usually call this kind
of narrative—the words or thoughts of a character presented without quotation
marks in language not quite the character's own, but not quite the narrator's
either—and it is now not at all unconventional. Jane Austen's mastery of it in
Emma may be her most important formal contribution to the novel; and since
Flaubert made it the chief instrument of his famous impersonality, it has been
the most important, most definitive mode of modernist narrative. Novelists as

---

1. Thomas Pynchon, *Gravity's Rainbow* (New York, 1973), 177.

different as James and Lawrence have used it with great success to very different ends; Joyce has used it with characters as unlike each other as Stephen in the opening chapter of *A Portrait* and Gerty McDowell in the Nausicaa chapter of *Ulysses*. But it is Virginia Woolf—the previous writer who in many ways is most like Pynchon—who is singled out by Erich Auerbach, in the final chapter of *Mimesis,* to represent the profoundly disturbing effect free indirect discourse has on the physical world and the realm of public events.[2] We need not share Auerbach's fear to appreciate his insight. For more important than free indirect discourse's manifold is the natural ambiguity of its "incorporeality": as Auerbach points out, it dissolves substantive bodies and physical boundaries into consciousness and writing. Free indirect discourse is free and indirect because it cannot be located in or confined to the consciousness and diction of the character or the mind and voice of the narrator. Character and narrator share the style without exchanging it: it is not a form of communication between them, nor is it expressive of either one. Its most important effect is that it blurs the conventional ontological line we suppose between them and erases the formal independence they would have as persons. In other words, free indirect discourse exposes our assumptions about the ontology of character. And the importance of it is hard to overestimate in the history of the novel, especially in relation to recent theory. This theory, which would make character merely a text—in Jonathan Culler's words, "a space in which forces and events meet"[3]— is not unanticipated by the novel's own practice, but it is that same practice which keeps affirming, in the structure of character itself, the equally important counterprinciple, which Peter Brooks articulates this way: "the rise of materialism as a philosophical position made the body, in the absence of any transcendent principle beyond nature, the substance to which any metaphysical speculation must ultimately return as the precondition of mind."[4]

A character in a novel we conventionally understand to be a representational human being, an individual with a determining psychology, a proper name, a social intelligibility (a reputation or character in the other common sense), and of course a body. Within the ontology of language, none of this is a problem, except of course "a body." As we will see, Roland Barthes in *S/Z* is exemplary of a certain kind of thinking that seems to begrudge the body's presence in

2. Erich Auerbach, *Mimesis: The Representation of Reality in Western Literature,* trans. Willard R. Trask (Princeton, 1953), 535–41.

3. Jonathan Culler, *Structuralist Poetics: Structuralism, Linguistics, and the Study of Literature* (Ithaca, 1976), 230.

4. Peter Brooks, *Body Work: Objects of Desire in Modern Narrative* (Cambridge, Mass., 1993), 34.

novelistic fiction, where it constitutes a limit to interpretability. But novelists as radical as Woolf and Pynchon, who redefine character by reorganizing the relationship of consciousness and matter, never repudiate character's entailment of the physical. They can't imagine characters without bodies, and what they point to is this: the ontologies of writing and matter may be categorically opposed, but character is never merely one or the other. The ontology of character is the ontology of the sign, in which there is always a physical component, an aural event or a graphic mark, in the make-up of the signifier. So, as the text of a novel is supported but not contained by the book, as the idea of writing has been fostered and affected by the history of print, the literary subject is misconstrued without its concomitant object.

Nonetheless, *as a sign*, character does not depend on the idea of substance as the basis of meaning, but on the play of similarity-and-difference; and as a sign a character does not exist of itself, but exists to be read. Any literary character who reads another's soul needs eyes to read through, and we need characters on the page to read them. What we are reading, moreover, as we read free indirect discourse, is writing. Dialogue and first person narration may represent speech, but free indirect discourse does not. It is the novel's writing, a purely textual event, a relationship that takes place only on the page, but still in reference to characters who, even as signs, must be attributed a physical reality, too. This is a duality we cannot get around or theorize away from the novel. It is exactly its solicitation and resistance, as we can see by returning to the passage from *Gravity's Rainbow* with which we began.

The first meaning of the passage I have quoted expresses the silent plea of Roger Mexico to Jessica Swanlake to stay with him, to save their union from the war's disintegrating forces and from the intrusion of her British lover, Jeremy. Roger's feelings here echo an earlier passage in the novel, also printed without quotation marks, which is a more complete statement of some of the novel's major themes:

> And there've been moments, more of them lately too—times when face-to-face there has been no way to tell which of them is which. Both at the same time feeling the same eerie confusion . . . something like looking in a mirror by surprise but . . . more than that, the feeling of actually being joined . . . when after—who knows? two minutes, a week? they realize, separate again, what's been going on, that Roger and Jessica were merged into a joint creature unaware of itself. . . . In a life he has cursed, again and again, for its need to believe

so much in the trans-observable, here is the first, the very first real magic: data he can't argue away.[5]

Union, as opposed to division, and the intuition that is opposed to the kind of analysis that means both division and death, are important in *Gravity's Rainbow*, and so is magic as a means of union, intuition, and nontechnological power. Pynchon seems to take magic as seriously as any major writer since Yeats, and this seriousness is in keeping with his ideas about character's instability, its vulnerability to all kinds of interference, and the uncertain permeability of its boundaries. The ways in which Yeats characterizes magic, moreover, characterize the experience of Pynchon's personnel quite aptly. Yeats says in "Magic," in *Beyond Good and Evil*, that its basic doctrines are:

(1) That the borders of our mind are ever shifting, and that many minds can flow into one another, as it were, and create or reveal a single mind, a single energy.
(2) That the borders of our memories are as shifting, and that our memories are part of one great memory, the memory of Nature herself.
(3) That this great mind and great memory can be evoked by symbols.[6]

There is probably no more dramatic demonstration of this great mind being evoked by symbols than in the episode of Franz Pökler's dream of Kekulé's dream of the benzene ring, which we will look at in greater detail later. But what makes Pynchon's characters often different from Yeats himself, working with these symbols even as he strolls among school children, is that the shifting borders of the mind accomplish more than merely psychological or visionary shifts. They change the character's ontology. Yeats sometimes hints at this possibility in dealing with figures other than himself ("Her present image floats into the mind— / Did Quattrocento finger fashion it . . . ?"), but Pynchon is clear about the ontological differences all the time.

Therefore, what makes the first passage quoted above more than routinely interesting as an example of Pynchon's free indirect discourse, saying for Roger what Roger cannot quite say for himself "out loud," is the way in which the words can also be applied to Pynchon himself, to his own relation to his materials and characters and, ultimately, to his reader: "I'm no longer sure which of all the words, images, dreams or ghosts are 'yours' and which are 'mine.' It's past

---

5. Pynchon, *Gravity's Rainbow*, 38.
6. W. B. Yeats, "Magic," in *Essays and Introductions* (New York, 1968), 28.

sorting out. We're both someone new now." This confusion is probably not extraordinary, in light of all the novels from *Don Quixote* to *The Counterfeiters* that have tried to erase the distinctions between the real author and his merely realistic characters in order to question the concept of "fiction" with the same stroke the writer uses to create one. And E. M. Forster has a wonderful notion that the focus of many novels on the nature of relationship seems to result from the writer's occupational hazard, sensitivity: "The constant sensitiveness of characters for each other—even in writers called robust, like Fielding—is remarkable, and has no parallel in life, except among people who have plenty of leisure. Passion, intensity at moments—yes, but not this constant awareness, this endless readjusting, this ceaseless hunger. I believe that these are the reflections of the novelist's own state of mind while he composes, and that the predominance of love in novels is partly because of this."[7] In Pynchon in particular, the confusion also underlines his refusal of narrative authority, the kind of participation (not always healthy) that his characters have in each other's lives, his continuous invitation to the reader to recognize herself in the book and lend to it her own interpretive powers, and his refusal to let anything remain unquestioned, unexplored, or unexposed to his own bravura playfulness: "'Fungus fricassee!' screams Roger the Rowdy. Jessica is weeping on the arm of Jeremy her gentleman, who is escorting her, stiff-armed, shaking his head at Roger's folly, away forever. Does Roger have a second of pain right here? Yes. Sure. You would too. You might even question the worth of your cause."[8]

The reader has probably not been addressed so directly in any other major twentieth-century novel. Yet "you" is not merely the normal form of address to the second person, dear reader. Idiomatically, as Pynchon uses it here, "you" is a slightly stronger, more American version of the Anglo-American "one": as in, one finds this quite different, doesn't one? And as Dorrit Cohn has explained to us, "you" is also the pronoun we use in talking to ourselves.[9] "I" for some reason doesn't call itself "me": it says "you." In *Gravity's Rainbow*, a novel in which alienation is profound and identity uncertain, this play of pronouns just begins to indicate how thoroughly, how radically Pynchon has, as Virginia Woolf has also, thought through the novel's convention of character, and how deeply they have both come to challenge its status—not its legitimacy, but its basic makeup. For they do not propose to alter character by plumbing it to new depths of psychological energy and contradiction, as Dostoevsky has; or by making its

7. E. M. Forster, *Aspects of the Novel* (New York, 1955), 54–55.

8. Pynchon, *Gravity's Rainbow*, 716.

9. Dorrit Cohn, *Transparent Minds: Narrative Modes for Presenting Consciousness in Fiction* (Princeton, 1978), 90.

formerly mute self-address audible in interior monologue, as Dorothy Richardson and Joyce do; or by opening it to a new range of content, as Proust does with Marcel, Faulkner with Benjy Compson, Lawrence with John Thomas and Lady Jane. Pynchon and Woolf want to alter character ontologically, to change its relation to matter and therefore to being, in order to see what this does with traditional notions. They can do this because they make full use of the possibilities that free indirect discourse offers them. We will, therefore, refer continually to Woolf and Pynchon, and refer them to each other, as we investigate the concept of character and the related concepts of identity and individuality; explain further what we then mean by saying character is also a *sign;* trace an evolution of character's status from Austen through Eliot to Conrad, and by this route return then to Pynchon and Woolf.

In traditional usage, character has two related senses. It has meant a fictional being's quality of moral intelligence, its beliefs, values, judgments, motives, and behavior, and consequently its reputation for these qualities, its way of being perceived by other characters. Character is not, therefore, the equivalent of identity, a related notion which comes from the Latin word meaning "same" and which Erik Erikson defines as the internal sense of self-continuity, of sameness through time and different circumstance, which you feel in yourself and have to have confirmed by others.[10] Without this external confirmation, there often follows an "identity crisis," which is almost always painful, even when it can be turned to good uses. Since the novel has, both intrinsically and historically, dealt with the self's relation to society, identity has always been a central theme, and the climax of many realistic novels of the nineteenth century has been the social confirmation, or recognition, often by marriage, of the identity the heroine has discovered herself to have—Esther Summerson and Dorothea Brooke are good examples. Sometimes, when this identity is so private that the society cannot fully confirm it, the novel is tragic, and the heroine's "recognition" is achieved in her death—Emma Bovary and Anna Karenina are the famous examples here, but there are also Cathy Earnshaw, Maggie Tulliver, and Eustacia Vye. In comic rather than tragic characters, however, identity can prove so fluid and resilient that Becky Sharp is not finally determined or threatened by what Culler calls "those interpersonal and conventional systems which traverse the individual." And the roles a *picara* such as Becky plays are more important to her, more an expression of her nature, than is any manifestation of the deep asocial integrity we have come to call authenticity. A character such

10. Erik Erikson, *Identity, Youth, and Crisis* (New York, 1968), 22–23.

as Becky anticipates the much bolder experiments with the concept of identity that we find more recently in John Barth's Henry Burlingame (who is the Proteus figure of *The Sot-Weed Factor*), Woolf's Orlando, or Norman Mailer's "Mailer" in *Armies of the Night*. It is not simply that these last three play roles; it is that they all seem to be able to admit into themselves what is definitively *other* without feeling the threat of disintegration. And they in turn point to an even more remarkable experiment with identity in a character who feels most herself when she feels different ontologically. This character is Woolf's Mrs. Ramsay:

> For now she need not think about anybody. She could be herself, by herself. And that was what now she often felt the need of—to think; well, not even to think. To be silent; to be alone. All the being and the doing, expansive, glittering, vocal, evaporated; and one shrunk, with a sense of solemnity, to being oneself, a wedge-shaped core of darkness, something invisible to others. Although she continued to knit, and sat upright, it was thus that she felt herself; and this self having shed its attachments was free for the strangest adventures. When life sank down for a moment, the range of experience seemed limitless. . . . Not as oneself did one find rest ever, in her experience . . . but as a wedge of darkness. Losing personality, one lost the fret, the hurry, the stir; . . . and pausing there she looked out to meet that stroke of the lighthouse, the long steady stroke, the last of the three, which was her stroke, for watching them in this mood always at this hour one could not help attaching oneself to one thing especially of the things one saw; and this thing, the long steady stroke, was her stroke. Often she found herself sitting and looking, sitting and looking, with her work in her hands until she became the thing she looked at.

What is remarkable about this experience is that Mrs. Ramsay supposes everyone shares it with her: "And to everybody there was always this sense of unlimited resources, she supposed; one after another, she, Lily, Augustus Carmichael, must feel, our apparitions, the things you know us by, are simply childish. Beneath it is all dark, it is all spreading, it is unfathomably deep; but now and again we rise to the surface and that is what you see us by." And for whatever suggestion of death this experience holds, Mrs. Ramsay herself feels rather comforted by the unity it also accomplishes with the once nonhuman world. In the following passage, the word "one" is not only a personal pronoun (the equivalent of "you"), it is also a substantive adjective, a state of being: "It was odd, she thought, how if one was alone, one leant to inanimate things; trees, streams, flowers; *felt they expressed one; felt they became one; felt they knew one, in a sense were one,* felt an irrational tenderness thus (she looked at that long steady light) as for oneself. There rose, and she looked and looked with her needles suspended, there curled up off the floor of the mind, rose from the lake of one's being, a mist, a bride to meet her lover."[11]

In Woolf, therefore, character is not necessarily identity, sameness with oneself, an integrity closed at every border; but Mrs. Ramsay is not playing a role either: she is not impersonating the dark wedge; it is *reifying* her without reducing or dehumanizing her. And this phenomenon seems more remarkable still as we look back at it from the version of human reification that Pynchon has developed in his novels and brought to awful conclusion in *Gravity's Rainbow,* in which one of his principal themes is that Western man's desire for certitude in the mastery of nature has turned his civilization away from life toward the stone certainty of annihilation. Pynchon works this theme in countless ways—from the dirty rocket limericks to Gottfried's sacrificial death; from Pointsman's mechanistic behavioral theory to the book's pandemic sadomasochism. But Pynchon's theme of reification gathers itself onto the "dark thing" at the center of Tyrone Slothrop that connects his sexuality to the German rockets that seem to fall on London in the pattern his trysts describe: wherever he has made love, a rocket comes with death.[12] And when Slothrop discovers the source of this connection, which matches no explanation of a cause-and-effect relationship anyone else can imagine, what he finds in himself is this:

> Does this mean Slothrop has been under their observation—m-maybe since he was *born?* Yaahhh . . .
>
> The fear balloons inside his brain. It will not be kept down with a simple Fuck You. . . . A smell, a forbidden room, at the bottom edge of his memory. He can't see it, can't make it out. Doesn't want to. It is allied with the Worst Thing.
>
> He knows what the smell has to be: though according to those papers it would have been too early for it, though he has never come across any of the stuff among the daytime coordinates of his life, still, down here, back here in the warm dark, among early shapes

---

11. Virginia Woolf, *To the Lighthouse* (New York, 1955), 95–97, 96, 97–98 (italics and ellipses added). See also Rebecca Saunders, "Language, Subject, Self: Reading the Style of *To the Lighthouse,*" in *Novel: A Forum on Fiction,* XXVII (1993), 192–213.

12. See Bernard Dufyhuzen, "Starry-Eyed Semiotics: Learning to Read Slothrop's Map and *Gravity's Rainbow*" in *Pynchon Notes,* VI (1981), 7–33, for the argument that the maps may not be "accurate."

where the clocks and calendars don't mean too much, he knows that what's haunting him now will prove to be the smell of Imipolex G.

Then there's this recent dream he is afraid of having again. He was in his old room, back home. A summer afternoon of lilacs and bees, and warm air through an open window. Slothrop had found a very old dictionary of technical German. It fell open to a certain page prickling with black-face type. Reading down the page, he would come to JAMF. The definition would read: I. He woke begging It *no*—but even after waking, he was sure, he would remain sure, that It could visit him again, any time It wanted. Perhaps you know that dream too. Perhaps It has warned you never to speak Its name. If so, you know about how Slothrop'll be feeling now.[13]

For Slothrop, the location of the "other" within himself is horrifying, and nothing at all like Mrs. Ramsay's embrace of the inanimate; for Pynchon, too, is disturbed by the possibility that human being can be reduced by such mechanism, invaded and compromised by something so—the usual word is—inhuman: although, of course, it is literally not inhuman at all.

"The coupling of 'Jamf' and 'I'"[14] in Slothrop emphasizes, as I have said, the difference between character and identity. Slothrop, we might say, is still a character even though he does not feel the same as himself, and this is a way of defining his problem. Another way is by saying he is not simply an individual, a separate human unit, one. Individuality, another notion related to the concept of character, is maybe best understood as a physical correlative of identity, constituted by our body's separation in space from other bodies and individuated at the borders of our skin from other individuals, who by definition remain indivisible into smaller elements, so that neither a twin nor an amputation alters individuality. This physical independence links human beings to things, is the mode of substance that allows them to stand in the world on their own, among other things, and thereby affects our sense of literary character when we simply take it for granted and project onto these fictional names a concomitant physical *body*. It is this body, nonexistent in a purely linguistic ontology, but always entailed by the idea of the sign, that seems most violated by the theory that defines character as a space of interacting relationships, a nexus for other systems; and in the case of Slothrop, who is the victim of totalizing systems, the claim that character is merely an "ideological prejudice" seems ruthless. It is, therefore, more than very interesting what Pynchon does with Slothrop to answer

---

13. Pynchon, *Gravity's Rainbow*, 286–87.
14. *Ibid.*, 623.

his dilemma: he dis-integrates him: that is, breaks him down to what seems like the molecular level, by a process of "de-reification" that is not death.

With a past he cannot quite remember determining a future he cannot choose, Slothrop's quest through the Zone for his own identity is farce and tragedy. He cannot "find" himself because he is not himself; and rather than resolve this problem, Pynchon exacerbates it by allowing Slothrop to become even less himself, and therefore considerably less than any character in serious fiction ever has been. Slothrop does not die: he disperses into nature, or disseminates, remaining only in the memory of a few who knew him, such as Seaman Bodine, and even there becoming gradually more attenuated. Yet, in whatever way we may have of explaining this singularity to ourselves, we have to speculate that Slothrop has changed ontologically. It is not just our perception of him that has changed, not only his relation to the other characters that is different: Slothrop is different in his relation to being, and, therefore, a different *kind* of character, perhaps *only* language, but always related nonetheless to the body he does not occupy, which is no longer in visual space. Even so, his transformation is not entirely unprecedented, for in her own experiments with an idea of character that is not limited by the ego, nor simply constituted within the limits of the physical body,[15] Woolf also entertained ideas of dispersal that, like Pynchon's, seem to be desirable, affirmative, good. In what we may call their more social form, these ideas appear in *Mrs. Dalloway:*

> But everyone remembered; what she loved was this, here, now, in front of her; the fat lady in the cab. Did it matter then, she asked herself, walking towards Bond Street, did it matter that she must evidently cease completely; all this must go on without her; did she resent it; or did it not become consoling to believe that death ended absolutely? but that somehow in the streets of London, on the ebb and flow of things, here, there, she survived, Peter survived, lived in each other, she being part, she was positive, of the trees at home; of the house there, ugly, rambling all to bits and pieces as it was; part of people she had never met; being laid out like a mist between the people she knew best, who lifted her on their branches as she had

15. See Virginia Woolf, "A Sketch of the Past" in *Moments of Being,* ed. Jeanne Schulkind (2nd ed.; San Diego, 1985), 73: "It proves that one's life is not confined to one's body and what one says and does; one is living all the time in relation to certain background rods or conceptions. Mine is that there is a pattern hid behind the cotton wool." James Naremore, *The World Without a Self* (New Haven, 1973), has the best discussion of this aspect of Woolf's fiction. See also Daniel Albright, *Personality and Impersonality* (Chicago, 1978), chapter 3.

seen trees lift the mist, but it spread ever so far, her life, her-self. . . .

It was unsatisfactory, they agreed, how little one knew people. But she said, sitting on the bus going up Shaftesbury Avenue, she felt herself everywhere; not "here, here, here"; and she tapped the back of the seat; but everywhere. She waved her hand, going up Shaftesbury Avenue. She was all that. So that to know her, or anyone, one must seek out the people who completed them; even the places. Odd affinities she had with people she had never spoken to, some woman in the street, some man behind a counter—even trees, or barns. It ended with a transcendental theory which, with her horror of death, allowed her to believe, or say that she believed (for all her scepticism), that since our apparitions, the part of us which appears, are so momentary compared with the other, the unseen part of us, which spreads wide, the unseen might survive, be recovered some-how attached to this person or that, or even haunting certain places after death . . . perhaps-perhaps.[16]

There are a number of things to say about these passages. First, given the novel's commitment to social relations, there is nothing unusual about Mrs. Dalloway's belief that she is completed by others and may survive the death that she, unlike Mrs. Ramsay, fears so much, by remaining in others' memories. What is unusual, though, is the *physical* implication of her beliefs. Secondly, her feelings cannot be dismissed here as only hers, or merely sentimental, because Woolf uses the same words—especially the important pun "appari-tions"—later in the passages of *To the Lighthouse* that we have already exam-ined. And, finally, the transcendental quality of Mrs. Dalloway's belief is not to be easily dismissed either. Mrs. Ramsay does indeed return to "appear" to Lily Briscoe, and Mrs. Ramsay shares Clarissa Dalloway's sense that she will also endure *in things*. What is noteworthy about this next passage, which I must also quote at length, is how effectively it can also work as an apologia for Woolf's style, how aptly it explains why her beautifully fluid, seamless sentences strive to erase the boundaries between one thing and another, the inner world and the outer, the human and the inanimate. Mrs. Ramsay is leaving the dining room as dinner (which in her mind has been a success) is completed:

Not that she did in fact turn or hurry; she went indeed rather slowly. She felt rather inclined just for a moment to stand still after all that

16. Virginia Woolf, *Mrs. Dalloway* (New York, 1953), 12, 231.

chatter, and pick out one particular thing; the thing that mattered; to detach it; separate it off; clean it of all the emotions and odds and ends of things, and so hold it before her, and bring it to the tribunal where, ranged about in conclave, sat the judges she had set up to decide these things. Is it good, is it bad, is it right or wrong? Where are we all going to? and so on. So she righted herself after the shock of the event, and quite unconsciously and incongruously, used the branches of the elm trees outside to help her to stabilise her position. Her world was changing: they were still. The event had given her a sense of movement. All must be in order. She must get that right and that right, she thought, . . . Yes, that was done then, accomplished; and as with all things done, became solemn. Now one thought of it, cleared of chatter and emotion, it seemed always to have been, only was shown now and so being shown, struck everything into stability. They would, she thought, going on again, however long they lived, come back to this night; this moon; this wind; this house; and to her too. It flattered her, where she was most susceptible of flattery, to think how, wound about in their hearts, however long they lived, she would be woven; and this, and this, and this, she thought, going upstairs, laughing, but affectionately, at the sofa on the landing (her mother's); at the rocking chair (her father's); at the map of the Hebrides. All that would be revived again in the lives of Paul and Minta; "the Rayleys"—she tried the new name over; and she felt, with her hand on the nursery door, that community of feeling with other people which emotion gives as if the walls of partition had become so thin that practically (the feeling was one of relief and happiness) it was all one stream, and chairs, tables, maps, were hers, were theirs, it did not matter whose. And Paul and Minta would carry it on when she was dead.[17]

That Mrs. Ramsay is wrong about so many of the human consequences of the party is not so important here as her reliance on the nonhuman things in her house for stability and an enduring *presence*. For her entailment of these is not like the usual metonymic relationship between a character and her setting, such as there is between Darcy and his house in *Pride and Prejudice* or Mrs. Dalloway and her attic bedroom. Kenneth Burke, as we have seen, says the relationship between the two terms in a metonymy is one of *reduction* of the incorporeal to

---

17. Woolf, *To the Lighthouse*, 169–71 (ellipsis added).

the corporeal, the spiritual to the physical.[18] But it does not seem that Mrs. Ramsay views her continuing *presentation* by the furniture of their summer house as a reduction; and given her sense of herself as the dark wedge, the furniture does not stand as her representative or surrogate. She and it participate mutually in the same "stream" of being, and if the stream will be diminished by her departure or death, it will be diminished perhaps only as a river is by removing floating debris: that is, not essentially. Woolf's style, in some serious ways, often seems to be a strategy or technique of *animism*. She does not have the fierce primitive force that Dickens develops to animate "the view from Todgers's";[19] there is none of the allotropic mystery Lawrence develops in trying to convert psychology to physiology. Woolf's animism is more like that gentle force in Forster that unites the dead Mrs. Wilcox still with Howards End and brings Margaret Schlegel into affinity with old Miss Avery. All are hard to define exactly, but all demonstrate, in various ways, that the novel has questioned the ontology of its characters before the structuralists formulated their objections explicitly, and that grounding character in the ontology of the sign does not necessarily reduce or destroy it. Woolf and Pynchon show that human reality can be reconceived in what are normally nonhuman terms, and that this reconception has its advantages.

The *Oxford English Dictionary* has interesting historical information about the word "character." The first seven definitions concern character's nature as a *sign*, "a distinctive mark impressed, engraved, or otherwise formed"; "a sign or symbol"; "a graphic symbol standing for a sound, syllable, or notion used in writing or in printing; one of the simple elements of a written language; e.g. a letter of the alphabet." Now, we all know a sign is a signifier and a signified, which are an acoustical or graphic image and the idea it refers to, that are at best arbitrarily linked. Signifiers ultimately point only to other signifiers, for never does the sign really refer beyond itself to a perfectly presentable world. Another way of saying this is that a sign is both a means and an end of interpretation, something we read and read-with in order to read something else, which we can then read-with; and although it is only a convention and a function within the system of language rather than a substantive itself, the sign is what we have. So, the most interesting definition of character, with these other definitions in mind, is the fourteenth, where character is "a description, delineation,

18. Kenneth Burke, *A Grammar of Motives* (Berkeley, 1969), 503–509.
19. Dorothy Van Ghent, "The Dickens World: A View from Todgers's," in *Dickens: A Collection of Critical Essays*, ed. Martin Price (Englewood Cliffs, N.J., 1967), 24–38.

or detailed report of a person's qualities." Quite commonly, and long before the novel came to be, a character was something like a letter of recommendation: "a formal testimony given by an employer as to the qualities and habits of one that has been in his employ." Such a character is left in Perdita's basket, with a bundle of compensation for her rescuers, when she is abandoned on the coast of Bohemia in *The Winter's Tale* (III.iii.47–48). And by the time we get to this definition, which is still before we get character defined as the novelistic entity we are interested in (Fielding is cited as the exemplary usage, 1749), we have to realize that the definitions of character which propose it as "the face of features betokening moral qualities"; "the sum of the moral and mental qualities which distinguish an individual or a race, viewed as a homogeneous whole"; or "the estimate formed of a person's qualities"—these definitions of character are extrapolations, analogues, even metaphors of the word's first sense; they are signs themselves, signifiers attaching themselves to other signifiers. It is hard, therefore, to defend character as a substance, when historically it has always been a sign. Not a human being, but a mark in language to represent human qualities.[20]

So we can use this history to say: character is that about a human being, a person, which language gives us access to. This may or may not include physical aspects, *presence,* but it can, and it does not necessarily exclude those. When we read a novel, we read characters: characters placed along the lines of the book's physical page, *literally,* as well as the characters, the fictional beings, these literal characters *figuratively* represent or constitute. And not only do we read characters, characters themselves read other characters. In a linguistic medium, interpretation is the basic, or the principal, or perhaps the only form of action that finally counts, whether we call that action discovering one's identity or vocation, falling in love, embracing or rejecting the world, or making meaning of life. As an act of interpretation or of reading, character has, therefore, both an active and a passive aspect. Passively, it is the sum of attributes, motives, beliefs, and behaviors which we interpret in one another. Actively, it is the principle behind our own attributes, motives, beliefs, and behaviors which gives us the ability to make our interpretations as we do, and thereby be interpreted ourselves by others. Our characters read and are read by other characters. For

---

20. J. Hillis Miller, *Ariadne's Thread: Story Lines* (New Haven, 1992), also uses the *O.E.D.* to form his discussion of character, but with different emphases (see 55–63). His most striking definition, however, is of character as the effect of the rhetorical figure catachresis. See 36–55, his discussion of character in the context of Nietzsche's ideas. For a completely different take on the "truth" of catachresis, see Jean Radford, *Dorothy Richardson* (Bloomington, 1991), 122–23. Radford says that Richardson writes from a sense of self that makes catachresis too limiting, but Richardson can also be read as an essentialist for whom catachresis is simply insufficient.

it says something about ourselves, too, whether we pity or condemn Madame Bovary; find Constantine Levin irritating or noble; feel that Rupert Birkin's attitude toward Gerald Crich is like Lawrence's own—a petty *ressentiment*. Literary characters cannot read us literally, of course, but we are "read" through them, explained to ourselves by the explanations we make of their characteristics.

And, of course, it is not only literary characters we read and are read by. We read and are read by each other, in every way our relationships are constituted, enacted, or expressed in our language and social codes. We all have a physical ontology which places us in the realm of other material things, and we have a linguistic ontology which places us in the realm of meaning, intelligibility, interpretation. We are objects and subjects. And it is this linguistic ontology, this "subjectivity," that we share with Flaubert, Tolstoy, and Lawrence, who are dead, but who have presented themselves to us through the characters of their novels. In this sense, character is the novel's fundamental principle of mediation, rather than language itself. For what we share with both the author and his creations, even if we do not also share their French or Russian, is this mode of interpreting and interpretability we call character. Character, in this sense, translates pretty well. A poem such as "A Servant to Servants," by the Robert Frost who says poetry is exactly what gets left out in translation, would lose much less in translation than one of his epistemological lyrics, such as "For Once, Then, Something" with all its colloquial puns on perspectival vision.

To preserve character in this way is to rescue it from the extremes of New Critical and structuralist formalism, as William Gass tries to do in this definition of Henry James's character Mr. Cashmore: "Now the question is: what is Mr. Cashmore? Here is the answer I shall give: Mr. Cashmore is (1) a noise (2) a proper name (3) a complex system of ideas (4) a controlling conception (5) an instrument of verbal organization (6) a pretended mode of referring, and (7) a source of verbal energy. But Mr. Cashmore is not a person."[21] And Gass's demystification is not fully satisfying because those seven appositives could attach themselves, with the same alacrity, to Joyce's word "Dublin," Dickens's "London," or James's own "Paris." These city names are instruments of verbal organization, modes of reference, and sources of energy, but we do not think of them as naming characters. Cities are physically different, and Gass does not think to acknowledge the difference this can make.

More radical, because it is less language-bound and quite emphatically physical, is the definition Hugh Kenner throws away in his book on *Ulysses* (named *Ulysses* with no trace of anxiety at all) when he says: "A character in

---

21. William H. Gass, *Fiction and the Figures of Life* (Boston, 1979), 44.

Ulysses (in a city of talk) is an interference phenomenon between 'his' language and language not his, sometimes other characters', sometimes the author's."[22] An interference phenomenon is a known value, used in processes such as spectroscopy, to interfere with and thereby measure an unknown value. Kenner's metaphor suggests the languages of Dublin and of Joyce are prior to any character, who uses them by distorting their flow according to his own measure. It is a metaphor that allows us to visualize in physical terms the system of *langue* and the intervention of *parole;* and as a visual metaphor, it can help us "see" Bloom, for instance, in relation to the extraordinary style of Oxen of the Sun, with which he hardly interferes at all. Yet as radical as Kenner's perspective may be, he does not develop it as completely as Pynchon develops the similar idea of the radio engineer Kurt Mondaugen: "In his electro-mysticism, the triode was as basic as the cross in Christianity. Think of the ego, the self that suffers a personal history bound to time, as the grid. The deeper and true Self is the flow between cathode and plate. The constant, pure flow. Signals—sense-data, feelings, memories relocating—are put onto the grid, and modulate the flow. We live lives that are waveforms constantly changing with time, now positive, now negative. Only at moments of great serenity is it possible to find the pure, the informationless state of signal zero." This statement is important because it is helpful to our understanding later of what exactly happens to Slothrop when he begins his slow dis-integration. Pynchon says:

> Slothrop, as noted, at least as early as the *Anubis* era, has begun to thin, to scatter. "Personal density," Kurt Mondaugen in his Pee- nemünde office not too many steps away from here, enunciating the Law which will one day bear his name, "is directly proportional to temporal bandwidth."
>
> "Temporal bandwidth" is the width of your present, your *now*. It is the familiar "delta-t" considered as a dependent variable. The more you dwell in the past and in the future, the thicker your band- width, the more solid your persona. But the narrower your sense of Now, the more tenuous you are. It may get to where you're having trouble remembering what you were doing five minutes ago, or even—as Slothrop now—what you're doing *here,* at the base of this colossal curved embankment. . . .
>
> "Uh," he turns slackmouth to Närrisch, "what are we . . ."
>
> "What are we what?"
>
> "What?"

22. Hugh Kenner, *Ulysses* (London, 1980), 70.

"You said, 'What are we . . .' then you stopped."

"Oh. Gee, that was a funny thing to say."[23]

What are we, is a question novelists have been asking since Austen, at least, and the answers they give are answers that depend on how their characters read each other and are read, what they think they are reading, and what difference this makes to the ways in which we define character ontologically.

"Whatever I do is done in a hurry," replied he; "and therefore if I should resolve to quit Netherfield, I should probably be off in five minutes. At present, however, I consider myself as quite fixed here."

"That is exactly what I should have supposed of you," said Elizabeth.

"You begin to comprehend me, do you?" cried he, turning towards her.

"Oh! yes—I understand you perfectly."

"I wish I might take this for a compliment; but to be so easily seen through I am afraid is pitiful."

"That is as it happens. It does not necessarily follow that a deep, intricate character is more or less estimable than such a one as yours."

"Lizzy," cried her mother, "remember where you are, and do not run on in the wild manner that you are suffered to do at home."

"I did not know before," continued Bingley immediately, "that you were a studier of character. It must be an amusing study."

"Yes; but intricate characters are the *most* amusing. They have at least that advantage."

"The country," said Darcy, "can in general supply but few subjects for such a study. In a country neighborhood you move in a very confined and unvarying society."

"But people themselves alter so much, that there is something new to be observed in them for ever."

"Yes, indeed," cried Mrs. Bennet, offended by his manner of mentioning a country neighborhood. "I assure you there is quite as much of *that* going on in the country as in town."

Reading character in *Pride and Prejudice* (1813) is an act performed quite literally, and this fragment of conversation highlights the book's debate about

---

23. Pynchon, *Gravity's Rainbow*, 404, 509.

whether character is as fixed, as permanent, as engraved in ivory as it seems to be, or mutable, historical, and therefore less easily legible. Elizabeth Bennet defends her sport by claiming "people alter themselves so much," but she acts as though they do not, as though she can know them completely and at once by an intuition of their essence. And she acts this way not only with characters as charmingly simple as Bingley, she does it even to Darcy:

> "I remember hearing you once say, Mr. Darcy, that you hardly ever forgave, that your resentment once created was unappeasable. You are very cautious, I suppose, as to its *being created.*"
>
> "I am," said he, with a firm voice.
>
> "And never allow yourself to be blinded by prejudice?"
>
> "I hope not."
>
> "It is particularly incumbent on those who never change their opinion, to be secure of judging properly at first."
>
> "May I ask to what these questions tend?"
>
> "Merely to the illustration of *your* character," said she, endeavouring to shake off her gravity. "I am trying to make it out."
>
> "And what is your success?"
>
> She shook her head. "I do not get on at all. I hear such different accounts of you as puzzle me exceedingly."
>
> "I can readily believe," answered he gravely, "that report may vary greatly with respect to me; and I could wish, Miss Bennet, that you were not to sketch my character at the present moment, as there is reason to fear that the performance would reflect no credit on either."
>
> "But if I do not take your likeness now, I may never have another opportunity."

Darcy seems much more aware here that the truth of character is in discourse, whereas Elizabeth, despite what she says, does not act as though it is. Contradictory accounts of Darcy's character seem impossible to resolve because, since his character *is* fixed, it must also be unmistakably legible to everyone. And "taking" it now, as though it were a snapshot, is taking it forever, apparently.

Later in the novel, Elizabeth virtually admits her prejudice in favor of fixed, essentialist character—of characters who are, as we said of Fielding's, part of nature rather than of history—in this outburst to her sister Jane:

> "Nay," said Elizabeth, "this is not fair. *You* wish to think all the world respectable, and are hurt if I speak ill of any body. I only want

to think *you* perfect. . . . There are few people whom I really love, and still fewer of whom I think well. The more I see of the world, the more I am dissatisfied with it; and every day confirms my belief of the inconsistency of all human characters, and of the little dependence that can be placed on the appearance of either merit or sense. I have met with two instances lately; one I will not mention; the other is Charlotte's marriage. It is unaccountable! in every view it is unaccountable!"

Charlotte has married Mr. Collins, a comic type who is the easiest kind of character to read because he regards himself and the world *typically*. Charlotte's marriage to him, as we have noticed before, seems to violate her own character as well as Elizabeth's estimate of it; and the fact that Elizabeth has been wrong so often lately may be even more upsetting than Charlotte's behavior. Major characters in Austen's small world most often go wrong by making a wrong estimate of another; their most important changes come about, usually, when they change their minds. And when Elizabeth has changed her mind about Darcy, she is careful to explain to Wickham, *"In essentials* . . . he [Darcy] is very much what he ever was."[24] Because the mind might be the only thing that can change in this tight, traditional society, misreadings and rereadings are very important acts.

So, therefore, are letters. Darcy changes Elizabeth's mind by means of the long letter he writes exposing Wickham's lies and treachery. Letters that can achieve so much indicate the kind of characters who write and read them; for these letters mean, in effect, that each character has an almost unlimited access to his own character, the character of others, to character itself. These letters mean a character can say what he is. And characters who do not say what they are, such as Jane Fairfax in *Emma,* are almost as upsetting as liars such as Wickham. Slothrop clearly cannot say what he is. Most of the characters in the major novels of the modernist period cannot even begin to say what they are either, since they are articulated by the very difficult styles that Woolf, Lawrence, Joyce, and Faulkner have developed to expose those reaches of being and consciousness that would be otherwise unavailable. And if Bloom could read *Ulysses,* how much of it would he acknowledge as his own experience, as himself? He would be able to read the letters in *Ulysses,* for they are minor things. The only one we read in full is Milly's, but we do not feel we are missing much by not seeing Boylan's note to Molly, Martha's note to Bloom, or his note

---

24. Jane Austen, *Pride and Prejudice* (Harmondsworth, 1972), 88, 136, 173–74, 260 (italics added).

back to her, which he writes in the Sirens episode as he discovers his conviction that words, letters can more fully express human life than the notes of music can. This is a wonderful moment in the novel: Bloom writes a note that he is allowed to think is as important, essentially, as the virtuoso prose of the chapter he writes it in, which he probably could not "read." Nothing in Joyce is better than this kind of generosity.

By the time we get from Austen to George Eliot's *Middlemarch* (1872), character has become so certainly dynamic that there is no possibility of "taking" it in a single glance. "Signs are small measurable things," Eliot warns us, "but interpretations are illimitable. . . ." Moreover, character in Eliot can change significantly, and at least three of the major characters change much more than their minds—Dorothea, Lydgate, and Fred Vincy. Eliot says of this phenomenon: "The risk [of betting on Lydgate's future] would remain, even with close knowledge of Lydgate's character; for character too is a process and an unfolding." Time itself, therefore, as well as language, justifies the validity of different perspectives: for, in time, no character is ever complete at any given moment; in language, no single perspective or discourse is ever completely comprehensive; and it is clear in the world of Eliot's novel that the multitude of signs, which develop in time to the tune of multiple perspectives, never exhausts a character's full intelligibility: "For surely all must admit that a man may be puffed and be lauded, envied, ridiculed, counted upon as a tool and fallen in love with, or at least selected as a future husband, and yet remain virtually unknown—known merely as a cluster of signs for his neighbours' false supposition."[25]

The center around which these signs merely cluster is ambiguous. Eliot offers no suggestion that it is an ineffable essence, but neither does she suggest that it is the absence Derrida proposes against Western logocentrism, nor does it mean that her world is, like Dickens's, essentially unknowable, limitlessly dispersive, a darkness we can only circumlocute. Eliot's world seems one of inexhaustible intelligibility, a middle of signification without origin or end, so rich with the potentiality of interpretation, it is an almost heroic labor to encompass it. And Eliot's narrator works heroically herself to remove from the reader whatever hinders knowledge, to undermine delimiting conventions and to distribute points of perspective at several different angles. In *The Mill on the Floss* (1860), there is a moment when she does this quite neatly.

> Whence Mr. Stelling concluded that Tom's brain being peculiarly impervious to etymology and demonstrations, was peculiarly in need

25. George Eliot, *Middlemarch* (Harmondsworth, 1965), 47, 178, 171.

of being ploughed and harrowed by these patent implements: it was his favorite metaphor, that the classics and geometry constituted that culture of the mind which prepared it for the reception of any subsequent crop. I say nothing against Mr. Stelling's theory: . . . I only know it turned out as uncomfortably for Tom Tulliver as if he had been plied with cheese in order to remedy a gastric weakness which prevented him from digesting it. It is astonishing what a different result one gets by changing the metaphor! Once call the brain an intellectual stomach, and one's ingenious conception of the classics and geometry as ploughs and harrows seems to settle nothing . . . we can so seldom declare what a thing is, except by saying it is something else?[26]

Then, if lessons such as these fail, Eliot can always importune the reader into following her own good example as she does in recommending Casuabon to our special tolerance.

But at present this caution against a too hasty judgment interests me more in relation to Mr. Causabon than to his young cousin. If to Dorothea Mr. Causabon had been the mere occasion which had set alight the fine inflammable material of her youthful illusions, does it follow that he was fairly represented in the minds of those less impassioned personages who have hitherto delivered their judgments concerning him? *I protest against any absolute conclusions,* any prejudice derived from Mrs. Cadwallader's contempt for a neighboring clergyman's alleged greatness of soul, of Sir James Chettam's poor opinion of his rival's legs—from Mr. Brooke's failure to elicit a companion's ideas, or from Celia's criticism of a middle-aged scholar's personal appearance. I am not sure that the greatest man of his age, if ever that solitary superlative existed, could escape these unfavourable reflections of himself in various small mirrors; and even Milton, looking for his portrait in a spoon, must submit to have the facial angle of a bumpkin. Moreover, if Mr. Casaubon, speaking for himself, has rather chilling rhetoric it is not therefore certain that there is no good work or fine feeling in him. . . . Suppose we turn from outside estimates of a man, to wonder, with keener interest, what is the report of his own consciousness about his doings or capacity: with what hindrances is he carrying on his daily labours;

26. George Eliot, *The Mill on the Floss* (Harmondsworth, 1979), 208–209.

. . . and with what spirit he wrestles against universal pressure, which will one day be too heavy for him, and bring his heart to its final pause. Doubtless his lot is important in his own eyes; and the chief reason that we think he asks too large a place in our consideration must be our want of room for him, since we refer him to the Divine regard with perfect confidence; . . . Mr. Casaubon, too, was the centre of his own world; if he was liable to think that others were providentially made for him, and especially to consider them in the light of their fitness for the author of a *Key to all Mythologies,* this trait is not quite alien to us, and, like the other mendicant hopes of mortals, claims some of our pity.

Certainly this affair of his marriage with Miss Brooke touched him more nearly than it did any one of the persons who have hitherto shown their disapproval of it, and in the present stage of things I feel more tenderly towards his experience of success than towards the disappointment of the amiable Sir James.

The italics I have added mark the heart of George Eliot's theory of character, which is, in effect, her theory of realism, too. There are no absolute conclusions, nothing final to say, for there are no absolutes in any sense because meaning is never entirely present. There is always another way to look at something, perhaps a perspective later that may even be better, but no end is in sight. Such conviction makes a novel difficult to end, and even the nine hundred pages of *Middlemarch*—a title that is certainly a spatial and narrative pun—just begin to tell the full story of Dorothea's subsequent life in all its circumstance and possibility. And it does not, I think, do equal justice to the character of Lydgate, but what it does is crucial.

Like Rosamund, Casaubon, and Bulstrode, Lydgate's moral flaw is a failure of intellectual breadth. He is not the overtly selfish egotist the others are, nor the kind of manipulator of others they are, nor is he someone whose version of life is reductive. His is a failure to connect, to bring that "distinction of mind which belonged to his intellectual ardour" to bear upon his "feeling and judgment about furniture, or women, or the desirability of its being known (without his telling) that he was better born than other country surgeons." Yet Lydgate is the only character in the book who shares anything like Eliot's intellectual interest in the science that grounds her metaphor of the web in something other than language: "he longed to demonstrate the more intimate relations of living structure and help to define men's thought more accurately after the true order." Yet again, since this aspiration is apparently not enough, the behavior and example of the narrator become even more important, not only to her readers, as we have seen already in the passage on Casaubon, but also in her characters as well. If there is a moment in the book when one of them is allowed to share in the narrator's power and meet the standard she sets, it is in the late scene in which Dorothea comes to Lydgate and offers her financial aid and, much more important, her belief in his character, an interpretation of him no one else is eager to bestow:

> "Not because there is no one to believe in you?" said Dorothea, pouring out her words in clearness from a full heart. "I know the unhappy mistakes about you. I knew them from the first moment to be mistakes. You have never done anything vile. You would not do anything dishonourable."
>
> It was the first assurance of belief in him that had fallen on Lydgate's ears. He drew a deep breath, and said, "Thank you." He could say no more: it was something very new and strange in his life that these few words of trust from a woman should be so much to him.

Dorothea once showed a more naive version of this faith to Casaubon, who did not know how to believe in it. Lydgate does by this time, and Eliot comments: "The presence of a noble nature, generous in its wishes, ardent in its charity, changes the lights for us: we begin to see things again in their larger, quieter masses, and believe that we too can be seen and judged in the wholeness of our character. That influence was beginning to act on Lydgate, who had for many days been seeing all life as one who is dragged and struggling amid the throng. He sat down again, and felt that he was recovering his old self in the consciousness that he was with one who believed in it."[27]

Character is a passive sum and an active principle, what we read and read-with, which is what is read in us, and these two aspects of character are inseparable. Lydgate's character, which as we read it includes his heretofore unadmitted dependency and his just self-esteem, is revived here as he sees it is being seen correctly. He can reinterpret himself as one who is not among the throng because Dorothea recognizes his distinction.

There is nothing quite like this kind of possibility in Austen's world, where there is nothing like the huge web of interrelated circumstances that no one but the narrator can know; and there is nothing either like the Middlemarch gossip, which is a parody of the narrator's vision, that brings down Bulstrode by inference but also brings down Lydgate with him. Wickham may fool many people,

27. Eliot, *Middlemarch*, 110–11, 179, 178, 819.

but never Darcy, who may not at first be appreciated by all the Bennets, but is known by Bingley. And while Emma can misconceive herself and Frank Churchill, Knightley sees right through her pride and his letters. Austen's world is too small, too public, and too highly defined for character to be so misperceived or change to be so dramatic. Bigger mistakes can take place in *Middlemarch* because there is simply more to know; the original context of each sign opens it to more interpretations; every signifier has more signifieds (and other signifiers) in its field of possible relations. And as we come to understand the nature of character as a sign, it is important that we see it with many signifieds. For instance: Dorothea and Lydgate seem linked because to both of them a career is a question of great importance. Marriage is important to them too. And for both of them, even though Dorothea tries to make her career her idealistic marriage to Casaubon, career and marriage conflict. Will Ladislaw sometimes seems out of place in the book because the themes of marriage and its relation to career do not initially attach themselves to him, as they do even to less important characters such as Fred Vincy and Farebrother. So Will seems an indefinite character, less meaningful, vaguer because he is not related to the major themes of the novel, the central signifieds. For this same reason, the great Darcy would be a minor character such as Sir James, whose career is his class, because what Darcy signifies is not so important in Eliot's world as it is in Austen's. And a character such as Heathcliff could refer to almost nothing in the *Middlemarch* scheme of themes and values. To this extent, every novel is a closed system in which its signifiers are related to its signifieds: what marriage means to Dorothea and to Emma are two very different things, although both of them would agree to many of marriage's public attributes and advantages. For this reason, therefore, it is hard to imagine successfully one novelist's character in another's novel; although vagueness may be a disadvantage to Ladislaw, in Kurtz's case it need be no handicap at all.

Kurtz, in a way, defines a limit of the traditional conception of character as a substance by remaining so long offstage it seems as though he is being proposed as pure interpretability. For he is the dead center of *Heart of Darkness*'s (1902) narrative about the possibilities of narrative truth; he is also a self-created fiction that is the destination of Conrad's narrative of the frame-narrator's narrative of Marlow's narrative, which all deal very self-consciously with the way embedding expands rather than closes in on meaning and with the problem of interpretation posed by the fact that initially everyone, except Marlow himself, has an idea of what Kurtz means—means to the voyage, to the company, to the evangelistic ideal the company pretends to stand for, to imperialism and the white man's burden, to the spiritually famished heart of the Russian harlequin, to the community of natives Kurtz rules, to nothing less than the whole mind of

Europe. We are, at this point on the river, far beyond the limits of Austen's country world, in a situation Elizabeth Bennet would find literally unimaginable. And the only thing around him that Marlow regards as real is the impenetrable jungle he has never seen before.[28] He finds human beings and behavior so absurd, inexplicable, unreal, that he has to redefine the situation in order to give himself the stability necessary to make some sense.

> "If you so much as smiled, he would—though a man of sixty—offer to fight you. I would not have gone so far as to fight for Kurtz, but I went for him near enough to a lie. You know I hate, detest, and can't bear a lie, not because I am straighter than the rest of us, but simply because it appalls me. . . . Well, I went near enough to it by letting the young fool there believe anything he liked to imagine as to my influence in Europe. I became in an instant as much of a pretence as the rest of the bewitched pilgrims. This simply because I had a notion it somehow would be of help to that Kurtz whom at the time I did not see—you understand. He was just a word for me. I did not see the man in the name any more than you do. Do you see him? Do you see the story? Do you see anything? It seems to me I am trying to tell you a dream—. . . ."

When Marlow asks, "Do you see him?"—meaning Kurtz—neither the pronoun nor the name has yet a clear reference for his audience, who are literally in the dark. And this lack of limiting reference is exactly what generates Marlow's narrative method and his anxiety. He keeps talking to dramatize both his quest for meaning *in* Kurtz and his quest for the meaning *of* Kurtz, which are not the same thing. And if it were not for the clearly defined physical and dramatic situation in which Marlow is asked to tell his story, it would be possible for us to say that Marlow's speech about the unseen, unknown Kurtz encloses itself into a system without reference, where it becomes a performance such as those in Beckett's narrative soliloquies in which an isolated character seems to speak in a kind of pure writing.

On the next page in *Heart of Darkness*, Marlow pauses to ruminate over the impossibility of conveying a dream—"We live, as we dream—alone. . . ."—then begins again by saying:

> "Of course, in this you fellows see more than I could then. You see me, whom you know. . . ."

28. Joseph Conrad, *Heart of Darkness* (Harmondsworth, 1973), 20, 33, 48–49, for instance.

It had become so pitch dark that we listeners could hardly see one another. For a long time already he, sitting apart, had been no more to us than a voice. There was not a word from anybody. The others might have been asleep, but I was awake. I listened, I listened on the watch for the sentence, the word, that would give me the clue to the faint uneasiness inspired by this narrative that seemed to shape itself without human lips in the heavy night-air of the river.

Inevitably, ironically too, Marlow has become to his auditor what Kurtz has been for him: a bodiless voice, language itself ungrounded and unattached, which is shaping meaning without apparent reference to anything except Meaning.

"The point was in his being a gifted creature, and that of all his gifts the one that stood out pre-eminently, that carried with it a sense of real *presence*, was his ability to talk, his words—the gift of expression, the bewildering, the illuminating, the most exalted and the most contemptible, the pulsating stream of light, or the deceitful flow from the heart of an impenetrable darkness."

"I was cut to the quick at the idea of having lost the inestimable privilege of listening to the gifted Kurtz. Of course I was wrong. The privilege was waiting for me. Oh, yes. I heard more than enough. And I was right too. A voice. He was very little more than a voice."[29]

In *S/Z*, Barthes accepts the concept of character he had once rejected and says not that it is an essence, but a construct: "character is a product of combinations: the combination is relatively stable (denoted by the recurrence of semes) and more or less complex (involving more or less congruent, more or less contradictory figures); . . . The proper name acts as a magnetic field for the semes; referring in fact to a body, it draws the semic configuration into an evolving (biographical) tense."[30] Character, in other words, is not simply language, but has a body, a physical component as the signifier does. Moreover, it is important to notice again how *physical* poststructuralist metaphors necessarily become and how fully dependent on spatial concepts the metaphors are. Those that aren't creating magnetic fields are causing rifts, ruptures, or margins— despite the fact that the basis of this discourse is an ontology of presence at odds with empirical experience and substantive bodies that stand of themselves, in space, among other things.

---

29. *Ibid.*, 38–39, 39, 67–68 (italics added), 68–69.
30. Roland Barthes, *S/Z*, trans. Richard Miller (New York, 1974), 67–68. See also 190–91.

The historical basis of this discourse against physical necessity Peter Brooks explains in *Body Works:* "Cartesian 'dualism,'—positing a thinking essence distinct from corporeality—creates a body that is no longer 'in' language but rather the object of discourse: 'The Cartesian body is "outside" language; it is given to discourse as an object (when it is not, in its absent moment, exiled altogether) but it is never *of* language in its essence.'" This attitude, however, has never been that of realism; for the other side of this Cartesian dialectic, the traditionally novelistic side, is implicit in another of Brooks's explanations: "If the sociocultural body clearly is a construct, an ideological product, nonetheless we tend to think of the physical body as precultural and prelinguistic: sensations of pleasure and especially of pain, for instance, are generally held to be experiences outside language; and the body's end, in death, is not simply a discursive construct."[31] It is always good to be reminded that death is impervious to deconstruction. It is also germane to note that even simpler sensations than pleasure and pain are outside language too. The heft and texture of this book in your hand are, as I have said, not completely representable by the text held by the book—which, to be fair, is a container that can't possibly "contain" what it seems to. Realism has always acknowledged a reality beyond language's reach; the novel has always explored the different, complex relationships of consciousness to matter. So Barthes seems to be coming to his senses exactly when he uses the phrase "referring in fact to a body."

For it is impossible to imagine Austen or Conrad imagining Elizabeth or Marlow without bodies. And when Marlow claims to do that with Kurtz, to disembody him and thereby elevate and reduce him to language, which is both Kurtz's own voice and Marlow's voice performing his interpretation of Kurtz, Marlow does so in order to remove Kurtz from the shared physical world in which Kurtz has other interpreters. On the left, there are the skeptics who want to remove Kurtz; on the right, the true believers such as the harlequin and the Intended. These are discrepant enough. More difficult of reconciliation, however, are the disparate claims of Kurtz's reputation as a universal genius and the physical evidence of the skulls staked around his hut. And this is to say nothing of the body, "savage and superb, wild-eyed and magnificent," of his African queen.[32]

Character is easier to read in *Pride and Prejudice* than it seems to be in *Heart of Darkness*, although both novels dramatize its difficulty because that is what

---

31. Brooks, *Body Work*, 5, 7. See also Elaine Scarry, *The Body in Pain: The Making and Unmaking of the World* (New York, 1985), for another study of the body's sometimes ineffable relation to language.

32. Conrad, *Heart of Darkness*, 87.

novels are traditionally about: characters reading other characters, human subjects and objects at play in their undecided similarity-and-difference. But the
difference Conrad represents is still more historical than ontological because it
is the difference between Austen's classicism and Conrad's modernism—which
is "the idea that in twentieth-century literature, difficulty is particularly necessary and virtuous."[33] For Marlow and Conrad both, Kurtz is still a human
figure; and though there is no hint that his essence is there to be read in his
eyes, his psychology is not unimportant: as he loses his mind, it seems he is
also losing his soul; he has an id rather than a dark wedge; and he does die
rather than disperse as Slothrop does. Marlow's own language is suggestive,
however, of another way to read Kurtz. He is a presence, Marlow says, because
he is a star: compelling, charismatic, and unavoidable. But he is also a presence
because at the moment that Marlow says he is, he is absent. And he is a voice,
a signifier without a specific signified or a signifying function without content,
because this makes him more susceptible to Marlow's control and evasions. So
Kurtz is finally more important for his discursive possibilities than his identity,
and the meaning *of* Kurtz more important than the meaning *in* him: although
Kurtz's body, living and dead, does seem to pose some limits to the authority
Marlow would like to arrogate to himself in managing Kurtz's significance.

> "What are we what?"
> "What?"
> "You said, 'What are we . . . ,' then you stopped."
> "Oh. Gee, that was a funny thing to say."

To this question in *Gravity's Rainbow*, "What are we," we have seen quite
different answers from these three mainline novelists, but all of them entail
assumptions about a character's legibility according to the degree of presence
it emanates. Elizabeth wants to be able to read fixed essences in facial features
as though she is reading a letter as authoritative, unambiguous, and firmly
intended as Darcy's. Austen herself does not argue for such essentialistic fixity,
but she does not suggest, as Eliot does, that character, as a cluster of signs, is
illimitably open. But Eliot herself is not arguing that those signs cluster around
an empty absence: it would be hard to argue that *Middlemarch*, suffused as it
is with spirituality, disbelieves in the soul; and hard to argue as well that the

---

33. Richard Poirier, *The Renewal of Literature: Emersonian Reflections* (New York, 1987),
98. His chapter "Modernism and Its Difficulties" makes an argument consonant with Walter L.
Reed's that literature is always testing within itself the claims of other forms of discourse.

signs cluster around a center of unintelligibility. Eliot is neither the nominalist nor the mystifier Marlow seems to be in his statement that Kurtz "was just a word for me. I did not see the man in the word any more than you do," but then Conrad isn't either. Marlow may try to disembody Kurtz; Conrad, however, is more interested in demonstrating that character as a sign, as a principle we read and read-with, is always an interpretation of consciousness's relation to matter. There are, in other words, limits represented by Kurtz's body and the bodies of his other interpreters or attendants. It is not hard to see, however, that in the "progress" from Austen to Conrad, character does become more problematic as it more explicitly questions the relationship between words and bodies (the issue itself in any construal of representation) and that the "progress" tends to favor the formalistic claims of language and the needs of interpretation, which a purely linguistic ontology facilitates.

The most radical questions about the nature of character, however, come from the writers who emphasize the physical component of character that opposes language. Mrs. Ramsay's "dark wedge" is not her body or her unconsciousness, but her inexpressible self, and the point on which the traditional relationship between im-manence and ex-pression is re-ordered. It is probably not as challenging a proposition as Pynchon's figuration of the self as an electromystical triode, but Pynchon's proposal is not without its analogues either. In *Elective Affinities* (1809), Goethe entertains a number of ideas for defining the nature of *relationship;* chemistry and the naturalism implicit in chemical explanations of adultery are obviously featured, but the most remarkable moment in the book may be the scene in which Eduard explains why he does not like anyone to read over his shoulder and the very unusual relationship between inner and outer, thought and its traditional bodily container, his explanation sets up:

> Only, one evening when he had sat down without thinking about where, he noticed Charlotte was reading over his shoulder. His old impatience came to life again and he rebuked her for it rather roughly, saying bad habits of that kind, like so many others that were an annoyance to society, ought to be broken once and for all. 'If I read aloud to someone,' he said, 'is it not as if I were speaking to him and telling him something? What has been written down and printed takes the place of my own mind and my own heart; and would I ever take the trouble to speak at all if a window were constructed in my forehead or in my chest, so that he to whom I want to expound my thoughts one by one, or convey my feelings one by one, could always know long in advance what I was getting at?

Whenever anyone reads over my shoulder it is as if I were being torn in two.'[34]

This is a sensitive guy, his whole inner being displaceable by someone else's prose and vulnerable then to the female gaze. His opposite is Andrei Bely's character Apollon Apollonovich Ableukhov in *Petersburg* (1916), whose own inner being can displace the world:

> Oh, better that Apollon Apollonovich should never have cast off a single idle thought, but should have continued to carry each and every thought in his head, for every thought stubbornly evolved into a spatiotemporal image and continued its uncontrolled activities outside the senatorial head.
>
> Apollon Apollonovich was like Zeus: out of his head flowed goddesses and genii. One of these genii (the stranger with the small black mustache), arising as an image, had already *begun to live and breathe* in the yellowish spaces. And he maintained that he had emerged from there, not from the senatorial head. This stranger turned out to have idle thoughts too. And they also possessed the same qualities.
>
> They would escape and take on substance.

There is a serious anti-Kantean comedy going on in *Petersburg*, a critique exemplified in passages such as this that also have another aspect. For what Bely grants to his characters is a power in physical terms that a writer has in language. Apollon's projection is not hallucinatory; it's creative "writing" in the manner of his own creative writer. And Bely's narrator says at the end of this chapter:

> You Will Never Ever Forget Him!
> In this chapter we have seen Senator Ableukhov. We have also seen the idle thoughts of the senator in the form of the senator's house and in the form of the senator's son, who also carries his own idle thoughts in his head. Finally, we have seen another idle shadow—the stranger.
> This shadow arose by chance in the consciousness of Senator Ableukhov and acquired its ephemeral being there. But the con-

---

34. Johann Wolfgang von Goethe, *Elective Affinities*, trans. R. J. Hollingdale (Harmondsworth, 1971), 49.

sciousness of Apollon Apollonovich is a shadowy consciousness because he too is the possessor of an ephemeral being and the fruit of the author's fantasy: unnecessary, idle cerebral play.

The author, having hung pictures of illusions all over, really should take them down as quickly as possible, breaking the thread of the narrative, if only with this very sentence. But the author will not do so: he has sufficient right not to.

Cerebral play is only a mask. Under way beneath this mask is the invasion of the brain by forces unknown to us. And granting that Apollon Apollonovich is spun from our brain, nonetheless he will manage to inspire fear with another, a stupendous state of being which attacks in the night. Apollon Apollonovich is endowed with the attributes of this state of being. All his cerebral play is endowed with the attributes of this state of being.

Once his brain has playfully engendered the mysterious stranger, that stranger exists, really exists. He will not vanish from the Petersburg prospects as long as the senator with such thoughts exists, because thought exists too.

So let our stranger be a real stranger! And let the two shadows of my stranger be real shadows!

Those dark shadows will, oh yes, they will, follow on the heels of the stranger, just as the stranger himself is closely following the senator. The aged senator will, oh yes, he will, pursue you too, dear reader, in his black carriage. And henceforth you will never ever forget him!

End of the First Chapter[35]

This is a passage as skeptical, as self-exposing as anything in Cervantes or Diderot and very close in its manner of play to the kinds of erasure and redisposition that go on throughout *Gravity's Rainbow*. The narrator here is not the author, whom the narrator both criticizes and defends; both have granted the character Apollon a correlative autonomy and power; the "stranger" later in the novel acquires a name, Dudkin, and a continuing role; all four characters have a different original ontology, and there are five of them, actually, if the author the narrator refers to is *not* Bely; and the "you," dear reader, of the text's direct address is something else entirely as you hold in your hand this book that holds within its language that of Bely.

35. Andrei Bely, *Petersburg*, trans. Robert A. Maguire and John E. Malmstad (Bloomington, 1978), 20, 35–36.

Although the writer in English who most resembles Pynchon and his attitude toward character is Woolf, the writer Pynchon resembles even more is Bely, whom he may well have read at Cornell under Nabokov's influence. For in Pynchon, character has several different styles. Mrs. Dalloway and Mrs. Ramsay are rather similar, and they differ from other, solider characters such as their husbands in much the same way. But Slothrop is not the only character in *Gravity's Rainbow* who takes strange leave of his ordinary body or has an extraordinary relationship to the transcendental sources of meaning Pynchon wants to interrogate. So on our way back to a further look at free indirect discourse, and what it establishes of the *meaning* of a character in ontological terms, it is of some profit to look at the characters who provide us with a context for Slothrop. The one thing all these characters have in common is that they are role-players, and I mean this term in both common senses: they play roles, as actors and actresses do; and they function in a system, play a role, over which they do not have complete control.

The social and cosmic orders in *Gravity's Rainbow* are obviously not stable, but whether they determine everything or nothing is one of the book's central concerns. Yet, in this uncertainty, Slothrop is free to play a number of roles, in emulation of his favorite comic-book hero, Plasticman, who is to Slothrop what the god Proteus is to Telemachus. As he goes into the Zone, Slothrop becomes the journalist Ian Scuffling, then the actor Max Schlepzig, then to his own mind a "silly" Tannhauser. He is, for reasons that are still funny, more serious about himself in the role of Rocketman, then a somewhat unwitting river-god or Orpheus-figure when he boards the *Anubis*, and then he becomes the lucky pig-god Plechazunga, a costume part that eventually saves him from Pointsman's final stroke. Penultimately, Slothrop also plays a crossroads, not as a wandering band of minstrels would play a crossroads, but insofar as he becomes an intersection. It is hard to know if his final state of dis-integration is also a role, or what space in the unknown molecular script Slothrop eventually inhabits. In any case, he is obviously luckier than at least two of the other characters in *Gravity's Rainbow* whose roles lead them to ends of utter emptiness.

These two are Katje Borgesius and Margherita Erdmann: they have both acted in movies; they have both been sexually involved with Slothrop; and they are identified with each other by a slip of the tongue Blicero makes. Quite early in the novel, after he has rescued her from Grigori, the trained octopus, Slothrop, who is not distinguished by his insight into women, sees the rest of Katje's life in an intuition that then turns back onto himself:

> Back in a room, early in Slothrop's life, a room forbidden to him
> now, is something very bad. Something was done to him, and it may

be that Katje knows what. Hasn't he, in her "futureless look," found some link to his own past, something that connects them closely as lovers? He sees her standing at the end of a passage in her life, without any next step to take—all her bets are in, she has only the tedium now of being knocked from one room to the next, a sequence of numbered rooms whose numbers do not matter, till inertia brings her to the last. That's all.

Naive Slothrop never thought anybody's life could end like that. Nothing so bleak. But by now it's grown much less strange to him— he's been snuggling up, masturbatorily scared-elated, to the dis- agreeable chance that exactly such Control might already have been put over him.

Greta Erdmann's case is different and more complex. She seems, in one way, taken over by her roles in Nazi films and acts them out in life by the ritualized slaying of Jewish children and by her need to persist in sadomasochistic routines, not unlike those Katje has played with Blicero and Gottfried. Greta's partner, however, is lately her daughter Bianca, which makes Bianca even more attractive to Slothrop than her mother has been. Around these women in particular, Slothrop is not the happy chucklehead he usually tries to be, and Greta's fate suggests a version of his own: "What Slothrop will be leaving Greta Erdmann to is not so clear. Along the Havel in Neubabelsberg she waits, less than the images of herself that survive in an indeterminate number of release prints here and there about the Zone, and even across the Sea." This is obviously only a psychological diminution, isn't it? Or an aging actress's occupational hazard, being less than her old images? Nothing ontological here. Yet Pynchon identifies Bianca with Ilse Pökler because they were both conceived under the power of the same movie fantasy; so Pynchon himself suggests otherwise: that there is another kind of ontology movies make and that Greta's fate, therefore, is not so different from Slothrop's dispersion.[36]

In any case, despite their roles, none of these characters has the freedom or the protection we have come to expect in the roles that comic characters and picaros are allowed to play. They all seem caught; and their malleability is evidence of their powerlessness, or evidence of a shaping power beyond their knowledge and perhaps beyond their comprehension. Their meaning, therefore, as human characters, is fundamentally different from the meaning of those

---

36. Pynchon, *Gravity's Rainbow*, 486, 208–209, 364. See also Susan Sontag, *On Photography* (New York, 1978). She discusses throughout her argument photography's effect on our under- standing of ontology, because photography, she argues, has redefined what's "real."

figures who are the free interpreters of their own experience; for Pynchon's characters may exist in an ulterior order, in a system that makes of their roles a function in another operation. For this reason exactly, these three—Slothrop, Katje, and Greta—are crucial characters in this novel about control, paranoia, Providence, and political totalization; but their situation also makes them, despite their political significance, not *realistic* characters in any traditional sense of that word. Or, perhaps, they alter the terms of the realistic equation that we will examine in the next chapter. In any case, they are hard characters to read because it is so difficult to establish their relationship to both the physical world and other systems of meaning.[37]

And they are not the only ones in the book who feel themselves to be functions in another plot. Franz Pökler does too, although at least part of that plot is a happier experience for him:

> Pökler may be only witnessing tonight—or he may really be part
> of it. He hasn't been shown which it is. Look at this. There is about
> to be expedited, for Friedrich August Kekulé von Stradonitz, his
> dream of 1865, the great Dream that revolutionized chemistry and
> made the IG possible. So that the right material may find its way to
> the right dreamer, everyone, everything involved must be exactly in
> place in the pattern. It was nice of Jung to give us the idea of an
> ancestral pool in which everybody shares the same dream material.
> But how is it we are each visited *as individuals*, each by exactly and
> only what he needs? Doesn't that imply a switching-path of some
> kind? a bureaucracy? Why shouldn't the IG go to séances? They
> ought to be quite at home with the bureaucracies of the other side.

In a book of astonishing speculation and device, this passage is one of the most important and radical. It is one thing to say the problem of the individual is resolved by "higher management," but quite another then to accept the implication of this resolution that life and death exist in a kind of complementarity which makes death just another interface and, therefore, the epigraph of the novel a proposition unalloyed by irony: "Nature does not know extinction; all it knows is transformation. Everything science has taught me, and continues to teach me, strengthens my belief in the continuity of our spiritual existence after death." The epigraph is a statement from Werner von Braun; and at first glance,

---

37. See Alec McHoul and David Wills, *Writing Pynchon: Strategies in Fictional Analysis* (Urbana, 1990), 23–66, for a deconstructive reading of these problems that closes Pynchon off entirely from the awkwardness of any realistic reference.

before we have read the rest of the book, it seems extraordinary and facetious. Science confirms spirituality? Death is only a higher continuity? This is a profound disorientation because it clearly changes our relationships to both our body and our supposititious soul and their relationship to each other. And this from the architect of the V-2 rocket? This is very hard to hear. And the way in which Pynchon goes on to extend his explanation of Kekulé's dream is no help at all because he talks to us—to "you" again—as though all this is something we have encountered before and are comfortable enough to joke about against those who aren't so comfortable:

> Kekulé's dream here's being routed now past points which may arc through the silence, in bright reluctance to live inside the moving moment, an imperfect, a human light, over here interfering with the solemn binary decisions of these agents, who are now allowing the cosmic Serpent, in the violet splendor of its scales, shining that is definitely *not* human, to pass—without feeling, without wonder (after you get a little time in—whatever *that* means over here—one of these archetypes gets to look pretty much like any other, oh you hear some of these new hire, the seersucker crowd come in the first day, "Wow! Hey—that's th-th' *Tree o' Creation!* Huh? Ain't it! Je-eepers!" but they calm down fast enough, pick up the reflexes for Intent to Gawk, you know self-criticism's an amazing technique, it shouldn't work but it does.

As he does so often in *Gravity's Rainbow,* at moments when we seem to need him the most with a serious explanation of what this means, Pynchon—"Je-eepers!"—starts goofing around. Yet if we ask at this point, as we have seen Slothrop ask, not who are we, but *what*, what does this conception of human character make us, Pynchon has an answer. We are "gates," a term he explains here and continues then to use throughout the rest of the book as though it were Navy slang.

> Once again it was the influence of Liebig, the great professor of chemistry on whose name-street in Munich Pökler lived while he attended the T. H. Liebig . . . inspired the young man to change his field. So Kekulé brought the mind's eye of an architect over into chemistry. It was a critical switch. Liebig himself seems to have occupied the role of a gate, or sorting-demon such as his younger contemporary Clerk Maxwell once proposed, helping to concentrate energy into one favored room of the Creation at the expense of

everything else (later witnesses have suggested that Clerk Maxwell intended his Demon not so much as a convenience in discussing a thermodynamic idea as a parable about the *actual existence* of personnel like Liebig.[38]

Roger Mexico, a statistician and relatively normal character, believes in the magic of union with Jessica that makes them "a joint creature unaware of itself." Pökler, the rocket engineer and also relatively normal, believes in his occult dream and in a system-function theory of human being that controverts most traditionally novelistic ideas of individuality. And Pynchon himself has obviously thought about human being and character in a number of different ways not usually pursued by novelists. Yet what forces us to take his speculation seriously is the power with which he can convey not only certain physical experiences of an unknown value, but also those of pain, dread, loss, death, and evil. For in no case does the characters' special ontology excuse them from suffering or guilt. Certainly, one of the most powerful moments in the book is Slothrop's discovery of Bianca's hanging body, and one of the most powerful sequences is the story of Pökler's discovery of what his life has really meant. This story reaches the kind of recognition we usually assign to tragedy and includes the suffering Pökler experiences as he sneaks into the Dora internment camp, which has been right next door to his laboratory all the time. "The odors of shit, death, sweat, sickness, mildew, piss, the breathing of Dora, wrapped him as he crept in staring at the naked corpses being carried out now that America was so close, to be stacked in front of the crematorium, the men's penises hanging, their toes clustering white and round as pearls . . . *each face so perfect, so individual.*"[39] Pökler has never looked at anything, except Ilse's face, so closely, and he only began to do that when he knew he was losing, had lost her. His belief that he functions in a higher system does not save him from pain and terrible guilt, and Pynchon's belief in a life after death does not keep *Gravity's Rainbow* from also recording the endlessness of anguish, emptiness, and loss, in the system of war.

There is, nonetheless, some hope in a completely different kind of character, whose relationship to physical reality seems most like Slothrop's own, especially in the novel's middle phases we can call the mode of Slothrop's mindless pleasures. The character is "Pirate" Prentice, who is open to the kind of magic

38. Pynchon, *Gravity's Rainbow*, 410–11 (italics added). "Gate" is a term used in thermodynamics as well as in both membrane physiology and the design of electric circuitry for computers.

39. *Ibid.*, 432 (italics added).

that shifts the mind into new wholes and different fields of energy. He is one of many, of course, at the White Visitation, who have special sensitivities; Slothrop is only the most extreme. Pirate's talent, which gives him his nickname, is his ability to play host to the otherwise debilitating fantasies of those who are more important to the War effort. His is a gift of vulnerability, his nature permeable to what can only be called, I guess, a psycho-osmotic flow. He is a gate; we can say he is, in a way, a healthy version of Woolf's Septimus Smith. But it is important to distinguish his states as a fantasist-surrogate from the magic Roger Mexico feels in union with Jessica; important also to distinguish him from the more traditionally endowed spiritualist, Carroll Eventyr, who can only contact the dead. Prentice seems to be able to organize his relation to the other with less self-loss and more control than most of the characters have, so he stands as a different, generally more affirmative version of those in the novel who seem driven toward their own destruction by something within them that it is possible to identify with, or even *as*, someone else, someone they do not possess. These characters ride the range of obsession from Roger's more or less conventional love of Jessica, to Weissmann's and Enzian's love and hate for each other, to Tchitcherine's hatred for Enzian, to Pointsman's obsession with Pavlov, and perhaps even Slothrop's with Jamf. There is not a lot of obvious good Prentice can do with his gift, but it does seem important to note that this gift is, like some of the other psychokinetic talents, charismatic in the archaic sense of the word— that is, of no personal benefit to the gifted person, but only to the others he serves with it; that it is also not unlike compassion, empathy, or imagination; and that it would not be useless to the kind of writer who says: "You go from dream to dream inside me. You have passage to my last shabby corner, and there, among the debris you've found life. I'm no longer sure which of all the words is 'yours' and which is 'mine.'" Prentice is Pynchon's portrait of the artist. He doesn't write, though, or make art; he *represents* Pynchon's writing.

In the modernist novels that are, in Woolf's words, "novels of consciousness" rather than of social reality, novels that in effect define consciousness as human nature, the figure of the artist is obviously going to be of crucial interest, even when he or she plays a secondary role. Lily is no Mrs. Ramsay, Stephen is no Bloom, Prentice is not even Slothrop. But Prentice is nonetheless important because, in this unsystematic book that does not fall into obvious patterns, he is at the center of the opening phase. He seems to be having the rocket dream; conscious, then, he is alert to the sky; by instinct, he saves the falling Teddy Bloat; by avocation, he cultivates the garden of bananas that tell Death to "fuck off"; by training, he can empty his mind. And when he stands "in the lavatory . . . pissing, without a thought in his head," he is too much like Slothrop, in his last integrated moment, to be accidental. For not everyone, by a long shot, can enjoy these moments of mindless pleasure.

Slothrop, of course, can: he goes out in one of them, as he is otherwise doing nothing: "And now, in the Zone, later in the day he became a crossroad, after a heavy rain he doesn't recall, Slothrop sees a very thick rainbow here, a stout rainbow cock driven out of pubic clouds into Earth, green wet valleyed Earth, and his chest fills and he stands crying, not a thing in his head, just feeling natural. . . ." "Not a *thing* in his head" is nice, a better way of saying, perhaps, that he has achieved "the pure, the informationless state of signal zero," where the "deeper and true Self" flows without the modulation of the ego and history, without interference, conditioning, or a function in any system.[40] Since Slothrop does not return from the state he enters here, it is obviously more than a momentary meditation and nothing at all like most of the other moments of similar texture and significance, because its issue is a change in ontology. Perhaps Lyle Bland's departure is analogous, but it is hard to tell because Bland's story is embedded, it seems, for sport. It is nothing we are prepared for; it is hardly mentioned again. Slothrop, on the other hand, we have watched from early on experiencing states such as Mrs. Ramsay's "reification" or Pirate's emptiness, as though he were testing his wings.

The first time we witness a similar change in him, Slothrop has an experience, like *déjà vu*, that feels more like a reintegration than it does dispersal: "They're reassembling . . . it must be outside his memory . . . cool clean interior, girl and woman, independent of his shorthand of starts . . . so many fading-faced girls, windy canalsides, bed-sitters, bus-stop good-bys, how can he be expected to remember? but this room has gone on clarifying: part of whoever he was inside it has kindly remained, stored quiescent these moments outside his head, distributed through the grainy shadows, the grease-hazy jars of herbs, candies, spices, all the Compton Mackenzie novels on the shelf." This is not unpleasant, it is just not as familiar as the normal sensation of bodily bliss.[41] "Breakfast is wine, bread, smiling, sun diffracting through the fine gratings of long dancer's hair, swung, flipped, never still, a dazzle of violet, sorrel, saffron, emerald. . . . For a moment you can let the world go, solid forms gone a-fracturing, warm

---

40. *Ibid.*, 10, 6, 626. See also the penultimate paragraph on 616 for a contrasting state.

41. *Ibid.*, 115. For contrast, see Woolf's "A Sketch of the Past," 67: "Now if this is so, is it not possible—I often wonder—that things we have felt with great intensity have an existence independent of our minds; are in fact still in existence?" In *Swann's Way* Marcel's tone is lighter and his metaphor almost self-subverting, but his point is the same: in another ontological dispensation, our inmost experiences, such as memory, persist in objects outside us. See Marcel Proust, *Remembrance of Things Past*, trans. C. K. Scott Moncrieff and Terence Kilmartin (New York, 1981), I, 47.

inside of bread waiting at your fingertips, flowery wine in long, easy passage streaming downward around the root of your tongue." And this kind of happiness is not the up-welling he can feel unexpectedly in the middle of bad news:

> Then in the morning Katje comes storming in madder than a wet hen to tell Slothrop that Sir Stephen's gone. Suddenly everybody is telling Slothrop things, and he's barely awake. Rain rattles at the shutters and windows. Monday mornings, upset stomachs, good-bys . . . he blinks out at the misted sea, the horizon mantled in gray, palms gleaming in the rain, heavy and wet and very green. It may be that the champagne is still with him—for ten extraordinary seconds there's nothing in his field but simple love for what he's seeing.

This is an important moment because it is so clearly one marked by the *absence* of meaning. Not a thing on his mind. What's there is there to be seen, simply, in a way like Strether with Madame de Vionnet in *The Ambassadors*. And Slothrop, in the moment of this purely empty poise, so much like Mrs. Ramsay's epiphanies, seems to feel no self-presence either. His state in the moment quoted above is blissfully different from those moments when an undefinable presence pressures him, and meaning looms:

> For a minute here, Slothrop, in his English uniform, is alone with the paraphernalia of an order whose presence among the ordinary debris of waking he has only lately begun to suspect.
>
> There may, for a moment, have been some golden, vaguely rootlike or manlike figure beginning to form among the brown and bright cream shadows and light here. But Slothrop isn't to be let off quite so easy. Shortly, unpleasantly so, it will come to him that everything in this room is really being used for something different. Meaning things to Them it has never meant to us. Two orders of being, looking identical . . . but, but . . .

At this point in the text, it would be nice to hear a word or two from Pynchon to the effect that it is Slothrop's special aptitude for thinning out and disintegrating that gives him this sensitivity to another "order" of presence, that *what he is* determines what he can *know*. Instead, Pynchon's narrative bursts into song:

> Oh, THE WORLD OVER THERE, it's
> So hard to explain!

Just-like a dream's got, lost in yer brain!
Dancin' like a fool through that Forbid-den Wing,
Waitin' fer th' light to start shiver-ing—well,
Who ev-ver said ya couldn't move that way,
Who ev-ver said ya couldn't try?
If-ya find-there's-a-lit-tle-pain,
Ya can al-ways-go-back-a-gain, cause
Ya don't-ev-ver-real-ly-say, good-by!

Why here? Why should the rainbow edges of what is almost on him
be rippling most intense here in this amply coded room? say why
should walking in here be almost the same as entering the Forbidden
itself—. . . what game do They deal? What passes are these, so
blurred, so old and perfect? . . .

He steps back out, backward out the door, as if half, his ventral
half, were being struck in kingly radiance: retreating from yet facing
the Presence feared and wanted.[42]

If Major Marvy is "in this primal American act, paying, more deeply himself
than when coming, or asleep, or maybe even dying," Slothrop is more deeply
himself when he is either terrified at ineffable presence or feeling mindlessly
empty, absent from himself. If the first state is one of absolute paranoia, the
second is antiparanoia, "where nothing is connected to anything, a condition
not many of us can bear for long." This radical discontinuity we can describe
as a state in which every thing is absent from everything else, the ground
condition for a metaphysics in which every object is so only and completely
itself that no abstraction, no transcendence of the individual thing is legitimate.
This immanence may also be the "informationless state of signal zero" in
Mondaugen's electro-mysticism; and while Slothrop can experience this state
as a peaceful joy, as we have seen in some of the quotations above, he can also
experience it as vague uneasiness:

Well right now Slothrop feels himself sliding onto the anti-paranoid
part of his cycle, feels the whole city around him going back roofless,
vulnerable, uncentered as he is, and only pasteboard images now of
the Listening Enemy left between him and the west sky.
Either They have put him here for a reason, or he's just here. He
isn't sure that he wouldn't actually, rather have that *reason*.

42. Pynchon, *Gravity's Rainbow*, 185, 221, 202, 203.

Slothrop, however, is only rarely like this; he is usually not resistant at all to the moments of emptiness, of the absence of meaning, that may be his only way out of a world so threatening, so completely overdetermined that it has no explanation. He certainly cannot explain it. Even Pynchon cannot explain it wholly. For when he comes to those moments of the most interesting and urgent mystery, Pynchon goofs off, breaks into song, turns to "you," the reader, in order to invoke once again your understanding and experience, as though your answers would get him off the hook. Here are three different, particularly interesting uses of the kind of indirect discourse in which Pynchon talks to himself, his characters, and his reader—all of whom are "you"—in the same breath. These passages show us again, as clearly as it can be shown, how character is the principal mediation the novelist, the novel, and the reader share; and they also return us to look again at indirect discourse itself:

> But these are rumors. Their chronology can't be trusted. Contradictions creep in. Perfect for passing a winter in Central Asia if you happen not to be Tchitcherine. If you *are* Tchitcherine, though, well, that puts you in more of a peculiar position. Doesn't it. You have to get through the winter on nothing but paranoid suspicions about why you're here. . . .
>
> You will want cause and effect. All right. Thanatz was washed overboard in the same storm that took Slothrop from the *Anubis*. He was rescued by a Polish undertaker in a rowboat, out in the storm tonight to see if he can get struck by lightning. The undertaker is wearing, in the hopes it will draw electricity, a complicated metal suit. . . .
>
> Now what sea is this you have crossed, exactly, and what sea is it you have plunged more than once to the bottom of, alerted, full of adrenalin, but caught really, buffaloed under the epistemologies of these threats that paranoid you so down and out, caught in this steel pot, softening to devitaminized mush inside the soup-stock of your own words, your waste submarine breath? It took the Dreyfus Affair to get the Zionists out and going, finally: what will drive you out of your soup-kettle? Has it already happened? Was it tonight's attack and deliverance? Will you go to the Heath, and begin your settlement, and wait there for your Director to come?[43]

"Buffaloed under the epistemologies," at the very least, you know?

43. *Ibid.*, 605, 434, 349, 663, 389–90.

As I said at the beginning of this chapter, free indirect discourse has been the most important form of modern narrative since Flaubert; and since he used it to discipline his own romantic longings, it has been used by writers as different as James, Joyce, Lawrence, Woolf, Faulkner, and Updike. What they have all found in free indirect discourse, what is exactly its most important quality, is a way of creating character that only the novel can realize, for free indirect discourse can't be imagined off the page. It is a style, therefore, that neither drama nor the narrative voice of epic can employ. It is, moreover, a style that deploys a boundary between narrator and character that can never be settled *physically,* for free indirect discourse is not a mode or type of speech. It is one of the novel's forms of writing.

First- and third-person narrators are imaginable as speakers. The kind of narrator that Scholes and Kellogg epitomize in Fielding is part inquiring *histor,* part discerning bard, and part creative maker. Full of "presence" and his own personality, he is a character who can be imagined as a living replica of the Homeric scop in performance, touring the country's campuses, performing the works he had written for the voice of the kind of living narrator he has become.[44] The first-person narrator such as Marlow, whose physical setting is so fully imagined a movie could be made of his recitation of the Kurtz legend, is also obviously dramatic, intimate, personal. These qualities we find in first-person narratives that say they are written out rather than told—think of John Dowling and Nick Carraway—and in the advanced version of first-person narrative we call the interior monologue. Molly Bloom's soliloquy has been recorded and performed.

Because its qualities are those of writing rather than speech, free indirect discourse implies no embodiment other than the prose on the page; it is no one's sole self-expression because it cannot be located in either the narrator alone or in the character either. It is, as I have said, the definitive style of the modernist principle of impersonality; and the absence it speaks from is always in reference to something else that isn't quite there, the reader, who often finds indirect discourse hard to interpret because there is no clear origin for it, no *expressive* intention, which makes the distance between the narrator and character hard to interpret and define yourself within. Free indirect discourse also changes, for all practical purposes, the relationship between the represented physical bodies in the novel's world; for it exists within the realm of language, and the characters it creates cannot have the kind of relationship with each other that each has with the narrator. Not, that is, unless they are built like Pirate Prentice and take onto themselves another's consciousness:

44. Robert Scholes and Robert Kellogg, *The Nature of Narrative* (London, 1966), 265–68.

Sitting on the floor with her arms round Mrs. Ramsay's knees, close
as she could get, smiling to think that Mrs. Ramsay would never
know the reason of that pressure, she imagined how in the chambers
of the mind and heart of the woman who was physically touching
her, were stood, like the treasures in the tombs of kings, tablets
bearing sacred inscriptions, which if one could spell them out, would
teach one everything, but they would never be offered openly, never
made public. What art was there, known to love or cunning, by which
one pressed through into those secret chambers? What device for
becoming, like waters poured into one jar, inextricably the same,
one with the object one adored? Could the body achieve, or the mind,
subtly mingling in the intricate passages of the brain? or the heart?
Could loving, as people called it, make her and Mrs. Ramsay one?
for it was not knowledge but unity that she desired, not inscriptions
on tablets, nothing that could be written in any language known to
men, but intimacy itself, which is knowledge, she had thought, leaning her head on Mrs. Ramsay's knee.[45]

What Woolf can do here, the presence she can extend, the access she can have
to Mrs. Ramsay's inner being and Lily's inmost, inexpressible emotion, the
characters themselves could never have in a moment such as this. Yet Woolf's
style here makes her feel not at all like a commentator, not the ironic author of
this essence-to-be-read metaphor we've already remarked, and in no way superior, but an equal in this intimacy and a participant in its yearning. And one
response to Lily's questions, which she could neither form nor answer in this
way—"What art was there, known to love or cunning, by which one pressed
through into those secret chambers? What device for becoming . . . inextricably
the same, one with the object one adored?"—is *this*, this art, this prose. There
is nothing like it, Lily dear, nothing like it that Mrs. Ramsay can tell you either.

The situation in *The Waves* is quite different. We can, of course, imagine the
characters with bodies in the world; we can complete for them what is not quite
there to begin with by the phenomenological act Seymour Chatman calls "reading out";[46] and we can understand the thematic importance of Percival, who is
their beautiful mute center even after he is absented in death. But they remain
so awkwardly, so completely the product of Woolf's *writing*—rather than of her
visual imagination—that when they "speak" they sound funny, especially when

45. Woolf, *To the Lighthouse*, 78–79.
46. Seymour Chatman, *Story and Discourse: Narrative Structure in Fiction and Film* (Ithaca,
1980), 39ff.

they try to deal with normal physical experience. Woolf does not try for the colloquial diction and tone which Pynchon does so brilliantly that they can disguise both the writing and the extraordinary kinds of experience he is presenting; and even though Pynchon writes about Slothrop almost always in the present tense, and has him undergo an experience of reintegration not less extraordinary than Bernard's, quoted here below, the prose of *Gravity's Rainbow* never sounds like this:

> "Yet behold, it returns. One cannot extinguish that persistent smell. It steals in through some crack in the structure—one's identity. I am not part of the street—no, I observe the street. One splits off, therefore. For instance, up that back street a girl stands waiting; for whom? A romantic story. . . . On the wall of that shop is fixed a small crane, and for what reason, I ask, was that crane fixed there? and invent a purple lady swelling, circumambient, hauled from a barouche landau by a perspiring husband sometime in the sixties. A grotesque story. That is, I am a natural coiner of words, a blower of bubbles through one thing and another. And striking off these observations spontaneously I elaborate myself; differentiate myself and listening to the voice that says as I stroll past, 'Look! Take note of that!' I conceive myself called upon to provide, some winter's night, a meaning for all my observations—a line that runs from one to another, a summing up that completes."

Although this passage *is* enclosed within quotation marks and Bernard, the speaker, ends the novel in a dramatized speaking part with an audience, like Marlow's, Woolf's language here betrays the great difficulty in writing about character and the world when they are not conceived in the usual substantive terms, when they are *written* in a style befitting the new ratio between matter and consciousness her conception of character assumes: "But how describe the world seen without a self? There are no words. Blue, red—even they distract, *even they hide with thickness instead of letting the light through.* How describe or say anything in articulate words again?—save that it fades, save that it undergoes a gradual transformation, becomes, even in one short walk, habitual—this scene also."[47] When *The Waves* works best, it is not in statements such as Bernard's aesthetic epistemology, but in passages, such as the one to follow below, in which Rhoda addresses only herself and the problem she experiences in the relationship of her body to her consciousness. This problem

47. Virginia Woolf, *The Waves* (New York, 1978), 115, 287 (italics added).

is the primal experience in Woolf and it is there as early as *The Voyage Out* in Rachel's final febrile state, where it is narrated as straight, third-person exposition to very different effect:

> The room also had an odd power of expanding, and though she pushed her voice out as far as possible until sometimes it became a bird and flew away, she thought it doubtful whether it ever reached the person she was talking to. There were immense intervals or chasms, for things still had the power to appear visibly before her, between one moment and the next; it sometimes took an hour for Helen to raise her arm, pausing long between each jerky movement, and pour out medicine. Helen's form stooping to raise her in bed appeared of gigantic size, and came down upon her like the ceiling falling. But for long spaces of time she would merely lie conscious of her body floating on the top of the bed and her mind driven to some remote corner of her body, or escaped and gone flitting round the room. All sights were something of an effort, but the sight of Terence was the greatest effort, because he forced her to join mind to body in the desire to remember something. She did not wish to remember; it troubled her when people tried to disturb her loneliness; she wished to be alone. She wished for nothing else in the world.[48]

Now listen to Rhoda in *The Waves:*

> "As I fold up my frock and my chemise," said Rhoda, "so I put off my hopeless desire to be Susan, to be Jinny. But I will stretch my toes so that they touch the rail at the end of the bed; *I will assure myself, touching the rail, of something hard. Now I cannot sink; cannot altogether fall through the thin sheet now. Now I spread my body on this frail mattress and hang suspended. I am above the earth now.* I am no longer upright, to be knocked against and damaged. All is soft, and bending. Walls and cupboards whiten and bend their yellow squares on top of which a pale glass gleams. Out of me now my mind can pour."

This next passage, for contrast's sake, is from Jinny, then Rhoda again follows in Woolf's text:

48. Virginia Woolf, *The Voyage Out* (San Diego, 1948), 347.

"Now we roar and swing into a tunnel. The gentleman pulls up the window. . . . My body instantly of its own accord puts forth a frill under his gaze. My body lives a life of its own. Now the black window glass is green again. We are out of the tunnel. He reads his paper. But we have exchanged the approval of our bodies. There is then a great society of bodies, and mine is introduced; mine has come into the room where the gilt chairs are. . . . We roar again through blackness. And I lie back; I give myself up to rapture; . . . I open my body, I shut my body at my will. Life is beginning. I now break into my hoard of life."

"It is the first day of the summer holidays," said Rhoda. ". . . Also, in the middle, cadaverous, awful, lay the grey puddle in the courtyard, when, holding an envelope in my hand, I carried a message. I came to the puddle. I could not cross it. Identity failed me. We are nothing, I said, and fell. I was blown like a feather. I was wafted down tunnels. Then very gingerly, I pushed my foot across. I laid my hand against a brick wall. I returned very painfully, drawing myself back into my body over the grey, cadaverous space of the puddle. This is life then to which I am committed."[49]

In "A Sketch of the Past," Woolf writes: "Again those moments of being. Two I always remember. There was the moment of the puddle in the path; when for no reason I could discover, everything suddenly became unreal; I was suspended; I could not step across the puddle; I tried to touch something . . . the whole world became unreal."[50] What, I wonder, did Woolf say *to herself* at the moment this happened? How did she sound? *What* was she?[51]

The French call free indirect discourse *le style indirect libre;* the Germans call it *erlebte Rede.* In *The Dual Voice,* Roy Pascal explains the important difference between what each implies, but uses himself the phrase "free indirect speech." In *Transparent Minds,* Dorrit Cohn gives this style a thorough consideration,

---

49. Woolf, *The Waves*, 27 (italics added), 63–64 (ellipses added).

50. Woolf, *Moments of Being*, 78.

51. Diane Filby Gillespie, in *The Sister's Arts: The Writing and Painting of Virginia Woolf and Vanessa Bell* (Syracuse, 1988), implicitly develops an answer in gathering Woolf's attitudes toward the physical objects of painting, the physical differences between painting and writing. Chapter 4 is important as are the not quite fully explored implications of this entry in Woolf's diary in 1935: "New combinations in psychology and body—rather like painting" (88). Lyndall Gordon discusses this passage in *Virginia Woolf: A Writer's Life* (New York, 1984), 231.

but she calls it "narrated monologue." In *Joyce's Voices,* Hugh Kenner calls it "The Uncle Charles Principle," thereby winning the game of terminology he does not have to admit he is playing, yet only Kenner seems to understand that free indirect discourse refers not to speech, but to writing.[52] I have stayed with the phrase free indirect discourse because it makes all the necessary distinctions. It is free of, or free with, the usual grammatical limitations of person and tense; indirect suggests as well that since it cannot be confined to narrator or character, it cannot be directed or addressed to anyone clearly either. Finally, it is discourse in exactly the sense in which we have employed the term in the preceding chapter: language that is always doubly self-conscious that there is another way to say what it is saying, the narrator's way or the character's way, neither of which it is. Its function in constructing character's ontology, however, should not lead us to overlook its great variety, its range of tones and applications.

Jane Austen's free indirect discourse allows her to move much closer to her characters than Fielding could, and yet remain more removed than Richardson, to stay in sympathy with Emma and yet still close enough to the reader to point out Emma's flaws. The delicacy of Austen's control is underlined by a technique like Flaubert's, who often seems to use free indirect discourse in *Madame Bovary* to stay as far away from his own Emma as he can in order to play his superior sensibility off her innocence or vulgarity. This technique also gives Flaubert's prose its inimitable, sometimes brutal speed. He has said in his letters: "Nor does it seem to me impossible to give psychological analysis the swiftness, clarity, and impetus of a strictly dramatic narrative." And: "I like clear, sharp sentences, sentences which stand erect, erect while running—almost an impossibility."[53] In *Madame Bovary,* he writes:

> . . . one could hear the clear clink of the louis d'or that were being thrown down upon the card tables in the next room; then all struck in again, the trumpet uttered its sonorous note, feet marked time,

52. Cohn, *Transparent Minds;* Roy Pascal, *The Dual Voice* (Manchester, 1977); Hugh Kenner, *Joyce's Voices* (Berkeley, 1978). See also Karen Lawrence, *The Odyssey of Style in Ulysses* (Princeton, 1981), especially the first chapter; and M. M. Bakhtin, *The Dialogic Imagination: Four Essays,* ed. Michael Holquist, trans. Caryl Emerson and Michael Holquist (Austin, 1981), especially the fourth essay, "Discourse in the Novel," for a contrasting description of a kind of discourse which includes speech forms but is not free indirect discourse as I describe it here. Finally, Leo Bersani, *The Culture of Redemption* (Cambridge, Mass., 1990) in chapter 5 argues, as I do, that free indirect discourse alters a character's ontology.

53. Gustave Flaubert, *The Letters of Gustave Flaubert, 1830–1857,* selected, ed., and trans. Francis Steegmuller (Cambridge, Mass., 1981), 166, 160.

skirts swelled and rustled, hands touched and parted; the same eyes that had been lowered returned *to gaze at you again.*

A few men (some fifteen or so), of twenty-five to forty, scattered here and there among the dancers or talking at the doorways, distinguished themselves from the crowd by a certain family-air, whatever their differences in age, dress, or countenance.

Their clothes, better made, seemed of finer cloth, and their hair brought forward in curls towards the temples, glossy with more delicate pomades. They had the complexion of wealth,—that clear complexion that is heightened by the pallor of porcelain, the shimmer of satin, the veneer of old furniture, and that a well-ordered diet of exquisite food maintains at its best. . . . Their indifferent eyes had the appeased expression of daily-satiated passions, and through all their gentleness of manner pierced that peculiar brutality that stems from a steady command over half-tame things, for the exercise of one's strength and the amusement of one's vanity—the handling of thoroughbred horses and the society of loose women.[54]

This is gossip of great precision, but there can be no doubt that though Emma (the "you" I have italicized) may be able to register many of these details on her retina, it is Flaubert who is explaining to us, over her "half-tame" head, what these details mean, without having to admit that they dazzle him too.

D. H. Lawrence uses free indirect discourse on behalf of his characters when they are passing through moments of intense, usually sexual, almost ecstatic experiences of fear and discovery, tension and joy, that bring them to ineffable states that their own speech, and any attempt to use their own language, would cancel. Here is a passage from *The Rainbow* that dramatizes Tom and Lydia Brangwen, in which it is very important to note how different Lawrence's tone is from Woolf's or Pynchon's, whom we have also read at those moments of their characters' "ecstasy":

"My love!" she said,

And she put her arms round him as he stood before her, round his thighs, pressing him against her breast. And her hands on him seemed to reveal to him the mould of his own nakedness, he was passionately lovely to himself. He could not bear to look at her.

54. Gustave Flaubert, *Madame Bovary*, ed. and trans. Paul De Man (New York, 1965), 36.

It is worth pausing a moment to try to imagine his saying to her, "You reveal to me, my love, the mould of my own nakedness, which is passionately lovely to me." Lawrence himself has to articulate what would, if it were spoken, sound absurd—and sometimes still does, even when he writes it. The distance he has to maintain from his characters and their experience, in order to preserve the silence, is perhaps more difficult to calibrate than the distance either Woolf or Pynchon has to have, because Lawrence writes of states more commonly experienced. In any case, his tone has to remain perfect, or the rest is bathos. The passage continues:

> "My dear!" she said. He knew she spoke a foreign language. The fear was like bliss in his heart. He looked down. Her face was shining, her eyes were full of light, she was awful. He suffered from the compulsion to her. She was the awful unknown. He bent down to her, suffering, unable to let go, unable to let himself go, yet drawn, driven. She was now the transfigured, she was wonderful, beyond him. He wanted to go. But he could not as yet kiss her. He was himself apart. Easiest he could kiss her feet. But he was too ashamed for the actual deed, which were like an affront. She waited for him to meet her, not to bow before her and serve her. She wanted his active participation, not his submission. She put her fingers on him. And it was torture to him, that he must give himself to her actively, participate in her, that he must meet and embrace and know her, who was other than himself. There was that in him which shrank from yielding to her, resisted the relaxing towards her, opposed the mingling with her, even while he most desired it, he was afraid, he wanted to save himself.
>
> There were a few moments of stillness. Then gradually, the tension, the withholding relaxed in him, and he began to flow towards her. She was beyond him, the unattainable. But he let go his hold on himself, he relinquished himself, and knew the subterranean force of his desire to come to her, to be with her, to mingle with her, losing himself to find her, to find himself in her. He began to approach her, to draw near.[55]

Tom cannot articulate his bodily experience without altering the value of its sublimity. That Tom and Lydia's physical positions suggest oral intercourse, however, means that we can now read this experience in terms less exalted and

55. D. H. Lawrence, *The Rainbow* (Harmondsworth, 1976), 89–90.

unspeakable. Lawrence himself has helped to change the cultural conventions and censors' tolerance; but nothing has happened yet to normalize Slothrop. So Lawrence's electric sexuality, like Orlando's gender and Norman Mailer's use of reincarnation in *Ancient Evenings,* is finally a thematic or psychological state, brilliantly realized, but not as basic to being as Mrs. Ramsay's silence within the dark wedge or Slothrop's reassembly of what he had been in that room from memories *outside* his head.

I don't want to suggest that, because Woolf and Pynchon, Flaubert and Lawrence, have used free indirect discourse to explore the frontiers of characterization and extraordinary moments, the style is useless closer to home. John Updike's use of free indirect discourse is interesting precisely because it is so domestic. This is his Rabbit Angstrom, the ex-basketball player with nothing much to recommend him but the physical grace, the touch, he is losing:

> With loving deftness, a deftness as complimentary to the articulation of his own body as to the objects he touches, he inserts the corners of the hanger into the armholes of the coat and with his long reach hangs it on the printed pipe with his other clothes. . . .
>
> . . . He has broken through the barrier of fatigue and come into a calm flat world where nothing matters much. The last quarter of a basketball game used to carry him into this world; you ran not as the crowd thought for the sake of the score but for yourself, in a kind of idleness. There was you and sometimes the ball and then the hole, the high perfect hole with its pretty skirt of net. . . .
>
> . . . A big bubble, the enormity of it, crowds his heart. It's like when he was a kid and suddenly thought, coming back from somewhere at the end of a Saturday afternoon, that this—these trees, this pavement—was life, the real and only thing.[56]

I have used the first example to set off the other two because the first may be purely Updike's description, if we cannot grant to Rabbit the consciousness of his own "deftness," "articulation," and "complimentarity." He can have the experience, of course, whether he commands the diction or not; but a lot of our reading turns on whose "loving" we decide it is, on whether we think Updike loves watching Rabbit more or less than Rabbit loves hanging up his coat. The ontology of the sign never allows character to become simply language, immaterialized as writing; but free indirect discourse reminds us constantly of how hard discrete physical experience is to verbalize. And it may as well be Updike

56. John Updike, *Rabbit, Run* (Greenwich, Conn., 1960), 11, 35, 60.

that Hugh Kenner is talking about (with unwitting echoes of Barthes's electro-magnetic formulations, too) when he writes of Joyce:

> This is a small instance of a general truth about Joyce's method, that his fictions tend not to have a detached narrator, although they seem to have. His words are in such delicate equilibrium . . . that they detect the gravitational field of the nearest person. One reason the quiet little stories in *Dubliners* continue to fascinate is that the narrative point of view unobtrusively fluctuates. The illusion of the dispassionate portrayal seems attended by an iridescence difficult to account for until we notice one person's sense of things incon-spicuously giving place to another's. The grammar of twelve of the stories is that of third-person narrative, imparting a deceptive look of impersonal truth. The diction frequently tells a different tale.[57]

When Elizabeth Bennet stands before Darcy and prosecutes his character with her bright eye, we are entitled to suspend our disbelief and believe in character as a body with an essential soul within, a nature native to us all, as Stevens would say, and therefore there for the taking. We are encouraged toward the same credulity by Balzac, when he presents us in *Eugénie Grandet* with this: "The glance of a man accustomed to drawing huge sums as interest on his capital, like the glance of the sensualist, the gambler, or the toady, necessarily contracts certain indefinable characteristics, a furtive, greedy, secret flicker, which do not pass unnoticed by his fellows who worship at the same shrine. This language of secret signs which they alone can interpret forms, as it were, a freemasonry among people of like passions."[58] We may not get this kind of self-confidence again until Norman Mailer describes the southern peace-keepers who arrest him in *The Armies of the Night.*[59] What we get in between begins, perhaps, with Eliot, who says in *The Mill on the Floss,* as though to correct Balzac for his semiotic enthusiasm: "But it is really impossible to decide this question by a glance at his person: the lines and lights of the human countenance are like other symbols—not always easy to read without a key. On an *a priori* view of Wakem's aquiline nose which offended Mr. Tulliver there was not more rascality than in the shape of his stiff shirt collar, though this too,

57. Hugh Kenner, *Joyce's Voices,* 16.

58. Honoré de Balzac, *Eugénie Grandet,* trans. Marion Ayton Crawford (Harmondsworth, 1977), 40.

59. Norman Mailer, *The Armies of the Night* (New York, 1968), 171–72.

along with his nose, might have become fraught with damnatory meaning when once the rascality was ascertained."[60]

It is useful to think of character as a sign because we read characters literally along the lines of the novel's pages, and we read the figurative characters the literal ones constitute. And in recognizing this alphabetical origin for the term we have taken to mean a fictionalized human being, a human being presented to us in the fiction of language, we acknowledge the relationship the word, character, has always had to language, *to writing in particular,* to physical marks and inscription. Character is, we can say, all that language gives us access to in either a realistic character or a real person. Character is intelligibility, however far that goes and whatever that admits, as it is our own intelligence of all of these. We read other characters, and what we read them with is our own character, which is what they read in us and is, therefore, our reputation, the cluster of signs we gather to present, how we are known and for what: our *character.* And in strict terms, character has never been, cannot ever be, substantive, our whole person. There is more to each of us than there is to our character because our character need not comprehend our autonomic nervous system, red cell count, taste for Chinese food, memory for song lyrics, or Kirlian aura. All of these can, of course, be raised into language's play and made an aspect of our character, a part of all we signify, but what does this is an act of interpretation by another character.

When this happens, it is as though we are acquiring more signifieds, a process that Barthes describes as happening to Sarrasine:

> Thus, from a classic viewpoint (more psychological than symbolic), Sarrasine is the sum, the point of convergence, of: *turbulence, artistic gift, independence, excess, femininity, ugliness, composite nature, impiety, love of whittling, will,* etc. What gives the illusion that the sum is supplemented by a precious remainder (something like *individuality,* in that qualitative and ineffable, it may escape the vulgar bookkeeping of compositional characters) is the Proper Name, the difference completed by what is *proper* to it. The proper name enables the person to exist outside the semes, whose sum nonetheless constitutes it entirely. As soon as a Name exists (even a pronoun) to flow toward and fasten onto, the semes become predicates, inductors of truth, and the Name becomes a subject: we can say that what is proper to narrative is not action but the character as Proper Name: the semic raw material (corresponding to a certain moment of our

60. Eliot, *Mill on the Floss,* 334.

history of the narrative) *completes* what is proper to being, *fills* the name with adjectives.[61]

Yet what this passage also reveals is the logical difficulty an ontology of language encounters. For "Proper Name" is Barthes's implicit admission that character needs some kind of core reality, some "precious remainder" he posits and makes fun of in the same phrase. It is impermissible to use "soul" in a secular age and materialist discourse, and embarrassing to use "body" in a linguistic ontology, but difficult to construct the subject over a void, without foundation or armature. So Barthes gives us the "Name," capitalized for greater gravity, to "flow toward and fasten onto," and he tries to finesse the matter of the substantive by a mixed and unarticulated metaphor of the electromagnetic field. (And at this point we are not too far removed from the physics behind Julien Sorel's nose.)

"The proper name enables the person to exist outside the semes" as a body permits one to exist outside language. But Barthes doesn't quite say that because between the historical person with a biological body and the Cartesian subject, extant as a textual site or discursive construct, there is not much compromise. Character, however, construed as a sign, acknowledges the pull of both extremes. The signifier has a necessary physical element, the signified doesn't, and the relationship between them remains provisional, negotiable, changing, because a character can always be reread and rewritten. Barthes himself does it, as we will see, in his autobiography, *Roland Barthes by Roland Barthes.* It is one thing as a critical theorist to define character solely as a linguistic function, but something else to represent your own in an autobiography that aspires to the conditions of a novel and has pictures of you too, physical images of your face and its seams as well.

What is more valuable about this passage, however, is Barthes's proposal that what is "proper to narrative is not action but the character as Proper Name." Every novel, therefore, is the story of character's accumulation of attributes, adjectives, interpretations, relationships of similarity-and-difference, signifieds and more signifiers, some of them from within the novel, some from without, none of them final, all of them the effect of some other character acting to characterize, to interpret. This explains why Elizabeth Bennet and Leopold Bloom, so different in so many ways, are recognizably similar: not because of their psychological representation, but because each is presented as a model of interpretation, of how interpretation within *their* specific limits works, of how they are to be interpreted as they interpret themselves. A character is also a sign: its signifier we may call its proper name, its signified, however, is nothing

61. Roland Barthes, *S/Z,* 191.

less than the world.[62] What Bloom interprets of it is different from what Elizabeth does; he is a different discourse, he gives reality a different character. That both of them can characterize the world without closing it off to the other, and without exhausting its interpretability, is what we mean when we say their epistemology is realistic, which is the topic of the next chapter. That they can interpret the world differently without exhausting its meaning is also what we mean by "the world."

62. This means we can also call a character a metaphor for the world, in the way Kenneth Burke defines metaphor in *A Grammar of Motives*. Seymour Chatman's implicit definition of character as metaphor is quite different; see *Story and Discourse*, 126–36. However, the best discussion of character as metaphor is in Wesley Morris, *Friday's Footprint: Structuralism and the Articulated Text* (Columbus, 1979), 64–71.

4

THE IDEAL OF REALISM

*Some things know their own story and the stories of other things, too; some
know only their own. Whoever knows all the stories has wisdom, no doubt. I
learned the story of some of the animals from them. They had all been
men, before. They were born speaking, or, to put it a better way, they were
born from speaking. Words existed before they did. And then, after that,
what the words said. Man spoke and what he said appeared.
That was before. Now a man who speaks speaks, and that's all.
Animals and things already exist. That was after.*
 —MARIO VARGAS LLOSA, *The Storyteller*

*Thanks to art, instead of seeing one world only, our own, we see that world
multiply itself and we have at our disposal as many worlds as there are
original artists, worlds more different one from the other than those which
revolve in infinite space, worlds which, centuries after the extinction of the
fire from which their light first emanated, whether it is called Rembrandt or
Vermeer, send us still each one its special radiance.*
 —MARCEL PROUST, *Time Regained*

REALISM IS FUNDAMENTAL to the novel, both historically and formally,
but it is not a simple principle. For the novel's realism is a combination of
attitudes, practices, and conventions, formalized by history, in which there are
conflicting allegiances and contradictory goals.[1] So realism is not simply con-

1. See Michael McKeon, *The Origins of the English Novel, 1600–1740* (Baltimore, 1987), for
an account of how disparate elements become "formalized" by history, 1–22. Toward the same
end, a different kind of argument is made by J. Paul Hunter in *Before Novels: The Cultural Contexts
of Eighteenth Century English Fiction* (New York, 1990), 29–58. McKeon and Hunter are both
still responding to and developing the positions of Ian Watt, *The Rise of the Novel: Studies in
Defoe, Richardson, and Fielding* (Berkeley, 1964). Hunter, however, is closer to Linda Nochlin's
study of nineteenth-century French painting in *Realism* (Harmondsworth, 1971). For its necessary
differences, Nochlin's argument is very instructive to readers of the novel interested in defining
realism. Finally, Walter L. Reed's concept of the "protocol" is also germane here. See *An
Exemplary History of the Novel: The Quixotic Versus the Picaresque* (Chicago, 1981), 49–50, where
he points out how discrete, provisional arrangements can become established narrative clichés.

stituted by a mimesis of the characters and furniture of the world with a degree of detail or a level of description that particularizes them in place and in time. And it is not the psychological representation of character that dramatizes perception within the conditions and limitations of the individual's affective life and consciousness. Realism is an epistemology that entails not only the relationship between knower and known, characters and things, but also the structural relationship within any particular novel between the characters themselves. As these characters interpret the world of the novel they share, the full play of their similarity-and-difference withholds from any one of them a final authority over either his or her own meaning or the world's. This is a fundamental property of the novel: it grants to every character an interpretive authority that is always resisted or qualified by the authority of every other character, and therefore resists the idea of authority itself with its necessary implications of a single origin, fixed center, or totalizing closure. Realism, in other words, resists transcendence.

On the other hand, realism as the aspiration of some of the great realistic novelists has often entailed an ideal which may never be realized but is nonetheless there. It is there, of course, in different ways in the descriptions of this ideal that we will see from Joyce, Flaubert, and Dostoevsky. For all their differences, however, what they have in common is very interesting: first, a doubleness of focus in themselves that points to both "higher principles" and the depth of matter; and second, an apparent indifference, at least in the statements I quote, to any specific stylistic technique. Because realism in the novel is ultimately a matter not of character itself, but of characters and their relationships, realism is also possible in different styles, no one of them authoritative either.

However, this realism entails another factor that all novels necessarily share, regardless of their construction of character and the world in a prose style: every novel is a book, an object itself, which is a fact of reading not immaterial to the individual reader and one of the themes by which Cervantes establishes the realism of *Don Quixote*. Cervantes's novel, Dickens's *Bleak House,* and Joyce's *Ulysses* are the major examples I want to use in illustrating my description of realism and how it works. But before coming to them, I want to backtrack a bit, begin again with some basic statements and examples, then discuss the ideal of realism expressed by Joyce, Flaubert, and Dostoevsky, and set up the other issues at stake in the ensuing discussion. Some of these are the relationship of romance and naturalism to the novel's realistic mode, the concept of impersonality as a feature of both realism and modernism, and realism's resistance to neat definitions, its practical excess and variety of measures.

As an epistemology, realism implicitly assumes the traditional, essentialist position that things have an ontological status independent of human perception, that they are present to themselves first and meaningful in themselves. They are, therefore, resistant to any final appropriation by language and are a limit to the mind's immaterial grasp and rhetoric's desire. Within classical realism, truth is the ultimate value and is constituted by the fit of the word to the thing, the adequacy of the imitation, the accuracy and completeness of reference. Representation, as it is distinguished from mimesis, is not essentialist but rhetorical; its ultimate value is the power that determines what will be represented and how, what will not be represented and why. I want to argue, however, that the realism of the novel is something else and that the ontology of language is, in this case, an adequate ground on which to make my explanation. For what things mean in human terms is a process, an experiment, an always open question whose answer entails a correlative question about the nature of character. In its simplest terms, within the novel's realism, the concept of character must be commensurate with the theory of things. For, generically, realism establishes a relationship of reciprocal intelligibility: what any character can read of the world is implicitly a reading of that character which the particular novel makes, puts into play with other characterizations, and offers to other readings. Different novels, of course, offer different protocols or versions of this relationship of intelligibility; and individual novels often offer different conceptions of character within their own narratives, which keeps the meaning of that novel's world open and in play. In my mind, the ultimate value of novelistic realism is neither truth nor power but the endless availability of the world and its characters to another interpretation, the authority of every character to signify the world and each other. For within the ontology of language, the relationship of the signifier to the signified does not have the same determinate relationship that the subject has to the object; the pairs look symmetrical but aren't. The following examples from four different novelists can illustrate what I mean by the relationship of intelligibility between characters and things and also how variously each of these realistic texts defines its realism.

First the opening paragraph of James's *The Portrait of a Lady:*

> Under certain circumstances there are few hours in life more agreeable than the hour dedicated to the ceremony known as afternoon tea. There are circumstances in which, whether you partake of the tea or not—some people of course never do—the situation is in itself delightful. Those that I have in mind in beginning to unfold this simple history offered an admirable setting to an innocent pastime. The implements of the little feast had been disposed upon the lawn of an old English country house in what I should call the perfect

middle of a splendid summer afternoon. Part of the afternoon had waned, but much of it was left, and what was left was of the finest and rarest quality. Real dusk would not arrive for many hours; but the flood of summer light had begun to ebb, the air had grown mellow, the shadows were long upon the smooth, dense turf. They lengthened slowly, however, and the scene expressed that sense of leisure still to come which is perhaps the chief source of one's enjoyment of such a scene at such an hour. From five o'clock to eight is on certain occasions a little eternity; but on such an occasion as this the interval could be only an eternity of pleasure. The persons concerned in it were taking their pleasure quietly, and they were not of the sex which is supposed to furnish the regular votaries of the ceremony I have mentioned. The shadows on the perfect lawn were straight and angular; they were the shadows of an old man sitting in a deep wicker-chair near the low table on which the tea had been served, and of two younger men strolling to and fro, in desultory talk, in front of him. The old man had his cup in his hand; it was an unusually large cup, of a different pattern from the rest of the set and painted in brilliant colours. He disposed of its contents with much circumspection, holding it for a long time close to his chin, with his face turned to the house. His companions had either finished their tea or were indifferent to their privilege; they smoked cigarettes as they continued to stroll. One of them, from time to time, as he passed, looked with a certain attention at the elder man, who, unconscious of observation, rested his eyes upon the rich red front of his dwelling. The house that rose beyond the lawn was a structure to repay such consideration and was the most characteristic object in the peculiarly English picture I have attempted to sketch.[2]

This description of a place and a moment obviously says a lot about the character who offers it—about his taste and experience, his appreciative sensibility, his attitude toward the privilege that he does not have. It also records what we may call his "ekphrastic deference" to the art of painting and a mode of visual representation implicitly superior to his "attempted . . . sketch." Like any truly self-conscious discourse, James's realism recognizes its limits, particularly the limits of language in representing the full reality of visible physical things. It strains against these limits, too, particularly in the oxymoronic phrase "a little eternity," which suggests transcendence into a realm of ideal, timeless essence

2. Henry James, *The Portrait of a Lady* (Harmondsworth, 1963), 5–6.

in which a sovereign self is capable of essential knowledge, of presence transparent and unconditioned. But this longing of the narrator's is qualified by his
recognition that not every character in the scene shares his desire. And we of
course may step back, too, and wonder if this narrator would be as appreciative
of tea-time at the home of the Garth family in *Middlemarch* or among the Bagnets
of *Bleak House*.

The opening paragraphs of Robbe-Grillet's *Jealousy* offer us a different realism:

> Now the shadow of the column—the column which supports the
> southwest corner of the roof—divides the corresponding corner of
> the veranda into two equal parts. This veranda is a wide, covered
> gallery surrounding the house on three sides. Since its width is the
> same for the central portion as for the sides, the line of shadow cast
> by the column extends precisely to the corner of the house; but it
> stops there, for only the veranda flagstones are reached by the sun,
> which is still too high in the sky. The wooden walls of the house—
> that is, its front and west gable-end—are still protected from the sun
> by the roof (common to the house proper and the terrace). So at this
> moment the shadow of the outer edge of the roof coincides exactly
> with the right angle formed by the terrace and the two vertical
> surfaces of the corner of the house.
>
> Now A . . . has come into the bedroom by the inside door opening
> onto the central hallway. She does not look at the wide open window
> through which—from the door—she would see this corner of the
> terrace. Now she has turned back toward the door to close it behind
> her. She still has on the light-colored, close-fitting dress with the
> high collar that she was wearing at lunch when Christiane reminded
> her again that loose-fitting clothes make the heat easier to bear. But
> A . . . merely smiled: she never suffered from the heat, she had
> known much worse climates than this—in Africa, for instance—and
> had always felt fine there. Besides, she doesn't feel the cold either.
> Wherever she is, she keeps quite comfortable. The black curls of
> her hair shift with a supple movement and brush her shoulders as
> she turns her head.[3]

The first paragraph reveals very little of the narrator, except that he seems to
aspire to the impersonal accuracy and patience of a photograph rather than to

---

3. Alain Robbe-Grillet, *Two Novels*, trans. Richard Howard (New York, 1965), 39.

the painterly expressiveness of James's narrator. The representation of the veranda at a moment in time is indicated by the shadows, but this narrator's use of the present tense indicates his design to render the veranda's materiality in all of its presence, as unmediated as it can possibly be, in words, by any film of interpretation or interference from his own consciousness, which Robbe-Grillet would also render to us with an immediacy and opacity commensurate with the porch's column. In the second paragraph, the narrator is more revealing of his own interior as he describes the woman, her behavior, and even her consciousness as well; but it is still worth noting that her self-containment, her apparent indifference at the moment to her own physical circumstances, indicates a gulf between the human and the nonhuman that Robbe-Grillet wants to emphasize. As we read further into *Jealousy,* we "naturalize" or "psychologize" this narrator, if only to accommodate the austerity of this point of view to our reading experience of more traditional novels, but we cannot fail to recognize here how different Robbe-Grillet has made the ratio between characters and things.

> In the morning it was raining. A fog had come over the mountains from the sea. You could not see the tops of mountains. The plateau was dull and gloomy, and the shapes of the trees and houses were changed. I walked out beyond the town to look at the weather. The bad weather was coming in over the mountains from the sea.[4]

As the final, "redundant" sentence of this third example indicates, Jake Barnes, the narrator of Hemingway's *The Sun Also Rises,* is not so much interested in issuing a weather bulletin as he is in establishing a kind of certitude by making a contact with the world that has none of the chaos and uncertainty of the Pamplona festival. By the time we get to this opening paragraph of chapter 16, we have a sense of both Jake's character and Hemingway's style, so this passage does not have the starkness of Robbe-Grillet's first paragraph in *Jealousy.* And, in fact, it strives for an effect quite different: not to question, but to stabilize character and reference on the ground of a world that is meaningful in itself. Jake's description here is almost void of interpretation because Hemingway's style suggests that the perception behind this description is a discipline against mere psychology and the abysses of consciousness. And Jake is alone at the moment: the "you" he uses, talking to himself in a fake mode of indirect discourse, attempts to universalize his perception against the possibility of

4. Ernest Hemingway, *The Sun Also Rises* (New York, 1970), 170. See also Terrence Doody, "Hemingway's Style and Jake's Narration," *Journal of Narrative Technique,* IV (1974), 212–25, for a more complete discussion of this passage and its implications.

another interpretation that another character may offer, a character both included and obviated in the "you," which has no other say. Getting "the real thing" exactly right is one goal of Hemingway's heroic, purgative style, but it is also the most stringent limitation he puts on the characterization of his male protagonists.

The anxiety that Hemingway's style defends Jake against is not always the effect of this kind of delimiting description. In Kafka's anecdote "On the Tram," the narrator's anxiety is fully self-conscious and articulate, and the style of his description offers a far richer representation of the problematic status of the object in realistic prose.

> I stand on the end of the tram and am completely unsure of my footing in this world, in this town, in my family. Not even casually could I indicate any claims that I might rightly advance in any direction. I have not even any defense to offer for standing on this platform, holding on to this strap, letting myself be carried along by this tram, nor for the people who give way to the tram or walk quietly along or stand gazing into shopwindows. Nobody asks me to put up a defense, indeed, but that is irrelevant.
>
> The tram approaches a stopping place and a girl takes up her position near the step, ready to alight. She is as distinct to me as if I had run my hands over her. She is dressed in black, the pleats of her skirt hang almost still, her blouse is tight and has a collar of white fine-meshed lace, her left hand is braced flat against the side of the tram, the umbrella in her right hand rests on the second top step. Her face is brown, her nose, slightly pinched at the sides, has a broad round tip. She has a lot of brown hair and stray little tendrils on the right temple. Her small ear is close-set, but since I am near her I can see the whole ridge of the whorl of her right ear and the shadow at the root of it.
>
> At that point I asked myself: How is it that she is not amazed at herself, that she keeps her lips closed and makes no such remark?[5]

In the silence that attends this scene, the girl, who is so present to the narrator that his visual experience becomes tactile, is reified by the same gesture that

5. Franz Kafka, *The Complete Stories*, ed. Nahum N. Glatzer (New York, 1976), 388–89. See also Peter Brooks, *Body Work: Objects of Desire in Modern Narrative* (Cambridge, Mass., 1993), 88–96, where he discusses visual representations of Madame Bovary and her reification. In *American Silences: The Realism of James Agee, Walker Evans, and Edward Hopper* (Baton Rouge, 1985), J. A. Ward argues that silence itself can indicate the essence of the real.

idealizes her as so completely self-possessed she is beyond the need to speak, express, or interpret herself. She is no longer a character but a thing perfectly and essentially silent.

Not many characters in the novel are reduced to the status of this objectified young woman. Even Percival, at the still center of Woolf's *The Waves,* is more open and "alive" because of the other characters' readings of him. And in fact, not even many *things* are reduced to the status of Robbe-Grillet's veranda or Hemingway's weather. In the novel, as Bakhtin points out, objects are never so isolate, singular, or pure of a significance anterior to any character's first perception:

> But no living word relates to its object in a *singular* way: between the word and its object, between the word and the speaking subject, there exists an elastic environment of other, alien words about the same object, the same theme, and this is an environment that it is often difficult to penetrate. . . .
>
> Indeed, any concrete discourse (utterance) finds the object at which it was directed already as it were overlain with qualifications, open to dispute, charged with value, already enveloped in an obscuring mist—or, on the contrary, by the "light" of alien words that have already been spoken about it. . . . The word, directed toward its object, enters a dialogically agitated and tension-filled environment of alien words, value judgments and accents, weaves in and out of complex interrelationships, merges with some, recoils from others, intersects with yet a third group: and all this may crucially shape discourse, may leave a trace in all its semantic layers, may complicate its expression and influence its entire stylistic profile.[6]

And what Bakhtin says of the object is true of any character as well: in the traditional novel, even a character-narrator as elevated as James's in *The Portrait of a Lady* is not the first or only one to experience what he describes. The world has a history. When Robbe-Grillet and Hemingway try to resist that history or efface it with style, they enact a moral decision, as though they would rescue and reconstitute the self by recasting alienation as a kind of sovereignty and sheer perception as the first step to a truer form of consciousness. In this sense, Kafka's narrator is more traditionally moral, and his wonder at the silence of the young woman he has nonetheless reified himself is a form of self-criticism,

6. M. M. Bakhtin, *The Dialogic Imagination,* ed. Michael Holquist, trans. Caryl Emerson and Michael Holquist (Austin, 1981), 276.

for he does recognize her as an ideal. The moral element implicit in "On the Tram" is quite explicit in the statements to follow from Joyce, Flaubert, and Dostoevsky for they all recognize something beyond themselves, a limit to their own authority or achievement. And what this leads to, in the novelistic practice of Dickens, Joyce, and Cervantes that we will go on to examine, is other characters who matter, who are not silenced, who possess an authority not their authors'.

In conversation with his friend the painter Arthur Power, who was trying to defend romanticism, Joyce once said:

> —Maybe, but in realism you are down to facts on which the world is based: that sudden reality which smashes romanticism into a pulp. What makes most people's lives unhappy is some disappointed romanticism, some unrealizable or misconceived ideal. In fact you may say that idealism is the ruin of man, and if we lived down to fact, as primitive man had to do, we would be better off. That is what we were made for. Nature is quite unromantic. It is we who put romance into her, which is a false attitude, an egotism, absurd like all egotisms. In *Ulysses* I tried to keep close to fact. . . . That is why we admire the primitives nowadays. They were down to reality—reality which always triumphs in the end.

Yet, in another mood in another moment, he also said to Power:

> But a writer must maintain a continual struggle against the objective: that is his function. The eternal qualities are the imagination and the sexual instinct, and the formal life tries to suppress both. Out of this present conflict arise the phenomena of modern life.
> —In my Mabbot Street scene I approached reality closer in my opinion than anywhere else in the book except perhaps for moments in the last chapter.[7]

In the first passage, Joyce is the Catholic, classically tempered writer who took Flaubert's ideal of stylistic impersonality and made it part of Stephen Dedalus's scholastic aesthetics in *A Portrait of the Artist;* in the second passage, he is the

---

7. Arthur Power, *Conversations with James Joyce*, ed. Clive Hart (London, 1974), 98–99, 74–75.

intensely private, openly defiant writer of a forbidden book that managed to be both obscure and obscene. And in the second passage, he makes the issue of realism even harder to resolve by apparently contradicting himself, for nothing in Circe, the Mabbot Street scene, seems to be like anything at all in Penelope. The Bunyan-like voice in Oxen of the Sun may as well be referring to Circe when it refers to Stephen's fears of the "land of Phenomenon." For in Circe, everything is reduced to a single phenomenal level of being: the self and the world interpenetrate with no distinction between the inner and the outer, the past and the future, the living and the dead; all clothing is costume; fantasies are immediately embodied and realized; buttons, among other things, talk; and Joyce's prose on the page often looks like a movie script in which the speed of montage is the most important value. Circe doesn't seem "down to fact" in any way, although it certainly affirms "the eternal qualities" of "the imagination and the sexual instinct."[8] Penelope, on the other hand, does seem "down to fact"; Molly, in her emphasis and anxiety, seems incapable of abstraction and recalls the realism of *Moll Flanders*. By the time we get to Penelope, moreover, after the taxing experiments of Oxen, Circe, Eumaeus, and Ithaca, its immediate interior monologue seems *normal.*[9]

Joyce's contradictions could be resolved, perhaps, if we knew exactly what "moments" in Circe he refers to, but his remarks are more valuable than a simple answer because they express the polarity that has always been intrinsic to the idea of realism, the conflicting allegiance to both the world and the self that he expresses in his desire to stay "down to fact" *and* to resist the "objective." Flaubert is more self-conscious in expressing the same conflict in a letter to Louise Colet:

> There are in me, literally speaking, two distinct persons: one who is infatuated with bombast, lyricism, eagle flights, sonorities of phrase and lofty ideas; and another who digs and burrows into the truth as deeply as he can, who likes to treat a humble fact as respectfully as a big one, who would like to make you feel almost

8. For a discussion of Circe's antirealism, see Marilyn French, *The Book as World: James Joyce's Ulysses* (Cambridge, Mass., 1976), 185–206. See also Hugh Kenner, "Circe" in *James Joyce's Ulysses,* ed. Clive Hart and David Hayman (Berkeley, 1974), for his study of what actually happens, 341–62. Also interesting are Alain Robbe-Grillet's remarks about the cinema's influence on prose fiction in *For a New Novel: Essays on Fiction,* trans. Richard Howard (New York, 1965), 149, 151. Richard Ellmann reports on Joyce's interest in the movies in *James Joyce* (Rev. ed., New York, 1982), 300–313, 561.

9. See Karen Lawrence, *The Odyssey of Style in Ulysses* (Princeton, 1981), 38–54.

physically the things he reproduces. The former likes to laugh, and enjoys the animal sides of man. . . .

What seems beautiful to me, what I should like to write, is a book about nothing, a book dependent on nothing external, which would be held together by the internal strength of its style, just as *the earth,* suspended in the void, depends on nothing external for its support; a book which would have almost no subject, or at least in which the subject would be almost invisible, if such a thing is possible.[10]

And Dostoevsky is perfectly aware of the contradictions that give this letter to the poet Maykov the conflicted energy with which he characterizes the Underground Man:

Ah, my friend. I have a completely different notion of actuality and realism than our realists and critics. My idealism is more real than theirs. God! If one were to relate meaningfully what we Russians have gone through in the last ten years of our spiritual development, wouldn't the realists exclaim that it was a fantasy! But that is the fundamental, basic realism. That's just what realism is, only deeper, while theirs merely skims the surface. Isn't Lyubim Tortsov really insignificant—and that's the only ideal thing their realism has allowed them. Realism is a profound thing—no question about it! You won't explain a hundredth part of real, actual facts through their realism. While we, with our idealism, have even predicted facts. It has happened.[11]

It is no accident—it is intrinsic to the problem of defining realism simply— that each of these writers is of two minds. And it is worth noting that their statements come in conversation and correspondence in which there is no need for a formal or aesthetic resolution, in which there is an openness equivalent to the division within their ideas. But it is more important to note the "direction" of their emphases: they all point to the belief that reality is down rather than up—"down to fact" in Joyce; not "eagle flights," but something to be burrowed into "deeply" in Flaubert; "fundamental, basic . . . only deeper" in Dostoevsky. Throughout his essays in *For a New Novel,* Robbe-Grillet refers to this traditional

10. Gustave Flaubert, *The Letters of Gustave Flaubert, 1830–1857,* selected, ed., and trans. Francis Steegmuller (Cambridge, Mass., 1981), 154 (italics added).
11. Reprinted in Fyodor Dostoevsky, *The Brothers Karamazov,* ed. Ralph E. Matlaw (New York, 1976), 751–52.

predilection as "the old myth of depth," and he argues that looking down in this way always turns the mind's gaze back up: "The idea of nature leads infallibly to that of a nature common to all things, that is, a superior or higher nature. The idea of an interiority always leads to the idea of a transcendence."[12] In explaining the history of the word "real" in *Keywords,* Raymond Williams points out that the word itself descends from the Latin *res,* which means "thing," and that it has always signified both the physical entity of a thing and the immaterial principle which stands behind, beneath, or above mere physical appearance.[13] The history of realism, therefore, as both Robbe-Grillet and Williams imply, has been the history of those changing attitudes toward what the thing really is, and it has obviously been a history of the traditional dualism in Western thought:

soul	body
spiritual	physical
form	matter
form	content
the signified	the signifier
presence	absence
the thing itself	its mimesis, representation

In this paradigm, there is a clear evidence of the cost involved or the sense that is sacrificed to the logic of those definitions of the real that link matter with absence and subordinate the material signifier such as a written word to the immaterial presence of the signified. Recent theory has, of course, exposed these hierarchies and their logic, but they have been very powerful, and even Joyce, Flaubert, and Dostoevsky can seem to lapse into their simplicities:

imagination	sexuality
rhetorical flights	burrowing
a realer idealism	the surface

12. Alain Robbe-Grillet, *For a New Novel,* 49, 58.
13. Raymond Williams, *Keywords: A Vocabulary of Culture and Society* (Rev. ed., New York, 1983), 257–62.

This scheme looks neat and has its force, but it is not quite accurate. Joyce does not oppose the imagination to sexuality even if he does not exactly equate them. Flaubert disparages the bombast and lyricism he loves, but he doesn't repudiate style itself in the name of an artless transparence. And although Dostoevsky argues his realism penetrates the surface to a more fundamental level, he circles back upward and claims a visionary power which shows his high, true religious colors. So there is more to their actual practice than any schematic abstraction allows for, and not one of them comes close to arguing the real is the already written (except, perhaps, in those "moments" when Joyce has written it himself). They also concur that the real is not to be captured easily, in any naive mimesis, simply expressed, but only re-presented—"approached . . . closer," in Joyce's words—in the alternate ontology of language. An obvious point, for writers, but worth remarking again: the real cannot exist within the language that defines it or without that language either. This way of formulating the problem suggests the structure not of subject and object but of signifier and signified, which keeps the quest for the real open and its best expression always the *next* novel.

Realism has not been a salient topic in any postsymbolist aesthetics that maintains the formal autonomy or self-reference of the text. Critics who have discussed it nonetheless have usually done so by emphasizing its dynamics rather than its fixed terms, its process, both formal and historical, rather than the particular nature of its content or local style. Here again is George Levine in *The Realistic Imagination* with a passage that exemplifies this method and implicitly addresses the anxiety we have already seen in the passages from Hemingway and Kafka:

> Realism exists as a process, responsive to the changing nature of reality as the culture understood it, and evoking with each question another question to be questioned, each threatening to destroy that quest beyond words, against literature, that is its most distinguished mark. . . . The impelling energy in the quest for the world beyond words is that the world be there, and that it be meaningful and good; the persistent fear is that it is merely monstrous and mechanical, beyond the control of human meaning. Realism risks that reality and its powers of disruption. And while it represses the dreams and desires of the self with the cumulative, formless energies of the ordinary, it seeks also the self's release—sometimes in the very formlessness of the ordinary, sometimes in the increas-

ingly complicated elaborations of the conventions and forms of the novel.[14]

In *On Photography*, Susan Sontag's version of the dynamics Levine describes has a different spin: "Photography is the paradigm of the inherently equivocal connection between self and world—its version of the ideology of realism sometimes dictating an effacement of the self in relation to the world, sometimes authorizing an aggressive relation to the world which celebrates the self. One side or the other of the connection is always being rediscovered or championed."[15] For the history of the novel, short as it is, Sontag's statement rings true, but it says something even more interesting about the complexities of impersonality. Is Robbe-Grillet's narrator more or less aggressive than James's? I'd say more aggressive because more unfamiliar, or defamiliarizing, than James's with his embracing nonchalance. Aggressive impersonality sounds like an oxymoron but isn't; it describes the thing—whatever it is—once and *for all*, closing off another interpretation as Jake Barnes does but Kafka's narrator doesn't. On the other hand, Robbe-Grillet's narrator isn't celebratory either. And my point is that however it is defined, realism in practice always exceeds neat definitions of it by its own openness to all the complexities in any relationship between consciousness and matter that language can formulate. Moreover, as characters in the same novel, the differences between James's narrator and Robbe-Grillet's wouldn't be any more challenging than the moral differences between the brothers Karamozov or the different epistemologies of the brothers Bundren. Realism is not a style of representation, a level of description, the degree of psychological complexity in the protagonist, or the reader's affinity with the author.[16] It is the structure by which any thing, every figure is kept open to interpretation: to another reading, a different point of view, a contending characterization—or contending characterizations within the same character,

14. George Levine, *The Realistic Imagination: English Fiction from Frankenstein to Lady Chatterley* (Chicago, 1981), 22.

15. Susan Sontag, *On Photography* (New York, 1977), 123.

16. See John W. Loofbourow, "Realism in the Anglo-American Novel: The Pastoral Myth," in *The Theory of the Novel: New Essays*, ed. John Halperin (New York, 1974), 257–70. Wayne C. Booth's *The Rhetoric of Fiction* (Chicago, 1961) is also a theory of realism, in which the real is the rhetorically consensual. The most interesting and sophisticated argument for this general position is in Elizabeth Deeds Ermath, *Realism and Consensus in the English Novel* (Princeton, 1983). Ermath's argument grows from her account of the rationalization of sight and consciousness as these have been explained, principally, by art historians. She is, perhaps, Robbe-Grillet's most exact opposite, and her consensus is neither social nor statistical, but phenomenological.

as we have seen in the double focus that Joyce, Flaubert, and Dostoevsky have directed on their work and the Canon of Toledo directs on *Don Quixote*. The Canon is useful to the novel he inhabits because he can explain from within the narrative some of the narrative standards it is to be judged by. His explanation goes into play with the standards and narrative values implicit in the different interpolated tales that *Don Quixote* accommodates, and his role excuses Cervantes and his narrator from having to make similar explanations, thereby imposing their authority and closing the debate.

At the end of The First Part, the Canon makes two long statements which pose in Renaissance terms a parallel to the remarks about realism that Joyce made to Arthur Power. The first passage is the Canon's own injunction against the egotism of the writer which produces distortions and romance. Like Joyce, the Canon invokes the norm of nature; unlike Joyce, however, he can still invoke a community of taste which makes the reader's own experience a standard of realism as well.

> If you reply that the men who compose such books write them as fiction, and so are not obliged to look into fine points or truths, I should reply that the more it resembles the truth the better the fiction, and the more probable and possible it is, the better it pleases. Fictions have to match the minds of their readers, and to be written in such a way that, by tempering the impossibilities, moderating the excesses, and keeping judgment in the balance, they may so astonish, hold, excite, and entertain, that wonder and pleasure go hand in hand. None of this can be achieved by anyone departing from verisimilitude or from that imitation of nature in which lies the perfection of all that is written. I have never seen a book of chivalry with a whole body for a plot, with all its limbs complete, . . .

This corporeal metaphor for a book's integrity is important because it affirms the physical reality that Sancho uses to oppose the Don's romantic ascesis; and it looks toward one of Joyce's most striking designs for keeping *Ulysses* "down to fact" by organizing the themes of each chapter according to a part of the body. The Canon also anticipates Joyce by apparently contradicting himself, forgetting the value of verisimilitude, and defending the epic for the *expressive* latitude it gives the writer.

> Yet he continued that, for all he had said against such books, he found one good thing in them: the fact that they offered a good intellect a chance to display itself. For they presented a broad and

spacious field through which the pen could run without let or hindrance, describing shipwrecks, tempests, encounters and battles; painting a brave captain with all the features necessary for the part; . . . now depicting a tragic and lamentable incident, now a joyful and unexpected event; here a most beautiful lady, chaste, intelligent, and modest; there a Christian knight, valiant and gentle; in one place a monstrous, barbarous braggart. . . . Sometimes the writer might show his knowledge of astrology, or his excellence at cosmography or as a musician, . . . and he might even have an opportunity for showing his skill in necromancy. He could portray the subtlety of Ulysses, the piety of Aeneas, the valour of Achilles, . . . and, in fact, all those attributes which constitute the perfect hero, sometimes placing them in one single man, at other times dividing them amongst many. . . . For the loose plan of these books gives the author an opportunity of showing his talent for the epic, the lyric, the tragic and the comic, and all the qualities contained in the most sweet and pleasing sciences of poetry and rhetoric; for the epic may be written in prose as well as in verse.[17]

This is a more generic, more discontinuous, and more modern theory, and even a description of many Odyssean aspects of *Ulysses*. But this last is only an accidental similarity between the two novels which share what all novels have: a definitive interest in the experience of the individual character and the interpretation of that experience, in a particular time and place, among other characters. But they also share an unusual self-consciousness of their own relation to other literature and a variety of styles that in each establishes a complicated satire or revision of other texts (strategies that are themselves a device of similarity-and-difference; or, as I said in the previous chapter, a new ratio of value between signifier and signified). Moreover, both *Don Quixote* and *Ulysses* also enact the novel's other fundamental realistic methods. If realism is an epistemology, if it depends on a relationship of reciprocal intelligibility between characters and things, and if it then finds its ultimate expression in the interpretive play of similarly authoritative characters, the novel promotes this epistemology *physically* by enacting three related principles: first, that a novel is a thing itself—not so much its author's self-expression as it is an object, such as Flaubert's object with "almost no subject"; second, that this kind of objective artifact entails the value of artistic impersonality; and third, that the novelist

17. Miguel de Cervantes Saavedra, *The Adventures of Don Quixote*, trans. J. M. Cohen (Harmondsworth, 1976), 425.

who wants to create this kind of thing and remain impersonal has to be willing to limit, distribute, or transfer authority in order to permit his or her novel the possibility of meaning we have seen arise among its characters as they are generated into interpretive paradigms.

Another way of saying this is that realism can achieve an "objectivity" by recognizing the inviolable subjectivity of every character, the potentially equal value and authority of every individual discourse, the possibility there is always another point of view, including the reader's. Cervantes first establishes a model of this practice by giving his protagonist a partner who is quite different but ambiguously equal and not a sexual or romantic mate.[18] The fact that the Don and Sancho, like Stephen and Bloom, cannot resolve their differences in marriage is important. Couples such as Elizabeth and Darcy can obviously embody the problems of interpretation at the heart of realism, and in Woolf's Ramsays there is a gulf that they cannot imagine between his way of looking at the world progressing all the way to Q and hers of settling into her dark wedge. But in Austen and Woolf, the couples' differences are covered under the bigger umbrella of love. In Cervantes and Joyce, the male partners keep the epistemological issues more open, more uncentered, and less accommodated by other *social* conventions. So, in this sense, the general narrator of *Bleak House* is a more equal and interesting partner to Esther Summerson than Allan Woodcourt or Inspector Bucket, because Esther and the narrator contest the exact value of an autobiography against the broader, louder voice of a social history. And the tragedy of Anna Karenina seems both harsher and more "significant" than Emma Bovary's because Anna is paired with Levin in the structure of the novel and loses her life in the same world where his open quest for meaning is not allowed to fail. Pairs of partners keep an openness that resists an easy identification by the reader and the absoluteness of a center.

A pair of characters, or a paradigm, also resists the closure of a single program of ontology, because the novel can accommodate naturalistic and romantic characters and their epistemologies in its scheme without abandoning its own realism. Naturalistic characters are impeded from knowing all of the world that another character can, even in the same novel, by the world's unintelligibility to them. Naturalism is usually understood as an impediment to power or action, a limit upon agency, or a discrepancy between cause and effect, but it can also

---

18. See Lowry Nelson Jr.'s introduction to *Cervantes: A Collection of Critical Essays,* ed. Lowry Nelson Jr. (Englewood Cliffs, N.J., 1969), 4. In including *Don Quixote* with *Ulysses* and *Gravity's Rainbow* in the genre of encyclopedic narrative, Edward Mendelson's "Gravity's Encyclopedia," in *Mindful Pleasures,* ed. George Levine and David Leverenz (Boston, 1976), has interesting remarks on its use of partners. See 165–66.

be understood as an impediment to the power of interpretation any character is afforded. In other words, under naturalism an object is less fully present as itself than it is as an entity in another system; it is determined by an ulterior principle, or overdetermined by several of them, and therefore beyond an intelligibility that fosters the kind of interpretation we consider an aspect of any character's freedom or control. In the novel, a pure naturalism hardly ever obtains because there is always another point of view against which the naturalistic character's limits are measured as limits. The superior perspective and interpretive power of the author and reader, for instance, are always in place as one set of these measures, and these same measures can also function in a critical way against romance epistemologies that suppose more interpretive freedom, more power for subsequent action in a world whose objects offer less intrinsic resistance to the romantic character's projections and transformations. In either case, naturalism and romance (and the allegories they both foster) are conditions of degree, or different degrees of the reciprocity allowed: the naturalistic world that she or he does not understand circumscribes the limited consciousness of naturalistic characters, and the world is often active against them in the form of drives they are not fully conscious of or can't control, or in the form of superior forces located in nature, history, or the social order that they cannot comprehend or oppose. The romance character's consciousness, by contrast, expands as a more malleable world expands under his or her metaphors, transformations, projections. Can't get away with murder, Rojack wonders. Just ensorcel the powers of the moon! Can't repeat the past, Gatsby challenges. Why, of course, you can. You buy it. But there is a confluence of lucky circumstance over which he has no control that allows Rojack to get away in spite of himself, and a realistic price to pay in paranoid anguish. And Gatsby, of course, is murdered, according to no principle his own plans include. But he can't repeat the past, really, because the one limit that is absolute in any realism is time. No character or thing is ever fully present to itself, or to each other, in any realistic temporality that acknowledges growth, change, decay. And even in Proust, loss is necessary in order that time be regained in the involuntary memory where the experience of the moment is idealized—and Marcel is, too, in the writing of it.

Dickens's *Bleak House* provides a nice mix of naturalistic, realistic, and even romance elements to examine as illustrations. Dorothy Van Ghent says that "the animation of inanimate objects suggests both the quaint gaiety of a forbidden life and an aggressiveness that has got out of control."[19] This aggressive animism not only energizes the world of things, it diminishes human characters; and if

---

19. Dorothy Van Ghent, "The Dickens World: A View from Todgers's," *Dickens: A Collection of Critical Essays*, ed. Martin Price (Englewood Cliffs, N.J., 1967), 24.

some of them are not reified in the way that Pynchon's characters can be, they are reduced emotionally and psychologically to an inanition or impotence little short of death. On the other hand, Dickens's desire often opposes to the naturalistic realm a powerful sentimentality that allows some characters to endure the world's immovable incomprehensibility, even if they cannot exactly triumph. We see this opposition in the situation of characters embroiled in plots they can never comprehend. For the problems his plots present are often much more interesting and important than the answers he finally delivers, and what Dickens chooses not to explain explicitly become obvious signs of his own evasions. He writes: "The one great principle of English law is, to make business for itself. There is no other principle distinctly, certainly, and consistently maintained through all its narrow turnings. Viewed by this light it becomes a coherent scheme, and not the monstrous maze the laity are apt to think it. Let them but once clearly perceive that its grand principle is to make business for itself at their expense, and surely they will cease to grumble." Despite its facetious irony, this passage from *Bleak House* is important. The physical metaphor of the maze suggests not only the city of London, but the Chancery Court, the endless slums, the bureaucracies of philanthropy that—like the bureaucracies of debt, finance, and circumlocution in *Little Dorrit*—work against individual characters and represent a naturalistic principle of determinism that no one can see above. "The one great principle" is a transcendent perspective no one, not even the narrator, holds. Elsewhere he exclaims: "What connexion can there be, between the place in Lincolnshire, the house in town, the Mercury in powder, and the whereabout of Jo the outlaw with the broom, who had that distant ray of light upon him when he swept the churchyard-step? What connexion can there have been between many people in the innumerable histories of this world, who, from opposite sides of great gulfs, have nevertheless, been very curiously brought together!" Dickens goes on to depict Jo, who "don't know nothink," and he would like us to catch the hint that the answer to his first question is implicit in "the distant ray of light," which suggests another transcendent principle and perspective, implicit with both more benevolence than the "great principle" of the law and a greater consciousness than the narrator has of the structure and meaning of Dickens's plot.[20] The second sentence sounds like a parallel construction, but it is not even posed as a question; in effect, it is a declaration of the narrator's evasiveness in the guise of impotent wonder. And neither he, nor the law's great principle, nor the ray of light offers us answers to some basic questions the plot poses. Why don't, or can't, Lady Dedlock and Captain Hawdon

20. Charles Dickens, *Bleak House* (Harmondsworth, 1971), 603–604, 272.

marry? And who asks Esther to write the autobiography that constitutes her sections of the narrative?

But this "omniscient" narrator, whose presence, knowledge, and discourse are often limited to the present tense and aloofness of the camera, is not the novel's only interpretive gauge. In the character of Esther herself, the other narrator, Dickens offers us another index of the realistic intelligibility of his world. We can measure the realism of any novel or character by asking: how much of that novelistic world can she know? If, like Elizabeth Bennet, she is capable of knowing everything, whether or not she actually does, the novel is realistic, and so is the character. She is even realistic if, like Dorothea Brooke, she could know the whole complex of the world of *Middlemarch,* if only she were allowed the narrator's altitude; Eliot's narrator is not superior in kind, only in degree, and this superiority is her pulpit and her hope for us. Esther cannot know everything in *Bleak House,* but neither does the general narrator. Esther knows a very great deal, however, and understands the good and evil in everyone almost exactly as we are allowed to. The timing is different. Hers is a retrospective story, so there is no opportunity for her to condemn, say, Skimpole when Jarndyce still thinks him harmless, although she has always doubted Skimpole's innocence. And if we are finally not convinced that Jarndyce himself is as healthy as Esther once thinks, this is a privilege of our interpretation. Jarndyce is a good man, even though he declines to understand himself and the world as well as Esther does. For whatever is intelligible in that world—and not everything is—she can know.[21] Moreover, Tulkinghorn, Bucket, and Woodcourt are realistic, too, and in fact are professional interpreters—of the law, of criminal evidence and behavior, of disease. (The courts, crime, and disease are structural synonyms in *Bleak House.*) The paranoid Mrs. Snagsby and the orotundistical Chadband, with the devotion he has to the "Terewth," are important as satirical figures in the novel's interpretive paradigm because they take their own limited knowledge to be certain and complete: they are, or want to be, what the general narrator and Esther never pretend: all-knowing.

However, the most telling and interesting "interpreter" in the novel is Jo, who is literally illiterate and claims he knows "nothink." He can however, read signs and character. The first time he encounters the disguised Lady Dedlock, he can see she is a lady. When she insists she is "not a lady. I am a servant,"

21. For another account of its "incoherence," of what cannot be known and why in *Bleak House,* see Christine van Boheemen, *The Novel as Family Romance: Language, Gender, and Authority from Fielding to Joyce* (Ithaca, 1987), 101–31. A completely different but equally basic take on Esther can be found in Alex Zwerdling's "Esther Summerson Rehabilitated," in *Dickens: New Perspectives,* ed. Wendell Stacy Johnson (Englewood Cliffs, N.J., 1982), 94–113.

he replies: "You are a jolly servant!" When Jo later recounts how he came by two half-crowns, all that is left of the sovereign Lady Dedlock gave him for his services as her tour-guide, the constable does not believe him. But Tulkinghorn and Bucket do. When they bring Jo to Tulkinghorn's rooms to confront Hortense dressed in the clothes Lady Dedlock has been wearing, Jo knows that, in the play of similarity-and-difference, the differences are critical. He says: "It is her and it an't her. It an't her hand, nor yet her rings, nor yet her voice. But that there's the wale, the bonnet, and the gownd, and they're wore the same way wot she wore 'em, and it's her height wot she wos, and she give me a sov'ring and hooked it."[22] What Jo does not have is the skill to *interpret* what he knows, the faculty for inference and abstraction, a knowledge of the context into which he's been forced, the habits of a lawyer or detective. Mr. Snagsby, who is there with them, can't interpret the scene either. Although he is closer in class to Tulkinghorn and Bucket, he is emotionally closer to Jo, more compassionate, less manipulative, and almost as helpless. He is, therefore, a good measure of both extremes.

Jo's helplessness is something Esther has felt, as she has been imposed upon by Miss Barbary and her moral order founded on denial and guilt, imposed upon even by Jarndyce and his need for a manager more competent than he is. So one of the things Esther gains by writing her autobiography is a sense of her own interpretive power. She writes as Esther Woodcourt, with a name that suggests she is a queen-figure and savior, now at peace in a sylvan realm. She was never Esther, the son of summer. And an important thing to understand about her character is that it does not integrate or resolve her many roles and the different identities from all the different relationships in which she has played. Her nicknames, for instance, limit and diminish her, but they multiply her, too. And as she is both child and mother, orphan and surrogate parent, so with Jarndyce, Richard, Woodcourt, Guppy, Bucket, and Jo, despite all their differences, she can be coupled in one function or another. She can play in triangles, too. Guppy, for instance, is the first to detect her resemblance to Lady Dedlock, and because he proposes, he displaces from Bucket any potential erotic interest the real detective might have as the three of them work toward the full meaning of Esther's resemblance. The triangle Esther, Ada, and Lady Dedlock form when they meet in the rain (in chapter 18) is symmetrical with the triangle Lady Dedlock forms with Hortense and Rosa, who represent the erotic and maternal aspects of herself that she cannot admit to or join. Dickens's characters often seem simplified by the architectural necessities of the plot and flattened by repressions, but they are best understood as constructed and dis-

22. Dickens, *Bleak House*, 277, 369.

tributed by displacements into roles, relationships, and differentiations that cast each of them into clusters; and major characters, such as Esther and Little Dorrit, for instance, exist in many, many different paradigms. These paradigms grow from the sheer length and population-density of Dickens's plots, but they also express his deepest assumptions about the nature of character itself.[23] Esther's name is a word that can be placed in many different sentences, in very different positions; yet even when she is writing these herself, there is no way she can know the meaning of the relationships between all her relationships. She cannot know herself completely, even though she can write her character as a writer into being.

In *Ulysses*, Stephen Dedalus has several roles and identities, as a figure of Telemachus, of Hamlet and Shakespeare, of Kinch the knife and Christ "the eternal son" (321), of Rudy Bloom and Blazes Boylan, too. These are most often structural roles—he doesn't know he is a Telemachus figure—and in this respect, Esther is often like him: cast in relational roles, clusters of characters, structural paradigms she cannot be fully aware of. But many of her roles are intentional and dramatic; and in them, she knows what she is doing. This is very important, for the general narrator is passive, spectatorial, and in a way as helpless as Jo, who is this narrator's other counterpart. Esther is active, engaged and beneficent, Jo's counterpart, too, but also his comforter. The narrator's power lies in rhetoric, hers in material efficacy, but he cannot *do* what she can. They are Dickens's double focus on the real, which is there not only to be known, but changed if possible, or at least ameliorated.

If we look back at Pynchon now with these standards in mind, we can examine his realism with these questions: Does he himself take seriously Mondaugen's electro-mystical concept of the self? Is that a model of character in which character can be more than a passive receiver? Is Pökler realistic? Does a dream count as an act of interpretation? What ontological status does a dream have, especially one that someone else has also had? Is it too simple to call such a dream an experience of intertextuality and leave it at that? Are the "bureaucracies of the other side" merely a metaphor or really a higher system of governance?

---

23. See Julian Moynahan, "The Hero's Guilt: The Case of *Great Expectations,*" in *Discussions of Charles Dickens*, ed. William Ross Clark (Boston, 1961), 82–92. In explaining Pip's excessive guilt, Moynahan aligns him with both Orlick and Drummle and points to the phenomenon of Dickens's "character-clusters." This essay, published in 1961, anticipates subsequent "structuralist" readings of Dickens, his doublings and splittings, and the roles of characters who are unintelligible without their cluster of complements. (I am indebted to Dennis Huston for pointing me to Moynahan's essay.)

How can Greta Erdmann feel "less than images of herself" unless she, like Slothrop, is thinning out? And is Slothrop's slow disintegration the reason he knows another order of presence? Does his different molecular status change his epistemology? If it does, if what he is able to know changes as he undergoes a change of state, it would be logical (but *merely* logical) to argue he is realistic.[24] The hitch is this: how would *we* know what he knows? How do you communicate from one such ontological state to a different one? Mrs. Ramsay, who is a realistic character, doesn't go so far away; Pökler and Prentice, who may also be realistic, don't either. But they are, finally, very different from Slothrop, for *Gravity's Rainbow,* like *Ulysses,* offers us several different orders of being in several different thicknesses. It would be interesting to know, therefore, at what moments in his narrative Pynchon himself (whom Salman Rushdie calls "the old Invisible Man")[25] thinks he "approached reality closer" as Joyce thought he did in the disparate episodes of Circe and Penelope. Tantivy's disappearance? Lyle Bland's? Pudding's humiliations? The vision of the cosmic Serpent? Slothrop's sighting of Mickey Rooney? Or Basher St. Blaise's apprehension of the Rilkean angel? Perhaps it is the description of Dora. Or Bianca's body. The Malcolm X episode. Or is it those moments of mindless pleasure?

24. The answers from other readers are very different. Peter L. Cooper, *Signs and Symbols: Thomas Pynchon and the Contemporary World* (Berkeley, 1983), argues that the epistemology of science no longer provides certitude about even the nature of the object it investigates; see chapter 5. For Brian McHale, *Postmodernist Fiction* (London, 1989), the question never comes up because he separates the epistemological concerns of modernism from the ontological concerns of postmodernism and obviates the problem in a flash. He does, however, refer to Maureen Quilligan's *The Language of Allegory: Defining the Genre* (Ithaca, 1979), which is interested in the real, but which she defines as the sacred, a standard that includes *Gravity's Rainbow* but not *Ulysses.* Her genre of allegory, however, is not concerned with the character who knows, but with the language that generates structure, meaning, and interpretation. The "sacred," according to Thomas H. Schaub, is a "whole" that no character can know from "This Side," for we could never get what would come to us from the four-dimensional space-time of the "Other Side." See Schaub's *Pynchon: The Voice of Ambiguity* (Urbana, 1981), 10–13. "Meaning," Schaub also says, "is always a medium, not an answer" (104). Like Schaub and many others, Hanjo Berressem, in *Pynchon's Poetics: Interfacing Theory and Text* (Urbana, 1993), adumbrates a kind of realism in *Gravity's Rainbow* by demonstrating that Pynchon can be read by playing off each other definitions of the real in Lacan, Derrida, and Baudrillard, whose "materialism" is important in opposition to Lacan's and Derrida's ontologies. Most interesting to me, however, is Leo Bersani's essay, "Pynchon, Paranoia, and Literature" in *The Culture of Redemption* (Cambridge, Mass., 1990). Bersani argues for a kind of realism in which his concept of paranoid character is matched to a theory of the paranoid order of things. For brilliance in a short span, this essay matches Edward Mendelson's "Gravity's Encyclopedia," which implies Pynchon's realism without defining it.

25. Salman Rushdie, "Thomas Pynchon" in *Imaginary Homelands: Essays and Criticism, 1981–1991* (New York, 1992), 352–57.

The best answer may be, all of the above. Pynchon does not have the neat double focus of Flaubert's bombast and burrowing, or Dickens's narrator and Esther, but in Bland's evanescent body and Bianca's corpse, Rilke's poetry and Mickey Rooney's movie musicals, rocket technology and Herero earth-worship, *Gravity's Rainbow*, which we could nickname *Entropy's Excess*, develops paradigm after paradigm of alternative sets of possibilities. There are so many, in fact, it is hard to focus in on a central pair, the paradigmatic paradigm, because there is no normative narrator, no character as comprehensive as, say, Esther and Bloom (in their different ways) are, no other half to the rainbow that would give this novel a discernible circumference and bound it as a whole. Nonetheless, I have an answer to propose, but I would like to hold it in abeyance until I have made my argument for the ways in which *Ulysses* and *Don Quixote* establish their own relationships between the concept of character and the theory of things. They practice realism in significantly different historical ways, and understanding these differences, and the ways in which Dickens fits between them, will be helpful in placing Pynchon and in describing what a postmodern ideal of realism might be.

Joyce offers us at least two primary relationships to the world in Stephen and Bloom. On this day on which he quits his place, repudiates his friends, and resigns his job to set out in search of the only thing he can ever find, which is himself, Stephen begins by establishing himself in the physical world, in the solitude in which Joyce's characters feel most conscious and possessed of themselves; this condition is the frame of their alienation and, therefore, the rationale for their style of interior monologue.

> Ineluctable modality of the visible: at least that if no more. Signatures of all things I am here to read, seaspawn and seawrack, the nearing tide, that rusty boot. Snotgreen, bluesilver, rust: coloured signs. Limits of the diaphane. But he adds: in bodies. Then he was aware of them bodies before of them coloured. How? By knocking his sconce against them, sure. . . . Shut your eyes and see.
> Stephen closed his eyes to hear his boots crush crackling wrack and shells. You are walking through it howsomever. I am, a stride at a time. . . . the *Nachbeinander*. Exactly: and that is the ineluctable modality of the audible. Open your eyes. No. Jesus! If I fell over a cliff that beetles o'er his base, fell through the *Nebeneinander* ineluctably! . . . My two feet in his boots are at the ends of his legs, *nebeneinander*. . . .
> Open your eyes now. I will. One moment. Has all vanished since?

If I open and am now for ever in the black adiaphane. *Basta!* I will see if I can see.

See now. There all the time without you: and ever shall be, world without end.[26]

Things in an "endless" world are not closed to interpretation by some holy telic code. Despite the phrase's allusion, the signs Stephen is there to read are signs, first, of the physical, of independent objects. These are the facts that must be "lived down to," and they are both elemental and trivial, nature's and culture's: "the nearing tide, that rusty boot." It is important to realize, too, that they are to be heard as well, and then spoken in his own voice, and "almosted" in phrases of free indirect discourse such as "his boots crush crackling wrack and shells." Seeing, hearing, touching, speaking, striding, he engages the world with great bodily emphasis, but entertains, perhaps a little unwittingly, Joyce's idea that identity is also socially constructed, often by costumes that dramatize relationships or roles: "My two feet in his boots are at the ends of his legs. . . ." But what is most important here is Stephen's desire to possess the world, with his eyes closed, in the dialectical aesthetics of Lessing's German, *as an idea.*

These opening passages are suffused, therefore, with Stephen's self-definitions as an artist and intellectual, isolate and original; not until later in the episode do we get his fears of death, his resentment of his father, his needy longing and willfulness: "As I am. As I am. All or not at all." And it is not until Scylla and Charybdis that he formulates a principle of character commensurate with his version of the nature of things, a formulation that suggests that the self contains ("All or not at all") as much variety as the physical world does in its endless differentiation and sensory plenum. "He found in the world without as actual what was in his world within as possible. Maeterlinck says: *If Socrates leave his house today he will find the sage seated on his doorstep. If Judas go forth tonight it is to Judas his steps will tend.* Every life is many days, day after day. We walk through ourselves, meeting robbers, ghosts, giants, old men, young men, wives, widows, brothers-in-love, but always meeting ourselves." Scylla and Charybdis, in its examination of theories of art, contains a number of ideas about the methods of *Ulysses*—explicitly in Stephen's doubly autobiographical theory of Shakespeare, implicitly in his theory of the inadequacy of paternity and its metaphoric relation to artistic creation, and offhandedly in such remarks as: "They remind one of Don Quixote and Sancho Panza. Our national epic has yet to be written, Dr. Sigerson says." Moreover, it contains more explicitly than

26. James Joyce, *Ulysses*, ed. Hans Walter Gabler with Wolfhard Steppe and Claus Melchior (New York, 1986), 31.

Proteus does Stephen's realization that the reciprocity he must maintain between the self and world is a relationship that exists in time. His opponents, such as AE, insist that we are eternal essences and that the truth is, too; against such an idealism Stephen has to assert that his personal identity is temporal, but that it is continuous despite its changes, and that it is not totally subject to mere circumstance. He says:

> Wait. Five months. Molecules all change. I am other I now. Other
> I got pound.
> Buzz. Buzz.
> But I, entelechy, form of forms, am I by memory because under
> everchanging forms.

And later he adds: "As we, or mother Dana, weave or unweave our bodies, . . . so does the artist weave and unweave his image. . . . [T]hat which I was is that which I am and that which in possibility I may come to be." As part of this intuition Stephen also realizes he is both the agent and the patient of his own life, and he says, "Act. Be acted on."[27] On this day in particular, this is an important and complicated pair of imperatives as well as a sign of Stephen's helpless rigidity. Nonetheless, Stephen's adaptation of Maeterlinck connects him to the novel's structural level in which he is not always just himself but a Telemachus and Hamlet figure, too. Proteus and the technique of interior monologue imply that we are what we *think;* chapters such as Oxen of the Sun, and *Ulysses'* whole structure, counter that we are not simply *what* we think we are, but identified within other systems under other auspices. These systems may not be as esoteric as Pynchon's "bureaucracies of the other side," but they are not conscious properties of *Ulysses'* characters, despite the unprecedented capaciousness of their minds.

Bloom formulates his version of the epistemology of realism in the Lestrygonians chapter as he is on his way to lunch. He is less abstract than Stephen and less tempted to idealism. If Stephen has to establish the world and himself within it by a bodily exercise in Aristotelian epistemology, Bloom's there by being hungry, which exacerbates his anxiety and loneliness. But it makes Bloom more economical, too. The reciprocal intelligibility of character and things, which is subject to changes in space and time, Bloom almost sums up with "Parallax." And the principle of his own continuity he debates with: "I was happier then. Or was that I? Or am I now I? Twenty-eight. She twenty three. . . . Could never like it again after Rudy. Can't bring back time. Like holding

27. *Ibid.,* 41, 175, 170, 158, 156, 159–60, 173.

water in your hand." More important, Bloom can admit to another principle of identity, one which Stephen has to defend himself against by insisting, "As I am." Bloom reflects: "Sad booser's eyes. Bitten off more than he can chew. Am I like that? See ourselves as others see us."[28] His ability to conceive of himself in this way also fosters Bloom's compassion: he can imagine himself Stephen's father, but Stephen can't imagine being Bloom's son.

Joyce's method never allows the parallels he draws to be strongly felt, but they are there, and at least three more should be mentioned. The counterpart of Stephen's use of Lessing is Bloom's meditation on the nature of beauty and its embodiment. It grows from his memory of the joyous seminal moment on Howth when he and Molly kissed and exchanged the seedcake. Stephen has to remind himself, in the abstract, not only to act, but to *be acted on*. Bloom simply remembers: "Kissed, she kissed me."

> Me. And me now.
> Stuck, the flies buzzed.
> His downcast eyes followed the silent veining of the oaken slab.
> Beauty: it curves: curves are beauty. Shapely goddesses, Venus, Juno: curves the world admires.

This complex of associations leads Bloom to inquire, with his eyes open, whether the museum's goddesses have anuses and therefore adequately represent humanity's material dependence on food. This is his Aristotelianism, alimentary and erotic, funny and naughty. However, Bloom's version of the self, which Stephen formulates through the adaptation of Maeterlinck, is not so sanguine. He makes a "structuralist" proposition of the self's interchangeability in a system that would never support Stephen's traditional, essentialistic individuality and romantic egotism:

> His smile faded as he walked, a heavy cloud hiding the sun slowly, shadowing Trinity's surly front. Trams passed one another, ingoing, outgoing, clanging. Useless words. Things go on same, day after day: squads of police marching out, back: trams in, out. Those two loonies mooching about. Dignam carted off. Mina Purefoy swollen belly on a bed groaning to have a child tugged out of her. One born every second somewhere. Other dying every second. Since I fed the birds five minutes. . . .
> Cityful passing away, other cityful coming, passing away too: other

28. *Ibid.*, 126, 137, 139.

coming on, passing on. Houses, lines of houses, street, miles of pavements, piledup bricks, stones. Changing hands. This owner, that. Landlord never dies they say. Other steps into his shoes when he gets his notice to quit. They buy the place up with gold and still they have all the gold. Swindle in it somewhere. Piled up in cities, worn away age after age. Pyramids in sand. Built on bread and onions. Slaves Chinese wall. Babylon. Big stones left. Round towers. Rest rubble, sprawling suburbs, jerrybuilt. Kerwan's mushroom houses built of breeze. Shelter, for the night.

No-one is anything.

Molly, who is as self-involved as Stephen is, nonetheless confirms Bloom's principle of substitution when she says: "and I thought well as well him as another."[29] Odysseus confirms Bloom, too, in his response to Polyphemus, "Outis is my name." That is: No man. I am no one.[30] Odysseus may as well have gone on to say: I'm therefore many, constituted by my roles and stories, as Bloom is. Bloom's depressed self-denial, in the face of the world's material multiplicity, is a version both of realism's impersonality and of Joyce's proposition that the nature of the individual is not in a singular essence but in the range and variety of its possible roles, versions of itself to be played against the versions of the world into which it is cast "as others see us," as no *one*. Therefore, in Bloom's case, the world within is much more capacious than Stephen's; in the actual world without, he can meet not only himself but Stephen, too, among many others, and take him home to Molly.

Had Stephen stayed, we might have discovered what Joyce means by the fact that Stephen's dream of an encounter in the street of harlots is a dream that Bloom has had, Molly has had, and the text of Circe has, too. The three characters are not symmetrically linked. A dream shared by Molly and Bloom we could chalk up to common experience, such as their shared memory of the moment of Rudy's conception; a dream shared by Bloom and Stephen, to their Homeric or Shakespearean symmetry, or to their textual coalescence as Stoom and Blephen.[31] The whole coincidence of their dreams, however, is hard to read by any conventional realism and tests the limits of Stephen's formula for the concept of character's reciprocity with the theory of things—"He found in the world without as actual what was in his world within as possible."—because it would be hard to imagine a conversation in which the three found in the outer world

29. *Ibid.*, 144–45, 134–35, 643–44.
30. Richard Ellmann, *Ulysses on the Liffey* (New York, 1979), 112–13.
31. Joyce, *Ulysses*, 39, 47, 311–12, 641, 359, 73–74, 640.

of each other the dream that each had had. Moreover, I don't think the coincidence is a narratological parody, *post hoc ergo propter hoc,* of the way in which Throwaway's victory makes Bloom a prophet; nor does it seem to be a hermeneutic joke such as the man in the mackintosh; nor is it a merely textual event, an effect of representation, such as the talking objects in Circe and Staggering Bob. In an ontology of language, the realism of the shared dream as a problem of reference is, of course, a nonissue. But it seems more fruitful to think of these dreams as actual events for which there is no established convention, which would make them "unrealistic," but not, therefore, unreal. This could then help us to think about similar events in *Gravity's Rainbow* in another way, and it gives a segué into *Don Quixote,* where dreams have a very different character.

The Don's crucial dream is a solitary experience, real but not "realistic" according to the conventions of the chivalric texts he orders his life by; and since *Don Quixote* is a novel precisely because it entertains and tests so many other kinds of narrative discourse, it is first of all a book about reading. Before he becomes a knight, the Don is a great bookman; and as Foucault says of him: "he is himself like a sign. . . . His whole being is nothing but language, text, printed pages, stories that have already been written down."[32] So Cervantes assumes, as the Canon does, an essential stability about the world in order to test the differences interpretation itself can make. In Joyce, these matters have been resolved: it goes without saying that Stephen and Bloom will characterize the world in entirely different ways; Joyce wants to explore just what differences his characters and prose styles can make. When Don Quixote reads the windmills as giants, there is no question about his mistake; but when Bloom walks through the meticulously recorded Dublin of 1904, there is no question he is also "*lisant au libre de lui-meme.*"[33] There is another way of putting this difference. At the start of the novel, the Don cannot be alone; he has to read the world against common sense and the sense of it that others have in common; he needs Sancho to say "No" to. Stephen, Bloom, and Molly can exist in a much more normative isolation because the novel has already confirmed and explored the social construction of the world, and alienation has become thematically advantageous. The vulnerability of the Don's madness is symmetrical with the strength of his self-conception, but he needs dramatic confrontations to enact them both. The characters of *Ulysses,* on the other hand, are most fully themselves in the formal privacy of their interior monologues, where the world has been made an aspect of consciousness by an historical turn inward that has at least one of its

32. Michel Foucault, *The Order of Things: An Archaeology of the Human Sciences,* a translation of *Les mots et les choses* (New York, 1973), 46.

33. Joyce, *Ulysses,* 153.

origins in *Don Quixote*. So Bloom would never have the kind of problem the Don has with the dream he has dreamed in the Cave of Montesinos. It is dreams that are in some way had in common that are a problem later.

This dream in the cave is a singular adventure for the Don because it is not an illusion or "enchantment," but the one experience he has which no one else witnesses and he cannot rationalize. (He does, however, have dreams that others are aware he is having.) Yet he is bothered by it so much that he later seeks a confirmation for it, or permission to experience such a private reality, when he tries to get Sancho to equate his experience in the cave with Sancho's own experience on the wooden horse Clavileno: "Sancho, if you want me to believe what you saw in the sky, I wish you to accept my account of what I saw in the Cave of Montesinos. I say no more." What he has dreamt, of course, is based like all his waking "visions" on what he has read, and these sources have been the paradigms of interpretation he has always been comfortable inserting himself into. The Don has not often debated Sancho's more "realistic" interpretations; he has simply dismissed them as erroneous, unchivalric, the foolishness of a nonreader: "No!" The modesty of this favor, therefore, makes Sancho's refusal even more poignant; for the story of what he has seen in the sky, which plays the height of his faked vision off the depth of the Don's real dream, is an elaborate, obsequious, and perfectly transparent fabrication, designed to appeal to the Duke and Duchess who are toying with Don Quixote. Sancho could only have learned to concoct a story such as this from the Don himself, and telling it makes him look like a fool in the eyes of the cynical Court. The Don is as simple and abashed as Sancho usually is, with no realization that his real dream is very different from Sancho's fake apology. And the dream remains so important to him that it is the only experience he has had that he is said to repudiate on his deathbed, where it still seems to him and to the narrator as well a mistake, perhaps because it was so authentically private.[34] (To us who have read the second part, it is also an awkward prolepsis.) For with his censor asleep, he has realized his ideal Dulcinea may not be above taking money from her devoted knight, himself, but there is no idea or convention by which he can "naturalize" this shocking realization.[35] It is his distinction that he always prefers to authentic experience the conventional representation of the chivalric code, the merely realistic to the actually real, which is for the Don, but not for Cervantes, the already written.

Don Quixote makes its essential propositions about the idea of realism by making a continual inquiry into the differences between the real and the real-

34. Cervantes, *Don Quixote*, 316–19, 735, 624.
35. Gerald Brenan, "Cervantes," in *Cervantes: A Collection of Critical Essays*, 25–26.

istic, the thing itself and the representational conventions by which any thing is given meaning and value. The barber's basin which becomes the helmet of Mambrino is an obvious counterpoint to the adventure in the Cave of Montesinos, for it is an example of a paradigm of interpretation which excludes Sancho, denies the authority of his perception, and limits reality to a single idea of it.[36] In order to gull the Don and have some fun with the barber whose basin it is, the priest and the barber from La Mancha, along with Don Cardenio and Don Ferdinand, all agree that the basin is Mambrino's helmet. The incredulous barber says:

"Well, if this basin is a helmet, then, this pack-saddle must be a horse's harness as well, as this gentleman said."

"It looks like a pack-saddle to me," said Don Quixote, "but, as I have already said, I am not interfering in that."

"Whether it is a pack-saddle or a harness," said the priest, "Don Quixote has only to say; for in these matters of chivalry all these gentlemen and myself defer to him."

This is not the first or only time something such as this happens; Sancho, for instance, is the victim of the same kind of conspiracy at the end of "The Tale of Foolish Curiosity" when the Don yells at him, "you are the most despicable rogue in Spain," for seeing through the Princess Micomicona's disguise. This scene shows, too, what the Don loses when he does not have his usual passionate belief in what he is doing. When he has discussed the helmet of Mambrino earlier, on his own initiative and according to his own principles, he offers an explanation of its mysterious variety that does not denigrate the potential good faith or interpretive authority of anyone involved:

---

36. For a "classical" reading of this episode, and an account of Cervantes's realism and impersonality different from mine, see Leo Spitzer, *Linguistics and Literary History: Essays in Stylistics* (Princeton, 1948), 41–86. The helmet of Mambrino, the dream in the Cave of Montesinos, the theme of the found manuscript, the automatic status as a liar that any Moorish narrator would have in the minds of the contemporary Spanish readership, and the relationship of Cervantes's second installment (1615) to the first (1605) after he had been plagiarized, are topics almost all readers treat as aspects of *Don Quixote*'s complex ontology. A brief, striking account of these complexities is in John J. Allen, *Don Quixote: Hero or Fool?* University of Florida Monographs, Humanities—No. 29 (Gainesville, 1969), 67–79. But more striking still is Marthe Robert's meditation and analysis, *The Old and the New: From Don Quixote to Kafka*, trans. Carol Cosman (Berkeley, 1977), for her ideas about imitation and the Don's sanctity.

"Is it possible that all this while you have been with me you have not discovered that everything to do with knights errant appears to be chimaera, folly and nonsense, and to all go contrariwise? This is not really the case, but there is a crew of enchanters always amongst us who change and alter all our deeds, and transform them according to their pleasure and their desire either to favour us or to injure us. So what seems to you to be a barber's basin appears to me to be Mambrino's helmet, and to another as something else. It shows rare foresight in the sage who is on my side to make what is really and truly Mambrino's helmet seem to everyone a basin."

The Don's explanation of the sage's foresight is not only one of the ways in which viewpoints other than his own are acknowledged, it is also one of those moments when the characters inside the book talk about the book itself, as though they actually are antecedent to it and independent: persons in history before they have become characters in a novel.[37]

This trespass across ontological frontiers first occurs when Sancho calls Don Quixote the Knight of the Sad Countenance. He explains that

"your worship has lately got the most dismal face I've ever seen. It must be either from weariness after the battle or from your worship's losing his teeth."

"It is from neither," replied Don Quixote, "but because the sage whose task it is to write the history of my deeds must have thought it right for me to take some title, as all knights did in the olden days. . . . That is why I say that the sage I mentioned has put it into your thoughts and into your mouth to call me now *The Knight of the Sad Countenance.*"

What's most preposterous about this explanation is that it's true. It does not obviate Sancho's explanation, which is true according to his sensory experience, but neither does it undermine the Don's prophecy, which is true to his visionary sense. And it emphasizes, perhaps most of all, the capaciousness of Cervantes's realism and the effect of his "modesty" here. ("It is so strange and rare," Cardenio says later, "that I do not know whether anyone trying to invent such a character in fiction would have the genius to succeed.")[38] At its heart, *Don Quixote* proposes that the full truth of reality resides not in an authoritative

37. Cervantes, *Don Quixote*, 404, 336, 204.
38. *Ibid.*, 147, 267.

closure, but in that open middle where no one's interpretive potential is denied and no single origin or end is privileged. Not even Cervantes himself, who is and is not the sage, who treats this book as Don Quixote treats this book—as a thing apart from himself, an object, among other things.

For the Don, the history the sage writes is a reification of even his most fantastic ideas, his most personal longings, and the object that confirms the meaning of his life as a knight errant—all knights errant have existed in books. Yet until the sage *writes* the Don's life, he is not a true knight errant, he is only real, and this reification is the necessary premise by which The Second Part becomes possible. The First Part is picaresque and centrifugal: Don Quixote wanders out to encounter the world. The Second Part is centripetal and "more realistic" in the sense that it is a chance for life, as it were, to correct the mistakes in a false art but only when life is also written. It not only criticizes the plagiarized history written as a sequel to The First Part, it records the Don's celebrity and the success that makes others seek him out. He becomes a center. For although he has an itinerary, which includes the Cave of Montesinos, in The Second Part the world really comes to Don Quixote to enter the circle of enchantment that he has created by the intensity of his idea of himself. And however ironic or condescending they are about their motives to be included in the next installment of the Don's history, figures such as the Duke and Duchess confirm the Don's reality, his vision of himself. Their public court is not the private cave in which the Don questions himself. Their court is actually his home field, where they all play by the book.

By the same token, the *thingness* of *Don Quixote* itself, its existence as an object, guarantees Cervantes that his fiction is not like the Don's self-delusions and uncertifiable dreams, and Cervantes goes to some lengths to *reify* his text in order to distance himself from creatures he does not claim. Although he is not the first author, Cide Hamete Benengeli is always designated the writer of the complete history; and between Cide Hamete and Cervantes—who says he is merely its "stepfather," but who is outraged by the plagiarist's insults—there are at least two translators, one of whom is hired on the spot when Cervantes finds a part of the manuscript in the Alacana at Toledo. This fragment contains pictures of Don Quixote and Rocinante, and Cervantes gives the manuscript even greater historicity by including himself within it as the author of *Galatea* and as the almost unidentified heroic rebel of "The Captive's Tale." In this way, Don Quixote is given the same ontological status as the historical character that Cervantes assumes, and Cervantes doubles this effect when he distinguishes between the Don's "authentic history" and "the tales and episodes set in it. For in some ways these are no less agreeable, ingenious, and *authentic* than the history itself."[39] Nor are the various narrators of the interpolated tales, the translators and commentators whom Cervantes is always referring to as his sources, any less authentic. Cervantes treats them as readers and as his equals, for they have become his collaborators in the job of explaining reality in a way completely unlike the Don's own explanation. They are, in a way, to Cervantes what the Duke and Duchess are to the Don: confirmation that *Don Quixote* itself is more like a windmill than a giant, a real thing rather than just a space of textuality.

In *Cervantes's Theory of the Novel,* E. C. Riley says: "Cervantes handles his work in such a way as to show his complete control over the creation he tries so hard to make seem independent."[40] But like Joyce and the Canon of Toledo, Riley can turn right around and praise Cervantes for his distance from his work and its autonomy. Nonetheless, Cervantes's control is not what is most interesting here: the control of form is exactly what we expect from art. What is most interesting is the effort he makes to make it not his, to resolve his artistry away, give his characters their freedom, and make the book seem autonomous. This is the effect, I think, of reading Penelope after the very self-conscious "literature" of the preceding chapters: in Molly's artlessness, Joyce tries to give his book away to life.[41] And the attitudes he shares with Cervantes—that there are many versions of the world, all of them authoritative, and none necessarily inferior to the author's—is at the heart of their common idea and the novel's ideal of realism.

The ideal of realism and the imperative of impersonality so intrinsic to it have affected modernist poetry as well. Robert Pinsky puts the case as quickly and clearly as anyone when he says in *The Situation of Poetry* that the tradition of using a persona, "a borrowed voice or alter-identity, as speaker or central character partly distinct from the poet, constitutes one of the most widely noted, perhaps over-emphasized, critically chewed, and fundamental aspects of modernism. . . . And 'the speaker' as a method stands in clear logical relation to the modernist goal of moving the poem away from the abstraction of a statement,

---

39. *Ibid.,* 25, 467–68, 76, 77, 62, 355, 236 (italics added).

40. E. C. Riley, *Cervantes's Theory of the Novel* (Oxford, 1962), 41.

41. One measure of his success is Molly's subsequent appearance in a dream that Joyce wrote down for Herbert Gorman. See Patrick McGee, *Paperspace: Style as Ideology in Joyce's Ulysses* (Lincoln, 1988), 172–73.

toward the being of an object."[42] What is operative behind Pinsky's statement is the presumption that lyric is utterance, poem is song, and lyric poems do not have to be written down to exist. Novels do have to be written down, however. Not every one of them has to insist on its physical reality as emphatically as *Don Quixote* does at the beginning; not many insist as *Ulysses* does later by means of the typographical maneuvers in Aeolus, Circe, and Ithaca that signal its own investigation of the new relationship between print and writing, technology and *écriture*. But novels have to be objects, things as well as texts, and what this means ultimately to the nature of character is what I want to explore before returning to Pynchon and my speculative conclusion.

My next starting point is unlikely, I think: a lovely and moving passage in Marx that is the best explanation I know of what is to be gained in the impersonality of an object that not only confirms the self but the self's communal nature as well:

> Supposing that we had produced in a human manner; each of us would in his production have doubly affirmed himself and his fellow men. I would have: (1) objectified in my production, my individuality and its peculiarity and thus both in my activity enjoyed an individual expression of my life and also in looking at the object have had the individual pleasure of realizing that my personality was objective, visible to the senses and thus a power raised beyond all doubt. (2) In your enjoyment or use of my product I would have had the direct enjoyment of realizing that I had both satisfied a human need by my work and also objectified the human essence and therefore fashioned for another human being the object that met his need. (3) I would have been for you the mediator between you and the species and thus been acknowledged and felt by you as a competition of your own essence and a necessary part of yourself and have thus realized that I am confirmed both in your thought and in your love. (4) In my expression of life I would have fashioned your expression of your

---

42. Robert Pinsky, *The Situation of Poetry: Contemporary Poetry and Its Traditions* (Princeton, 1976), 14. Fredric Jameson, in *The Political Unconscious: Narrative as a Socially Symbolic Act* (Ithaca, 1981), says "authorial depersonalization" is one of the "threefold imperatives" of "high" realism; the other two are "unity of point of view, and restriction to scenic representation" (104). But David Carroll argues that the premises of phenomenology make impersonality impossible: *The Subject in Question: The Languages of Theory and the Strategies of Fiction* (Chicago, 1982), 55–56. I should point out that impersonality can only be aspired to or achieved by a *person*, and not by the subject constructed by linguistic function, textuality, or discourse.

life, and thus in my own activity have realized my own essence, my human, my communal essence.[43]

We do not have to claim for this passage that it contains a theory of reading in order to remind ourselves that it implies, in this context, the novel's physical being. And Marx's notion that such a thing as a novel objectifies not only our individuality but our "species-being" as well reminds us again that our character is not our person, identity, or individuality, but our signal relationship to the manifold of interpretation. This experience of the self's variety, plurality, multiplicity is a very important correlative of the ideal of impersonality because it means, as novelists since Cervantes have known, even those as "primitive" as Richardson and Defoe, that the writer who does not want to speak *in propria persona* is not confined to a single other voice; and that the writer uses other characters not as prosthetic devices but as real aspects of the self, part of his or her own human nature, and all it can mean. Don Quixote says: "I know who I am, . . . and I know, too, that I am capable of being not only the characters I have named, but all the Twelve Peers of France and all the Nine Worthies as well, for my exploits are far greater than all the deeds they have done, all together and each by himself."[44] The Don's cry here is as important and as modern as Descartes's *cogito,* Montaigne's *que sais-je,* and Hamlet's "I could be bounded in a nutshell and count myself a king of infinite space—were it not that I have bad dreams." And more immediately it emphasizes that both the Don and Cervantes are distributing themselves throughout their various roles quite deliberately. Not all the role-playing in *Don Quixote* is so fully self-conscious or responsible; in fact, the moral lesson of the longest of the interpolated tales, "The Tale of Foolish Curiosity," is that the actor must guard against being overtaken by his act, that he ought to find rather than lose himself in this kind of play.

The moral aspect of role-playing is not a problem for Joyce—as some of it seems to have become for Pynchon. The variety of Joyce's obvious presence throughout the second half of *Ulysses,* after his attempt at magisterial invisibility throughout all of the first half but Aeolus, is an easy demonstration of one of the principles of modernism Stevens epitomizes in the "Adagia": "A change of style is a change of subject."[45] The play on subject is important and it points us to the fact that Joyce's virtuosity expresses quite directly his sense of what it means to be human. When he discussed the Ulysses theme with Frank Budgen and

43. Quoted in David McLellan, *Karl Marx* (New York, 1975), 31–32.
44. Cervantes, *Don Quixote,* 54.
45. Wallace Stevens, *Opus Posthumous,* ed. Samuel French Morse (New York, 1966), 171.

Georges Borach, he emphasized both Ulysses' *humanity* and his multiplicity, the variety of his roles, until the two seemed to mean the same thing. This long passage, which Richard Ellmann quotes from Borach's journal, should recall to us both the Canon's remarks in *Don Quixote* about the expressive latitude the epic offers a writer and Stephen's remarks in Scylla and Charybdis that "We walk through ourselves, meeting robbers, ghosts, giants, old men, young men, wives, widows, brothers-in-love. But always meeting ourselves."

J. J. thinks:

'The most beautiful, all-embracing theme is that of the Odyssey. It is greater, more human, than that of *Hamlet, Don Quixote,* Dante, *Faust.* The rejuvenation of old Faust has an unpleasant effect upon me. Dante tires one quickly; it is like looking at the sun. The most beautiful, the most human traits are contained in the Odyssey. I was twelve years old when we took up the Trojan War at school; only the Odyssey stuck in my memory. I want to be frank: at twelve I liked the supernaturalism in Ulysses. When I was writing *Dubliners,* I intended at first to choose the title *Ulysses in Dublin,* but gave up the idea. In Rome, when I had finished about half the *Portrait,* I realized the Odyssey had to be the sequel, and I began to write *Ulysses.*

'Why was I always returning to this theme? Now *in mezzo del cammin* I find the subject of Ulysses the most human in world literature. Ulysses didn't want to go off to Troy; he knew that the official reason for the war, the dissemination of the culture of Hellas, was only a pretext for the Greek merchants, who were seeking new markets. When the recruiting officers arrived, he happened to be plowing. He pretended to be mad. Thereupon they placed his little two-year-old son in the furrow. Observe the beauty of the motifs: the only man in Hellas who is against the war, and the father. Before Troy the heroes shed their lifeblood in vain. They want to raise the siege. Ulysses opposes the idea. [He thinks up] the stratagem of the wooden horse. After Troy there is no further talk of Achilles, Mene-laus, Agamemnon. Only one man is not done with; his heroic career has hardly begun: Ulysses.

'Then the motif of wandering. Scylla and Charybdis—what a splendid parable. Ulysses is also a great musician; he wishes to and must listen; he has himself tied to the mast. The motif of the artist, who will lay down his life rather than renounce his interest. Then the delicious humor of Polyphemous. "Outis is my name." On Naxos, the oldster of fifty, perhaps bald-headed, with Nausicaa, a girl who is barely seventeen. What a fine theme! And the return, how profoundly human! Don't forget the trait of generosity at the interview with Ajax in the nether world, and many other beautiful touches. I am almost afraid to treat such a theme; it's overwhelming.'

"It is not surprising," Ellmann comments, "that Joyce's description of Ulysses as pacifist, father, wanderer, musician, and artist, ties the hero's life closely to his own."[46]

This also, of course, ties Joyce to Bloom, but with slightly different consequences. It is obvious we are supposed to see Bloom as a father and as a son, husband and cuckold, pacifist, wanderer, inventor, companion, figure of the artist, and good gentle man. It is also important we see him eating and sleeping, going in Calypso and coming in Nausicaa, at work and at large, through his own eyes and through the eyes of other Dubliners, who have the mean-spiritedness of John Henry Menton and Davey Byrne's respect, the Citizen's anti-Semitism and Josie Breen's affection. Bloom knows it is inevitable, as we have seen, that we all have these other perspectives on ourselves: "Am I like that? See ourselves as others see us." And at his most dispirited he knows: "No one is anything." Bloom is no *one* in the sense that his character has a single identity defined simply by his body's delimiting boundaries. He is a version of Odysseus, God the Father, Shakespeare; he writes himself as Henry Flower; and he plays through several identities both in the prose encyclopedia of Oxen and in the cinematic dissolutions of Circe, where even the bodily limits of his gender no longer obtain. For in Joyce, the complement of impersonality is character's intrinsic multiplicity. If no one is any thing, one may as well be many. If not every character is like Bloom, every serious novelist is like Joyce insofar as every novelist exists and extends his or her existence in language.

Flaubert, as he said to Louise Colet, felt in himself, "literally speaking, two distinct persons," high and low, distinguished by their attitudes toward language. By this standard, Joyce could have felt himself to be as abundant as Odysseus, with his own "autobiography" inscribed in all the different styles of *Ulysses'* second half. Whether we want to say now that the different styles of Sirens and Circe amount to different "characters," as the personal narrator of Cyclops certainly is, is not important. That every character can be a different discourse does not mean every discourse must be a different novelistic character. What is important is that they are all Joyce's and to none of them does he give a special authority. The style of Calypso is not truer than Circe; the dreamy self-indulgence of the style in Nausicaa does not present us with a better Bloom than the cool, irrational catechism of Ithaca. Joyce does not distribute himself throughout Moorish historians and interpolated raconteurs, but he achieves the same value by adopting for himself a series of masks, voices, personae, characterizations, or styles, as easily, as fluently, as Stephen adopts new identities for himself in Proteus.

"The essential thing about the ever-living Proteus," says J. Mitchell Morse, is that "he doesn't *imitate* fire, water, animals, etc., but *is* and by turns *manifests himself as* fire, water, animals, etc. He is all nature, potent, latent; through changing forms he manifests the rolling, heaving neverchanging everchanging all."[47] Language signifies without imitating, unless language is itself the basis of protean reality, in which case Joyce imitates reality exactly. So, although not every one of the last nine chapters of *Ulysses* is realistic by any single definition, together they are realistic in their commitment to a truth based on the equality of difference, of different characterizations. These points of view, or different discourses, may be embodied in different characters, as I proposed in chapter 2; or they may be embodied in the several aspects, or different styles, or complementary perspectives of a single character. And, in light of this, it is easier now, I think, to grant that when Joyce said, "In my Mabbot Street scene, I approached reality closer in my opinion than anywhere else in the book except perhaps for moments in the last chapter," he was defining his idea of realism quite exactly: posing his spoken discourse at the moment against the objectified body of his work, and posing the discourse of one chapter against the character of another; claiming nothing absolute for any of the four different modes; leaving himself, with the phrase "in my opinion," open to Power's opinion as well; and leaving an exact definition of "reality" ideally out of reach. For the ideal of realism is not in its mimetic fidelity but in its belief in the world's, in being's recurrent abundance and in the matching plenitude of its human characterization. In this respect, impersonality is no limit, but a license that assures us we do not have to repeat even ourselves.

Realism is an epistemology in which characters and things must be commensurate ontologically, in a system that is not merely the linguistically determined relationship of signifier and signified. In the novel, realism is also a structural relationship among characters that keeps the meaning of any single thing open to other characterizations, including the meaning of any one of the characters, read by another, which means that the nature of character itself is not singular

---

47. J. Mitchell Morse, "Proteus," in Hart and Hayman, *James Joyce's Ulysses*, 29.

and decided but multiple. Don Quixote's representative *thing* is the helmet of Mambrino. Sancho sees it as the barber's basin; his take on it is sensory, empirical, realistic. Don Quixote reads the basin as the chivalric headpiece; his take is imaginative, textual, representational. Neither characterization is untrue; each version of the thing reads something of the character who makes it; the meaning of their relationship is more important to the novel than the basin or helmet is. There is no such single physical object in *Bleak House*. By the nineteenth century, society has become the ground of the novel's research into the real. So the relationship between Dickens's narrator and Esther is not only important for their epistemological or interpretive differences, but also for the differences that her gender, social status, and power make to the formal differences inherent in their narrative modes. Still, if there is a focal "object" in *Bleak House*, it may be Jo. Esther can care for him; the narrator can perform a scalding eulogy; neither can save his life. But even if the focal object is Chancery, or the identity and death of Lady Dedlock, or anything else, the relationship, the difference between the general narrator and Esther is still the nexus of *Bleak House*'s realism; and the fact that Esther cannot fully know herself or the narrator is a crucial limit.

The paradigm we have educed from *Ulysses* is symmetrical to those from *Don Quixote* and *Bleak House*, but even more reductive, as the things for a realistic style to comprehend have grown in number and the modes of knowing we now deem "realistic" have, too. Stephen looks at the elemental and trivial objects time and tide have brought to the natural scene of Sandymount strand, at the threshold of the earth and ocean. Bloom looks on a similar plenum in the site and symbol of civilization that he and Joyce think of as The City, "DEAR DIRTY DUBLIN." Stephen tries to think of himself expanded through a romantic perspectivalism; Bloom's self-conception is as an empty slot in a structural system of tenancy or, later, as merely one item in the series that cycles through Molly's bed. They do not confront each other to argue as the Don and Sancho do. Their encounter is subject to Bloom's mollifications in the style of Eumaeus and the separations of logic in the parody of Ithaca, where they do not, for instance, seriously discuss race or the reasons for Stephen's refusal to stay. And because of Bloom's relationship to Molly and her presence in his mind throughout the day, his opposition with Stephen is not as neatly focused as Esther's is with Dickens's narrator.[48] *Ulysses* is not as long as *Bleak House* which, in the Penguin editions, is not as long as *Don Quixote*, but *Ulysses* seems much thicker, thicker

---

48. For Molly as an interpretive principle herself, see Vicki Mahaffey, *Reauthorizing Joyce* (Cambridge, U.K., 1988), especially chapter 4.

with paradigms, thicker with the detail that the narrative structure, despite the orderly plot, keeps open from many different angles.

Gravity's Rainbow seems even more open because it does not have the plot *Ulysses* does, seems to have as many characters as *Bleak House,* and contains a range and context of information we are still in the early stages of organizing. It's hard, therefore, to know or decide that it has a representative thing. Slothrop, as I have tried to explain, enacts with his own body a reciprocal epistemology *if* his ultimate thinning out is what gives him his alertness to other modes of presence—not only to the rockets over London before they are there, but also to the presence of Jamf within him, and to the other intimations he has of Them, of Something Else at Work. But once he disperses, *what* he knows, how he knows it, and *what* he is to know it as—all the fussy protocols of commensuration—are hard to determine. Still, I think there is an object to propose. It is impossible to tell if Slothrop is enclosed in the embracing *you* of the narrative's free indirect discourse in the quotation below; impossible to explain logically how this object can be represented as something extant *before* the birth of human consciousness which has worked to mediate, represent, and therefore deny it.

> It's golden-dark, almost night. The region is lonely and Pan is very close. Geli has been to enough Sabbaths to handle it—she thinks. But what is a devil's blue bite on the ass to the shrieking-outward, into stone resonance, where there is no good or evil, out in the luminous spaces Pan will carry her to? Is she ready yet for anything so real? The moon has risen. She sits now, at the same spot where she saw the eagle, waiting, waiting for something to come and take her. Have you ever waited for *it?* wondering whether it will come from outside or inside? Finally past the futile guesses at what might happen . . . now and then re-erasing brain to keep it clean for the Visit . . . yes wasn't it close to here? remember didn't you sneak away from camp to have a moment alone with What you felt stirring across the land . . . it was the equinox . . . green spring equal nights . . . canyons are opening up, at the bottoms are steaming fumaroles, steaming the tropical life there like greens in a pot, rank, dope-perfume, a hood of smell . . . human consciousness, that poor cripple, that deformed and doomed thing, is about to be born. This is the World just before men. Too violently pitched alive in constant flow ever to be seen by men directly. They are meant only to look at it dead, in still strata, transputrefied to oil or coal. Alive, it was a threat: it was Titans, was an overpeaking of life so clangorous and mad, such a green corona

about Earth's body that some spoiler *had* to be brought in before it blew the Creation apart. . . .

. . . A few keep going over to the Titans every day, in their striving subcreation (how can flesh tumble and flow so, and never be any less beautiful?), into the rests of the folk-song Death (empty stone rooms), out, and through, and down under the net, down down to the uprising.

In harsh-edged echo, Titans stir far below. They are all the presences we are not supposed to be seeing—wind gods, hilltop gods, sunset gods—that we train ourselves away from to keep from looking further even though enough of us do, leave Their electric voices behind in the twilight at the edge of the town and move into the constantly parted cloak of our nightwalk till[49]

So this transhistorical, unembodied "voice" or "point of view," this characterization without a traditional character to tie it to, may be what and where Slothrop is now. And postmodernism's Helmet of Mabrino is, therefore, the earth. That is, it is every *thing* that has gone to make up the world and also every other thing that has been excluded in order to make the world the whole.[50]

49. Pynchon, *Gravity's Rainbow,* 720 (ellipses added).

50. "I have been trying to think of the earth as a kind of organism, but it is no go. I cannot think of it this way. It is too big, too complex, with too many working parts lacking visible connections. The other night, driving through a hilly, wooded part of Southern New England, I wondered about this. If not like an organism, what is it like, what is it *most* like? Then, satisfactorily for that moment, it came to me: it is most like a single cell." Lewis Thomas, *The Lives of a Cell: Notes of a Biology Watcher* (New York, 1974), 5.

5

FLAUBERT'S PARROT
POSTMODERNISM
ROLAND BARTHES

I think everybody is a realist. I do not think we have a choice.
—DONALD BARTHELME, Interview, *Gulf Coast*

. . . and if I were to tell you that this year, before going to Tokyo, I went to
Oxford, Ohio, and that I even bought some dental floss—that is to say,
an eolian harp—in a drugstore in Ithaca, you would not believe me.
You would be wrong; it is true and can be verified.
—JACQUES DERRIDA, "Ulysses Gramophone"

IN HIS REVIEW of Julian Barnes's *Flaubert's Parrot,* David Lodge calls it "an exemplary poststructuralist text."[1] In his review, John Updike is irritated by the things Lodge likes. The narrative's self-consciousness and skepticism, all the formal elements that seem to make *Flaubert's Parrot* a metafiction, Updike says are "arch, quarrelsome, curt, cute, and implausibly literary." He goes on: "While the novel as a form certainly asks for, and can absorb, a great deal of experimentation, it must at some point achieve self-forgetfulness and let pure event take over. . . . [H]is [the narrator's] real-life misfortune remains raw and rough, and resists sublimation by literature. But so much artifice in establishing the priority of the 'real' feels artificial, and leaves us cold."[2] "Implausibly

---

1. David Lodge, "The Home Front," *New York Review of Books,* May 7, 1987, p. 21. In *The Art of Fiction* (New York, 1993), however, Lodge does not mention *Flaubert's Parrot* in discussing metafiction, nor does he list Barnes with Barth, Borges, Calvino, Drabble, Fowles, and Vonnegut as one of the style's exemplars.

2. John Updike, "A Pair of Parrots" in *Odd Jobs: Essays and Criticism* (New York, 1991), 631, 632. Updike also says in *Odd Jobs* that he keeps reviewing foreign novels to rediscover the essential secret of the real: "The innovative power of American realism isn't what it was for Hemingway and Faulkner, and foreign solutions to the puzzle that fiction poses in this post-print, anti-teleological era held out to me hope of some magical formulae" (xxii). For more on Updike's realism, see Terrence Doody, "Updike's Idea of Reification," *Contemporary Literature,* XX (Spring, 1979), 204–20.

literary," "pure event," and "the priority of the 'real'" are bones to pick, but not here, because I don't agree with Lodge completely either. Metafiction is only one kind of postmodernist writing; it is, perhaps, the easiest to identify, and deplore, but it is not the most important kind of writing we find in recent fiction.

Flaubert's Parrot is actually a fairly traditional realistic novel. But it so conscientiously displays its assumptions and the limitations of its realistic epistemology, it can be read as though it wants to be something else—such as a theory of itself, not unlike *Roland Barthes by Roland Barthes*, a work it mentions in order to disparage. *Roland Barthes*, on the other hand, is an essay on the nature of writing and the subject, an experiment against normative narrative order and its implications, that wants nonetheless to be read as a novel. These two books share more, however, than just their cross purposes. *Flaubert's Parrot* is centered around an important writer and plays a variety of narrative and discursive methods against each other in order to develop the richness of the problem Flaubert represents. *Roland Barthes* is also centered around an important writer, and it, too, plays a number of discursive ideas against each other in order to develop and overcome the problem that the subject "Barthes" represents. Flaubert is represented by a number of stuffed parrots, physical objects that constitute a text over which he has no authority. And Barthes is represented by a number of photographs that render his body from points of view he cannot have on himself—shot from behind, for instance, as he writes at his desk—as a physical presence outside the authority of his own writing. The *punctum* of these photographs is Barthes's often unprotected and unposed openness to being "read."[3] But more important than anything else they have in common, and more significant to their status as "exemplary" texts, is the fact that they are both autobiographies.

"There is no theory," Valéry says, "that is not a fragment, carefully prepared, of some autobiography." Nor, it now seems, is there any autobiography that is not an attempt to enact or embody a theory. And to the extent that serious literary autobiography is often an act of renewal, it is congruent with postmodernism's effort to renew literature, again, by rereading it. "If today the problem of reading occupies the forefront of science, it is because of this suspense between two ages of writing. Because we are beginning to write, to write differently," Derrida says, "we must reread differently."[4] As an *academic* movement, literary post-

---

3. See Roland Barthes, *Camera Lucida: Reflections on Photography*, trans. Richard Howard (New York, 1981), for his definitions of *punctum* (25–27) and "posing" (10–12), which turns on the idea of his "essence."

4. Jacques Derrida, *Of Grammatology*, trans. Gayatri Chakravorty Spivak (Baltimore, 1976), 86–87. Two other accounts of what this kind of rereading accomplishes come from Derek Attridge,

modernism is no doubt a concerted rereading—Barthes rereading Balzac, Derrida rereading Rousseau, feminist critics rereading everyone—but whether postmodernist theory has sponsored a really different kind of writing is harder to decide. For recent theory has not so much influenced the novel as it has been influenced by it; and it would be hard to calculate whether experiments such as *Glas* and *Roland Barthes* mark a measurable advance beyond the experiments of *The Wild Palms, Tender Buttons,* or *Finnegans Wake.* Moreover, there are fine, important "nineteenth-century" novels still being written, such as *The Golden Notebook,* Updike's own Rabbit tetralogy, and the novels of Naguib Mahfouz. But autobiography is an inevitable form for writing that grows from theories that have transformed the individual into the subject and then placed the subject in question. "The origin and the end of autobiography converge in the very act of writing," says Michael Sprinker, "as Proust brilliantly demonstrates at the end of *Le temps trouvé,* for no autobiography can take place except within the boundaries of a writing where concepts of subject, self, and author collapse into the act of producing a text."[5] Sprinker's formulation is efficient and revealing. The historical self and the agency of that self as an author are subsumed into the linguistic ontology of the subject, which is the product of the text rather than its producer; the text "takes place," as though of itself, within implicitly spatial boundaries that confer upon the writing a physical reality it does not otherwise have, that it can't have *as a text;* and the example of this entire operation is a novel, which is *not* Proust's autobiography, but indicative of the intricate formal and historical relationship novels and autobiographies have had at least since the "real" Gines de Pasamonte discussed with the fictional Don Quixote the autobiographer's more-than-formal problems with closure.

Flaubert's Parrot and *Roland Barthes by Roland Barthes* are, therefore, useful starting points for a discussion of postmodernism and the situation of the recent novel. By treating *Flaubert's Parrot* at some length, I can recapitulate points I have made about the novel in previous chapters and apply them to a single book with at least the pretense of completeness, something I haven't done so far. By treating *Roland Barthes* in some detail also, I can establish background for the second part of my argument, which is not another theory of postmodernism, but

---

"Criticism's Wake," in *James Joyce: The Augmented Ninth,* ed. Bernard Benstock (Syracuse, N.Y., 1988), 80–87; and Richard Pearce, "What Joyce after Pynchon," in *James Joyce: The Centennial Symposium,* ed. Morris Beja, Phillip Herring, Maurice Harmon, and David Norris (Urbana, 1986), 43–46.

5. Michael Sprinker, "Fictions of the Self: The End of Autobiography," in *Autobiography: Essays Theoretical and Critical,* ed. James Olney (Princeton, 1980), 342.

a descriptive diagram of the kinds of writing that have been important to the novel since the end of World War II. The diagram looks like this:

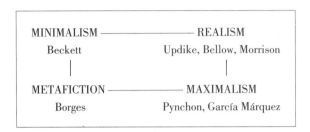

This is not a diagram of theory so much as it is a suggestion of the tensions between theory and practice. Metafiction and Realism, for instance, take a different stance toward the empirical world. Under Borges's general leadership, Metafiction casts language as ontology and does not refer beyond language's system in the library of Babel to anything else. Saul Bellow's realistic portrait of Mr. Sammler, however, refers quite powerfully to the Holocaust, racism, the violence in American culture, the Upper West Side of New York, the moon, and the inescapability of moral connection. Borges, therefore, is often favored by theorists who think Bellow is a reactionary still trying to write *Daniel Deronda*. The tensions between these two positions are real; they indicate the disparate tendencies in any literary era; and I have no wish to resolve them under a bigger umbrella. Postmodernism opposes totalizations and is, in fact, a misleading term unless it is put in the plural: there are only postmodernisms, ramifications of a center that doesn't exist, effects of an event that has never taken place.

Another way of putting it is that modernism is a name we have given to our inquiry into the problematic relationship of the part to the whole, and postmodernism is also a name we have given to the problem of the part and the whole—except that there are no wholes. This formula occurred to me as I was trying to reconcile explanations of modernism that emphasize the image, the fragment, and the alienated figure, such as Bloom, with those that emphasize originary myth, formalism's autonomy, and the intention of the heroic artist, such as Joyce. That both explanations fit many of the same works suggested the need to reformulate the matter. And although this formulation may sound as though it yearns for inclusion in The Apocrypha of Oscar Wilde, it has mnemonic efficiency in the classroom and a suggestive symmetry. For it obviously points to our habit of making a kind of history in which modernism and postmodernism are congruent with the differences between structuralism and poststructuralism and the autonomous integrity of formalism has given way to the deconstructive principles behind new versions of historical and material culture.[6]

We have become suspicious of modernist and formalist wholes for a number of reasons. One of them is that logically, as Gödel and Derrida have shown, they cannot contain the principle that defines or guarantees their own totality or integrity. They need to be proven whole by an ulterior principle, such as a metanarrative, or a supplement that by definition reveals them as incomplete. Another reason is that, politically, we now believe a whole that is integrated and harmonious, according to a law that is also psychoanalytic, must have repressed or excluded whatever foreign matter compromises its construction. Without a belief in wholes, moreover, it is no longer possible to believe that the beginning determines the end, that the artist's intention determines the artifact's meaning. In place of formal intention, we honor desire, which in Lacan's formulation is uniformly without the possibility of fulfillment and totalized as insatiable. By the same logic, absence is now a more important idea than presence and a more productive experience, since absence makes desire go farther. And the artist, who used to be able to mediate the discontinuity between the part and the whole and make something of it, new or not, is now the subject of the text or narrative sentence that produces a narrator as a function within its own operation. There are no supervisory signifieds any more, only signifiers; so in our rereading, we no longer look for the finished structure but for the seams of its construction in order to open it up to demystification and our own authority.

For the novel, there are many advantages to this new regime—the redefinition of the narrator as a character part and the redistribution, therefore, of interpretive authority; character itself construed as a sign rather than as the whole substance we have called a person; the opening of the middle of the narrative into something other than the line between the beginning and an end that closes the novel into a formally finished box; the realization that realism is not achieved by the disclosure of an object's essence or the exhaustive accumulation of descriptive data, but is practiced by keeping characters and things open endlessly to another reading, a new point of view, a different interpretation, nothing final or total, not even the whole earth's catalogue.

To propose, as I did in discussing Pynchon's realism, that the earth itself is postmodernism's helmet of Mambrino, is to suggest what any whole such as the novel now has to comprehend. Among these are the great range and variety of experience that the novel has to entertain to meet any "realistic" standard of inclusiveness: the number of different discourses, both academic and techno-

---

6. See Jonathan Culler, *Flaubert: The Uses of Uncertainty* (Rev. ed., Ithaca, 1985), 233–34, who argues against any distinction between structuralism and poststructuralism.

logical, competing with each other, with the novel, and for the novel's attention; the enormity of everything—the world's population, the proliferation of nuclear weaponry and diminution of natural resources, the ruthlessness of nationalist and religious crusades, the frequency of genocidal war, the longing for apocalyptic simplicities and deliverance—and the impossibility of representing it *all*. It is historical conditions such as these that preclude the adequacy of a single definition of postmodernism arising from any single principle, such as the metaphysics of the sign, the intransitivity of writing, the discourse of the other, the power of power in discursive and epistemic formations, or the decoding of formalism into race, class, and gender. To avoid any of these reductions, therefore, it seems necessary to talk about recent novels in a way that honors all their real differences.

I want to begin to explore these differences by contrasting two books as similar-and-different as *Flaubert's Parrot* and *Roland Barthes* for another reason as well. Autobiography is often a response to a crisis; and although neither of these is a reaction to any larger political issue, they do signify trouble. In *Flaubert's Parrot* Braithwaite elevates the failure of his marriage into a narrative and epistemological crisis; because he does not understand his wife and cannot face himself, he poses the impossibilities of historical knowledge and of sorting out Flaubert. Barthes does not seem to write from a crisis so personal—perhaps because it is hard to take *the subject* personally. But *Roland Barthes* points to a crisis nonetheless. If you do take seriously theories of the subject and want to write an autobiography regardless, you have to find a way, as he does, to escape the subject's theoretical limits.

That *Flaubert's Parrot* is a novel that aspires to be taken as something else, as more than merely the narrator's own story, is its most conventional sign. That *Roland Barthes* is an autobiography that aspires to the novel's values without in any way imitating the novel's traditional means is its most important novelty. And together they suggest why autobiography is postmodernism's exemplary form. When the subject is in question, in any way, for any reason, you write yourself the answer.

Flaubert's parrot is both a physical object and several texts. One of these texts is the novel by Julian Barnes he entitles *Flaubert's Parrot*. Another is the autobiography of Geoffrey Braithwaite, who is the narrator of *Flaubert's Parrot*, a novel he is unaware of. Braithwaite is a retired physician, the widower of an unfaithful woman, and an amateur Flaubert scholar who looks to the great writer for wisdom—a tribute you'd think would embarrass Flaubert. Braithwaite begins to comment explicitly on the relation between words and things in the novel's fourth paragraph, when he talks about the deterioration of certain statues of Flaubert around the city of Rouen.

> Perhaps the foundry's assurances can be believed; perhaps this second-impression statue will last. But I see no particular grounds for confidence. Nothing much else to do with Flaubert has ever lasted. He died little more than a hundred years ago, and all that remains of him is paper. Paper, ideas, phrases, metaphors, structured prose which turns into sound. This, as it happens, is precisely what he would have wanted; it's only his admirers who sentimentally complain. The writer's house at Croisset was knocked down shortly after his death and replaced by a factory for extracting alcohol from damaged wheat. It wouldn't take much to get rid of his effigy either: if one statue-loving Mayor can put it up, another—perhaps a bookish party-liner who has half-read Sartre on Flaubert—might zealously take it down.[7]

The easy irony that mere words, verbal texts can outlast metal and stone is not so important here as the theme that nothing whatsoever is stable, especially meaning, even if it is something so trivial as the meaning of Flaubert's parrot. Braithwaite first sees it at the hospital in Rouen, where the inscription explains that Flaubert had borrowed it to put on his work-table as he was writing "A Simple Heart." Almost immediately, Braithwaite sees "it" again in a cabinet in the pavilion in Croisset that is all that remains of Flaubert's house. "My initial response," he says, "was that the second seemed less authentic than the first." Of course: the "belated" is never authentic, a feeling Braithwaite has about himself. But long before he finally discovers that there are fifty of these stuffed parrots in a storage room of the Rouen museum, the reader has realized that Flaubert's parrot is many things, including of course Braithwaite himself, parroting Flaubert's ideas about life and art.[8]

The parrots represent a number of other things as well: the way in which matter multiplies and differentiates, subverting and exposing, therefore, the specious unity of any idealization that language sponsors; the specious idealization that there is a single source, an authentic origin that establishes an uncompromised authority; the authority of even Flaubert himself, the heroic figure from whom Braithwaite depends, as Marlow does from Lord Jim, and in whom he seeks an elevated identity. Lord Jim, Marlow keeps arguing, is "one

7. Julian Barnes, *Flaubert's Parrot* (New York, 1985), 2.
8. *Ibid.*, 14, 9.

of us," although what he means is that he has discovered himself to be one with Jim and a romantic. Braithwaite does not have the temerity to identify himself in such a way with Flaubert, but he would prefer not to be just another version of Charles Bovary. Moreover, he knows enough to realize that just as there are several versions of *the* parrot, there are several versions of Flaubert himself. "We no longer believe," he says, "that language and reality 'match up' so congruently—indeed, we probably think that words give birth to things as much as things give birth to words"—an effect of discursive formation he will demonstrate himself in the second chapter, "Chronology." He knows, too, that this discursive power is what renders the individual a subject: "Sartre himself rebuked Flaubert for passivity, for belief (or collusion in the belief) that *on est parlé*—one is spoken."[9]

But Braithwaite does not want to construe Flaubert as a subject because he would then have to construe himself as a subject too, and he does not want to do this, to relinquish whatever power he may still think he has. This would align him with Roland Barthes, who says of himself in the third person: "He wants to side with any writing whose principle is that *the subject is merely an effect of language.*"[10] It is as though Braithwaite has been the victim of his wife's infidelity and does not want to admit he is language's "victim" as well. This resistance to an idea he understands completely sets a limit to his narrative and keeps it within the normative tradition. Although he cannot know finally why his wife has been unfaithful, or all that her sexual life has meant to her, his problem is circumstantial and psychological. His cuckoldry is not an ontological condition; the fact he doesn't know his wife doesn't make her unknowable. And despite all that he does with his versions of Flaubert and his own different styles as a narrator, these uses of language do not alter him, do not change his relation to language itself, do not subject him to its other ontology. Braithwaite entertains some advanced ideas, but his own characterization prevents *Flaubert's Parrot* from being the kind of postmodernist text Lodge wants it to be. It is not even as radically skeptical as *As I Lay Dying*, for instance, and it does not take the matters of loss, memory, or displacement to the edge that Marilynne Robinson reaches in this extraordinary passage from *Housekeeping:*

> I could conjure her face as it was then, startled by the sudden awareness of our watching. At the time I think I felt only curiosity, although I suppose I remember that glance because she looked at me for signs of more than curiosity. And, in fact, I recall the moment

9. *Ibid.*, 90–91, 11.
10. *Roland Barthes by Roland Barthes*, trans. Richard Howard (New York, 1977), 79.

now with some astonishment—there was neither doubt nor passion in her destruction of the letter, neither hesitation nor haste—and with frustration—there was only that letter and never another one, and nothing else from him or about him at all—and with anger—he was presumably our father, and might wish to know what had become of us, and even to intervene. It occurs to me sometimes that as I grow older I am increasingly able to present to her gaze the face she seemed to expect. But of course she was looking into a face I do not remember—no more like mine than Sylvie's is like hers. Less like, perhaps, because, as I watched Sylvie, she reminded me of my mother more and more. There was such similarity, in fact, in the structure of cheek and chin, and the texture of hair, that Sylvie began to blur the memory of my mother, and then to displace it. Soon it was Sylvie who would look up startled, regarding me from a vantage of memory in which she had no place. And it was increasingly to this remembered Sylvie that I presented my look of conscious injury, knowing as I did so that Sylvie could know nothing of that letter.[11]

Flaubert's Parrot is, nonetheless, exemplary of what good novels always do: it makes the psychology of its narrator's interpretation a *formal* aspect of the narrative. And in Braithwaite's case in particular it allows him, and Julian Barnes, to suggest several paradigms, internal and external, that make the play of Braithwaite's similarity-and-difference with other narrators unusually broad. In *The Book of Laughter and Forgetting*, Milan Kundera says, using a musical analogy: "Variations also constitute a journey, but not through the external world. . . . The journey of the variation form leads to that *second* infinity, the infinity of internal variety concealed in all things."[12] This is a good idea by which to measure the richness of any novel and one that *Flaubert's Parrot* works out with some finesse. The paradigms I want to examine now are those of the parrot itself, the figure of Flaubert, and Braithwaite's narrative roles and arrangements. In some cases, these arrangements are the narrator's; in some others, they are the author's; in some, they belong to both, which would seem to add another dimension toward Kundera's internal infinity, but doesn't really. *Flaubert's Parrot* always withholds itself from the extremes it implies.

We may assume, I think, that the parrot is first a living animal. In chapter 4, "Flaubert's Bestiary," Braithwaite even goes so far as to say, "Parrots are human

11. Marilynne Robinson, *Housekeeping* (Toronto, 1982), 52–53.

12. Milan Kundera, *The Book of Laughter and Forgetting*, trans. Michael Henry Heim (New York, 1981), 164.

to begin with; etymologically, that is. *Perroquet* is a diminutive of *Pierrot; parrot* comes from *Pierre;* Spanish *perico* derives from *Pedro.*"[13] So the parrot is a character, in the sense that it is something to read, a sign with several significations, although it cannot read itself; and it is a character whose signification changes according to the discourse into which it is set, even when that discourse is taxidermy before it is art. When Flaubert moves the stuffed parrot he has borrowed from his worktable into his text, it becomes a living animal named Loulou, and his character Felicité accepts it because in the story it is from America and reminds her of her beloved absent Victor: "In her isolation, Loulou was almost a son or lover to her," the story says.[14] When Loulou dies, Felicité herself has it stuffed, which makes the parrot, once a symbol of Victor, now a representation of its living self as well, and then an icon of the Holy Spirit Felicité prays to as she is delirious and dying. In this discourse, Loulou represents Felicité's longing and her desire for transformation. Flaubert's parrot is also something like that for Braithwaite, as he tries to come to an understanding of Flaubert in order to understand and transform himself in doing so. Flaubert took the real parrot from the realm of history and revivified it in the discourse of fiction, but Braithwaite wants to take it out of Flaubert's art and insert it into the history of his own life. He knows that this makes it a kind of fetish, but he uses it as a focal point for his meditation on the connections between art and life, Flaubert and himself, fictions and the "truth." He does not know, of course, that Barnes has raised the parrot, as though he were embedding it "up," from Braithwaite's "history" into a superior fiction in which Barnes makes it the focus of Braithwaite's obsessions and evasions, parroting Flaubert and hiding from himself in research. There are several different ontological levels here—Flaubert's, Barnes's, and Braithwaite's, all of them textualized in different ways—but never are they confusing to us and at no time does Braithwaite lose himself as Charles Kinbote does in Nabokov's *Pale Fire,* in which at some points it is impossible to distinguish Kinbote's mad interpolations from the text's "facts."

As I said earlier, as soon as it is clear to Braithwaite that there is no authentic single parrot, he presents in "Chronology," the second chapter, three different versions of Flaubert's life, which are complementary but not exactly parallel. The first version resembles the positive account we might find in a biographical dictionary or literary encyclopedia:

1821 *Birth of Gustave Flaubert, second son of Achille-Cléophas Flaubert, head surgeon at the Hotel-Dieu, Rouen, and of Anne-*

---

13. Barnes, *Flaubert's Parrot,* 16, 20, 25.
14. Gustave Flaubert, *Three Tales,* trans. Richard Baldick (Harmondsworth, 1961), 47.

Justine-Caroline Flaubert, née Fleuriot. The family belongs to the successful professional middle class. A stable, enlightened, encouraging and normally ambitious background.

The second style of entry is decidedly pessimistic, derivative, and more critical:

1817   *Death of Caroline Flaubert (aged twenty months), the second child of Achille-Cléophas and Anne-Justine Caroline Flaubert.*

1819   *Death of Emile-Cléophas Flaubert (aged eight months), their third child.*

1821   *Birth of Gustave Flaubert, their fifth child.*

1822   *Death of Jules Alfred Flaubert (aged three years and five month), their fourth child. His brother Gustave, born entre deux morts, is delicate and not expected to live long. Dr. Flaubert buys a family plot at the Cimetière Monumental and has a small grave dug in preparation for Gustave. Surprisingly, he survives. He proves a slow child, content to sit for hours with his finger in his mouth and "almost stupid" expression on his face. For Sartre, he is "the family idiot."*

The third chronology is taken from Flaubert himself and reflects not only his own dour address, but also his inveterate, even compulsive resort to metaphor:

1842   *Me and my books, in the same apartment: like a gherkin in its vinegar.*

1846   *When I was young I had a complete presentiment of life. It was like a nauseating smell of cooking escaping from a ventilator: you don't have to have eaten it to know that it would make you throw up.*

1846   *I did with you what I have done before with those I loved best: I have showed them the bottom of the bag, and the acrid dust that rose from it made them choke.*[15]

15. Barnes, *Flaubert's Parrot*, 16, 20, 25.

Flaubert is a different character in these different discourses, the same historical person, of course, but read in different ways, as though the three versions of his life have come from different narrators. That Braithwaite has chosen every entry himself indicates his clear realization there is no self-substantial "versionless version" of Flaubert's life—no essential Flaubert to match a single parrot. Chapter 4, "The Flaubert Bestiary," extends this insight as Braithwaite constructs another kind of anatomy of Flaubert out of all the other animal metaphors with which "the bear of Croisset" has figured himself, and Braithwaite is clear that none of these animal metaphors is necessary, transformative, or totalizing. They are metonyms, and Flaubert's self-definition is distributed throughout them without a definitive beginning or summary end. Whatever his Romantic self-involvement may have led to, Flaubert's skepticism undercut; there is no apotheosis or transcendence.

And there is no single narrative position in which Braithwaite comes to rest. If he does not alter his own relation to language, nor let the ontology of language alter his relationship to himself, he does realize the possibilities in different narrative viewpoints. In the book's most impressive chapter, "Louise Colet's Version," Braithwaite invents a dramatic monologue in which Flaubert's mistress at the time he was writing *Madame Bovary* makes her retort. Embedded as she is in Flaubert's life and letters, so is she embedded now in this account of Flaubert's exemplary mastery, where her dissenting narrative is surrounded by Braithwaite's narrative, which at the moment is the story of her story and both Barnes's and Braithwaite's indication that the fullness of meaning is built out of the open middle of a novel's narrative, out of the possibility of other versions, the discourse of other characters who interpret their lives, the lives of the others in their orbit, and are offered to our interpretation as well.

There are two counterparts to "Louise Colet's Version," "Cross Channel" and "Pure Story." Braithwaite uses the phrase "pure story" in several ways. Ellen's is a pure story, he says, because she "wasn't corrupted." Her adultery did not "coarsen" her "spirit," so she didn't grow to be like Madame Bovary, is one thing he clearly means to argue. But it is also clear that he doesn't quite know what to think about the whole thing, and he plays many variations such as this:

> I loved her; we were happy; I miss her. She didn't love me; we were unhappy; I miss her. . . .
> My wife went to bed with other men: should I worry about that? I didn't go to bed with other women: should I worry about that? Ellen was always nice to me: should I worry about that? Not nice out of adulterous guilt, but just nice. . . . I didn't have affairs because I wasn't interested enough to do so; . . . Ellen did have affairs, because,

I suppose, she was interested enough. We were happy; we were unhappy; I miss her. "Is it splendid, or stupid, to take life seriously?"

"This is a pure story" also suggests it is pure because of Braithwaite's ignorance. "I have to hypothesise a little. I have to fictionalise (although that's not what I meant when I called this a pure story)," but that's what it means now. And this in turn raises the question, what is an impure story? And would its definition imply Braithwaite's corruption: Ellen's uncorrupt, her story's pure; he's corrupt, his story isn't? Or would an impure story, such as Braithwaite's, be a combination of fiction and historical facts such as *Flaubert's Parrot?* An autobiography he narrates within a novel he does not comprehend. Serious novels admit many different modes of discourse and generically, therefore, question the boundaries of the genre. Exemplary novels also question the boundaries of consciousness that determine traditional narrative character. *Flaubert's Parrot* does not quite go this far. Braithwaite's real limit is psychological not epistemological, and the ideas he entertains are also excuses and evasions. His final note is not one of transformation but of pathos, of his belatedness or diminishing authenticity. He says:

> Perhaps there was something else as well. Some people, as they grow older, seem to become more convinced of their own significance. Others become less convinced. Is there any point to me? Isn't my ordinary life summed up, enclosed, made pointless by someone else's slightly less ordinary life? I'm not saying it's our duty to negate ourselves in the face of those we judge more interesting. But life, in this respect, is a bit like reading. And as I said before: if all your responses to a book have already been duplicated and expanded upon by a professional critic, then what point is there to your reading? Only that it's *yours*. Similarly, why live your life? Because it's *yours*. But what if such an answer gradually becomes less and less convincing?[16]

"Cross Channel" is not more revealing of Braithwaite's pain, nor of the reasons his evasiveness can be transformed into scholarship. But it seems a stronger kind of argument and more to Braithwaite's credit, for it is the most "simply" autobiographical and most aggressive in repudiating Flaubert's imperative that art be impersonal. It is as though Braithwaite, or Barnes, is saying theory's fine, but the practice that grows from personal need and temperament is more binding.

16. *Ibid.*, 190, 184–85, 183, 184, 180, 187, 187–88.

In his simplest formulation of his method and purpose, in this chapter at least, Braithwaite says:

> The fat lorry-driver on the banquette is snoring like a pasha. I've fetched myself another whiskey; I hope you don't mind. Just getting braced to tell you about . . . what? about whom? Three stories contend within me. One about Flaubert, one about Ellen, one about myself. My own is the simplest of the three . . . and yet I find it the hardest to begin. My wife's is more complicated, and more urgent; yet I resist that too. Keeping the best for last, as I was saying earlier? I don't think so; rather the opposite if anything. . . . Ellen's is a true story; perhaps it is even the reason I am telling you Flaubert's story instead.

But in telling Flaubert's story—which is not "pure" like Ellen's, nor an auto-biography like his own—Braithwaite does not believe he is writing a metafiction either. In a playful, cranky list of critical rules he issues to his silent confessor in this chapter, he says: "There shall be no more novels which are really about other novels. No 'modern versions,' no reworking, sequels or prequels. . . . every writer is to be issued with a sampler in coloured wools to hang over the fireplace. It reads: Knit Your Own Stuff." But his own stuff in this chapter sounds like this:

> As for the hesitating narrator—look, I'm afraid you've run into one right now. It might be because I'm English. You'd guessed that, at least—that I'm English? I . . . I . . . Look at that seagull up there. I hadn't spotted him before. Slipstreaming away, waiting for the bits of gristle from the sandwiches. Listen, I hope you won't think this rude, but I really must take a turn on deck; it's becoming quite stuffy in the bar here. Why don't we meet on the boat back instead? The two-o'clock ferry, Thursday? I'm sure I'll feel more like it then. All right? What? No, you can't come on deck with me. For God's sake. Besides, I'm going to the lavatory first. I can't have you following me in there, peering round from the next stall.[17]

And this approach-and-retreat, as Braithwaite turns from trying to legislate the rules for closure to the solid fact of the seagull and then to the boundaries of his privacy, sounds like Woolf's Bernard in the loose final pages of *The Waves*. This is the strength of *Flaubert's Parrot:* it promotes paradigms in which

17. *Ibid.*, 87–88, 105, 92–93.

Braithwaite is played off against many other characters: Charles Bovary and Flaubert himself; the fictional critic Ed Witherspoon and the historical Enid Starkie; Sartre and his biographical style in *The Idiot of the Family* against the style of the narrator of *Bouvard and Pécuchet;* Woolf's Bernard and John Dowell of *The Good Soldier,* who even sounds like Braithwaite: "I console myself with thinking that this is a real story and that, after all, real stories are probably told best in the way a person telling a story would tell them. They will then seem *most real.*"[18] As I've said, Nabokov's Kinbote lurks in the shadows, Conrad's Marlow is apposite, and Braithwaite even alludes to *Roland Barthes by Roland Barthes* and Barthes's list, which he misnames "What I Like" and makes fun of.[19] The self-involvement of first-person narrators often means that they have few other characters to play off, that their isolation is the point they would like to make into their singularity. Braithwaite, as I have said, resists the extremes he implies and is never, on the one hand, the cipher Dowell has been nor, on the other, the linguistic subject Barthes analyzes; neither Beckett's savagely narcissistic Molloy, nor Nabokov's madman Kinbote. He is more like the Marlow who offers the men on the veranda not only his own version of Lord Jim, but the French lieutenant's, Stein's, and Gentleman Brown's versions to judge his by. Braithwaite is the author of his own autobiography and responsible for his eccentric displacements onto Flaubert, but he is also a character in Julian Barnes's novel and *not* responsible for his wife's morality or mystery, Enid Starkie's errors and accent, or Witherspoon's professional ethics. The world, in other words, is not resolved away into textuality, and Barnes's "exemplary poststructuralist text" is a sophisticated but "prestructuralist" novel most valuable for a surface self-consciousness that finally alters neither consciousness nor the self. There are limits in this book that language cannot erase. Braithwaite asks and tries to answer the traditional question, Who am I? But it never occurs to him, as it does to Barthes and Slothrop, to ask, *What* am I? This makes all the difference.

"'I' is harder to write than to read," Barthes argues in an aphorism,[20] but autobiography is still easier to write than define. For there are, according to

---

18. Ford Madox Ford, *The Good Soldier* (New York, 1989), 201 (italics added).

19. Barnes, *Flaubert's Parrot,* 85.

20. Quoted in "Deliberation" in *A Barthes Reader,* ed. Susan Sontag (New York, 1982), 487. This essay on keeping a journal, with its journal-like entries, resembles the later, posthumously published *Incidents,* trans. Richard Howard (Berkeley, 1992), as examples of the more traditional autobiographical style Barthes seems to have been moving toward.

James Olney, "no rules or formal requirements binding the prospective auto-biographer—no restraints, no necessary models, no obligatory observances gradually shaped out of a long developing tradition and imposed by that tradition on the individual talent who translates a life into writing." Consequently, "In talking about autobiography, one always feels that there is a great and present danger that the subject will slip away altogether . . . leaving behind the perception that there is no such creature as autobiography and that there never has been. . . . On the other hand, . . . there arises the opposite temptation (or perhaps it is the same temptation in another guise) to argue not only that autobiography exists but that it *alone* exists—that all writing which aspires to be literature is autobiography and nothing else."[21] Olney's formulations strongly resemble Bakhtin's formula for the novel as a "genre not in its formalistic sense, but as a zone and field of valorized perception";[22] but Olney also implies their differences. Autobiography has "no obligatory observances" and "no restraints." In my mind, in the novel, these obligations and restraints are the characters other than the author-narrator-protagonist, those other points of view that keep the narrative open, the principles of interpretation that provide the discipline of difference. The autobiographer is not required to provide these "distractions." So the values of realism and strategies of impersonality are not necessary either, as they are to the novel and to its deployment of characters in paradigms that develop the narrative's meaning in the play of similarity-and-difference. Against these and other restricting conventions, autobiography has often been used as an access to more authentic life, to a truer account of experience; and, of course, these autobiographical strategies have often been used in novels to achieve the same ends. There is a good example of this in *Jane Eyre*. She does not know, of course, that her autobiography has been written by Charlotte Brontë; but in changing the rules she is playing by, she mirrors Brontë's formal motives: "Hitherto I have recorded in detail the events of my insignificant existence: to

---

21. Jamey Olney, "Autobiography and the Cultural Moment: A Thematic, Historical, and Bibliographical Introduction," in Olney, *Autobiography: Essays Theoretical and Cultural*, 4. As the epigraph to this volume, Olney uses the principle from Valéry I have used earlier, "There is no theory that is not a fragment, carefully prepared, of some autobiography." Olney explores some of the ramifications of this principle in his essay "Some Versions of Memory/Some Versions of *Bios:* The Ontology of Autobiography." He is especially eager to show the difficulty of limiting the term and Valéry's disquieting use of it; see 249–59. A similar description of autobiographical writing's elasticity can be found in William C. Spengemann, *The Forms of Autobiography: Episodes in the History of a Literary Genre* (New Haven, 1980). See especially his treatment of *The Scarlet Letter*, 132–65.

22. M. M. Bakhtin, *The Dialogic Imagination*, ed. Michael Holquist, trans. Caryl Emerson and Michael Holquist (Austin, 1981), 28.

the first ten years of my life I have given almost as many chapters. But this is not to be a regular autobiography: I am only bound to invoke memory where I know her responses will possess some degree of interest; therefore I now pass a space of eight years almost in silence: a few lines only are necessary to keep up the links of connexion."[23] Jane Eyre's identity and autonomy arise from her decision not to be determined either by memory or by received conventions, not to accept herself as fated by her experience or her reading, but to identify herself only by those things she chooses to find interesting, and then to order her narrative accordingly. She is writing her version of herself into being, as Esther Summerson Woodcourt does, and the character we read is not the "person" known to others in her world who share her social life. Her character, those aspects of herself she has full access to only in her writing, is what we alone know by reading her.

As Olney says, autobiography has become so critical, or theorizing autobiography has become so problematic, because our general attention has shifted from the *bios* to the *autos:* from the life of the individual in time that even someone else, a biographer or historian, could write, to the nature of the self and the fluidities of self-consciousness and subjectivity. And these are complicated in turn by new definitions of writing and the conflicting constructions of the subject that theory has given rise to. It should be no surprise, therefore, that theorists whose theories compromise the autonomy of the subject or deny the existence of substantive individuality, should feel themselves compelled to write some form of autobiography in order to explain, if not who they are, *what* they are. And it is worth remarking again their use of the novel's conventions as a measure or format for these critiques of the theory of the subject.

Roland Barthes by Roland Barthes is not the only one of these experiments to do so. Derrida's *The Post Card* is another essay in autobiographical writing that wants to be a novel. The "I" of the text, the sender of the postcard, says to "you," its receiver, that their correspondence is "our Socratic novel," which follows the practice of all serious novels that define themselves from within as something singular. There are no other "Socratic novels" I know of, nor any that play with *The Post Card*'s revisionary premise, pictured on the postcard in its cover illustration, that shows Plato dictating to Socrates what to write. This image is an unexpected version of Derrida's grammatological argument against the primacy of speech and phenomenological self-presence, and this principle affects other aspects of this book, as we will see. But "Socratic novel" is not the only definition of *The Post Card*'s genre that he makes. He underlines its debts to earlier literature by referring to its obvious epistolary format and by aligning

23. Charlotte Brontë, *Jane Eyre*, ed. Q. D. Leavis (Harmondsworth, 1966), 115.

it to travel literature. "J. D.'s" obsessive summary on the book's back cover also calls it a *satire* of these conventions and of many other "modes, genres, and tones," and an "abuse" of the language itself. He has initially defined the whole form as an extended apostrophe, and he has said that "There will be several books in this book, I count four."[24] The several books he refers to are not only the several books this one grows from and comments on—books by Plato, of course, and by Joyce, Heidegger, Freud, Lacan, and Levinas—but the several kinds of books this could be defined as. In a novelistic way, he is playing with the permeable boundaries through which the novel receives the other forms of discourse it is always incorporating.

But unlike Braithwaite and Barthes, Derrida himself is never a character in this autobiographical writing. The "I" is always only a subject, the "you" its correlative function without any more identity than that, and this relationship has a significant effect on *The Post Card*'s fulfillment of its novelistic aspiration. "Listen," for instance, to this impassioned passage: "I understood that it was you. You have always been 'my' metaphysics, the metaphysics of my life, the 'verso' of everything I write (my desire, speech, presence, proximity, law, my heart and soul, everything that I love and that you know before me)."[25] Except for "my heart and soul, everything that I love," "you" is constituted here by some pretty funny appositives. My "proximity"? Linda Kauffman's suggestion, therefore, that *The Post Card* is written *to* literature itself is helpful.[26] I would prefer to say, however, that it is written to language. For language has been Derrida's metaphysics, the "verso" of everything he has written, and it has "known" everything before Derrida has come to it himself. If we take this one step further, we can begin to realize another theme, another book among the books of *The Post Card:* "Before all else I wanted, such was one of the destinations of my labor, to make a book—in part for reasons that remain obscure and that always will, I believe, and in part for other reasons that I must silence. A book instead of what? Or of whom?" Despite the obscurities here, making a book is also, simply, producing an object. The idea of the book for Derrida, as

24. Jacques Derrida, *The Post Card: From Socrates to Freud and Beyond*, trans. Alan Bass (Chicago, 1987), 176, 179, 153, 4, 178. See also Jonathan Culler, "Apostrophe" in *The Pursuit of Signs: Semiotics, Literature, Deconstruction* (Ithaca, 1983), 135–54. Culler argues that apostrophes are always self-referential and signs of fictionality.

25. *Ibid.*, 197.

26. Linda S. Kauffman, *Special Delivery: Epistolary Modes in Modern Fiction* (Chicago, 1992), 96. She also discusses our "avid appetite for autobiography" and how Derrida plays with the reader's expectations and status as he plays with the identities of his sender and receiver. See 85–103. She pairs Derrida's autobiographical writing with Barthes's, as I do, but uses Barthes's *A Lover's Discourse*.

we have seen, is the idea of a totalizing signified "profoundly alien to the sense of writing" he develops in *Of Grammatology*. The idea of the book is *not* a book, just as *écriture* is not printing. A book involves a writer, bodily agency, and the physical act of writing. The physicality that is missing from *The Post Card*'s metaphysics, the bodies absent from the ontology of language in writing such as this that honors the novel and its polymorphous capaciousness, but not its concept or representation of character and character's form of presence, can all be inferred from the *yearning* in this following passage, the yearning for something more than writing affords:

> I don't know if I'll send you this letter since you are here in so few days. I will give it to you. But I cannot stop myself, nor miss the chance of a pickup, I have to write to you all the time when you are not here—and even when you are here and I am still alone (the old impossible dream of exhaustive and instantaneous registration—for I hold to words above all, words whose rarefaction is unbearable for me in writing—the old dream of the complete electro-cardio-encephalo-LOGO-icono-cinemato-bio-gram. And flat—I mean first of all without the slightest literature, the slightest superimposed fiction, without pause, without selection either of the code or of the tone, without the slightest secret, nothing at all, only everything—and flat in the end because if such a card were possible, even if for only a very brief lapse of time (afterwards they would need centuries of university to decipher it), I could finally die content. Unless it sent me directly to hell, for there is nothing I fear more than this exposition without envelope [*pli*]. And for me to go away content it would still be necessary that I be able to send it to you registered, this final total card (my absolute *pancarte)*, that you be able to read it, hold it in your hands, on your knees, under your eyes, in you . . .

You're no*body* till some*body* loves you, the old song says; and it is hard to love this bodiless sender, the subject of this discourse, who is an auto graph without a life to fill its empty center.

> Sorry for the beginning of this somewhat dubious letter: It's always the same thing that comes back, the same wound, it speaks in my place as soon as I open the lips, my own, however.
> Promise me that one day there will be a world. And a body.[27]

27. Derrida, *Post Card*, 5, 68, 122.

In this plea is everything that the subject lacks, that theories of the subject resign, but that the novel's concept of character never relinquishes—a world in which characters take their place among other things. "Promise me . . . a world. And a body" sounds like something Slothrop might say, after his dispersal into the mere meaning Robbe-Grillet long foresaw as a danger. But the crucial difference between Slothrop and *The Post Card*'s sender is that Slothrop has had a body to begin with, whereas the sender has only the text's unusual typography for physical distinction. And *The Post Card* has its back cover, where there are no friendly blurbs, no ads for Derrida's other books, not even the publisher's name. The final page, the back cover of the book is more of the text still epitomizing itself, hectoring and desperate to be held in our hands. The back cover is the text's attempt to become a thing, the voice's attempt to assume the body it cannot have.

The body's relation to writing is not the same thing as the subject's relation to writing or the self's relation to the text a novel presents to the actual reader as a book. It is the strength of the novel that the subjects in question—authors, characters, readers—are always in another series of relationships to physical objects that raise other questions of presence, identity, signification: objects that disclose the limits of the language that represents them. If the book suggests to Derrida, as it has to many others, the totality of the signified, the book as *world,* a totality that we now argue no book or system can contain, the book as a thing cannot be contained, either, in a system that reduces it to something else. That the novel has always taken its place among other things, things other than language, is one of the reasons the novel has retained its utility and pleasure, its openness on every page to another reading, another character, the characterization of another actual reader, who is not merely the function that "you" signifies in *The Post Card.*

Another "you," more gracefully disposed and no less complex, is offered to us in an autobiographical experiment modeled on a novel that Gertrude Stein wrote as *The Autobiography of Alice B. Toklas.* In the passage I am going to quote below, the book's final paragraphs, the shifting signification of the pronouns "I" and "you," "she" and "me," convey a richness of possibility to the nature of the self, authority, identity and writing that the novel gives us for thinking about, but that Derrida's model of the Socratic novel does not approach.

> For some time now many people, and publishers, have been asking Gertrude Stein to write her autobiography and she had always replied, not possibly.
>
> She began to tease me and say that I should write my autobiography. Just think, she would say, what a lot of money you would

make. She then began to invent titles for my autobiography. My Life With The Great, Wives of Geniuses I Have Sat With, My Twenty-five Years With Gertrude Stein.

Then she began to get serious and say, but really seriously you ought to write your autobiography. Finally I promised that if during the summer I could find time I would write my autobiography.

When Ford Madox Ford was editing the Transatlantic Review he once said to Gertrude Stein, I am a pretty good writer and a pretty good editor and a pretty good business man but I find it very difficult to be all three at once.

I am a pretty good housekeeper and a pretty good gardener and a pretty good needlewoman and a pretty good secretary and a pretty good editor and a pretty good vet for dogs and I have to do them all at once and I found it difficult to add being a pretty good author.

About six weeks ago Gertrude Stein said, it does not look to me as if you were ever going to write that autobiography. You know what I am going to do. I am going to write it for you. I am going to write it as simply as Defoe did the autobiography of Robinson Crusoe. And she has and this is it.[28]

Barthes, as I have said, is always a character in *Roland Barthes by Roland Barthes;* like Derrida, he is also a subject, and an object, and the unmistakable referent of his album of photographs. He writes of himself, as we have read already, that "He wants to side with any writing whose principle is that *the subject is merely an effect of language."* And he says of the subject's moral and emotional life within the sentence: "The so-called personal pronouns: everything happens here, I am forever enclosed within pronominal lists: 'I' mobilize the image-repertoire, 'you' and 'he' mobilize paranoia."[29] On the other hand, the epigraph, the opening statement the book makes, is a photographic image of Barthes's handwriting. Before this is language, in which the subject is effected, it is an act of his own body. It entails and signifies a physical writing instrument and the motion of his hand, and this form of bodily presence in the manuscript that became the printed book, this presence *to* the book in our hands, is as

28. Gertrude Stein, *The Autobiography of Alice B. Toklas* (1933; reprint New York, 1961), 251–52. Toklas's real autobiography takes the inevitable postmodernist form of the cookbook, in which theory and practice necessarily intersect: Alice B. Toklas, *The Alice B. Toklas Cookbook* (1954; reprint New York, 1984).

29. Barthes, *Roland Barthes*, 79, 168.

important as any other aspect of *Roland Barthes by Roland Barthes* and the kind of exemplary poststructuralist text I think it is.[30] The book ends with another image of his handwriting; translated, transcribed, and printed in italics, it reads:

> *And afterward?*
> *—What to write now? Can you still write anything?*
> *—One writes with one's desire, and I am not through desiring.*

The deliberate play of pronouns, the importance and open-endedness of desire, the refined irresolution that refuses totalization, are important, but no more important than the handwriting itself. And so that we do not miss the point of these graphic bookends, the penultimate page is also an image of his hand's writing, this time not of words but of Arabic-looking lines, or an *hommage* to Cy Twombly, which Barthes captions, "Doodling . . . or the signifier without the signified," images which play off not only the image of his working notes, but also the cartoon he calls "The History of Semiology."[31]

What the handwriting in the epigraph forms is not unimportant either: *"It must all be considered as if spoken by a character in a novel."* But this "novel" then unfolds with forty pages of pictures from Barthes's collection—pictures that record his parents and grandparents; his childhood, youth, young manhood, and maturity; a picture of him a little too big to be in his mother's arms and clinging to her; another one of him, looking like a movie star, snapped lighting his cigarette, left-handed. The first long caption develops the theme of Barthes's differences from himself in history, in the pictures, in his written text; but this theme is more poignantly stated in the caption facing two pictures made twenty-eight years apart: Barthes as a young man in the tuberculosis sanitarium, then Barthes at the age of fifty-five, turning toward the photographer from his writing desk:

30. See Italo Calvino, "In Memory of Roland Barthes," *The Uses of Literature*, trans. Patrick Creagh (New York, 1986): "All of his work . . . consists in forcing the impersonality of the mechanisms of language and knowledge to take into account the physical nature of the living, mortal subject" (301–302). A more traditional reading, oblivious to the value of the physical in Barthes's writing, is in Paul Jay, *Being in the Text: Self-Representation from Wordsworth to Roland Barthes* (Ithaca, 1984), 174–83. Jonathan Culler's *Roland Barthes* (New York, 1983) is always attentive to physical values throughout Barthes's work and to the culminating place of *Roland Barthes* within it. D. A. Miller's *Bringing Out Roland Barthes* (Berkeley, 1992) focuses on Barthes's "homosexual body." This brief book is also an example of the kind of autobiographical criticism, inspired by *Roland Barthes*, that I treat below.

31. Barthes, *Roland Barthes*, 163, 128.

"But I never looked like that!" —How do you know? What is the "you" you might or might not look like? Where do you find it—by which morphological or expressive calibration? Where is your authentic body? You are the only one who can never see yourself except as an image; you never see your eyes unless they are dulled by the gaze they rest upon the mirror or the lens (I am interested in seeing my eyes only when they look at you): even and especially for your own body, you are condemned to the repertoire of its images.[32]

The condition of the self's plurality is an important theme in Barthes and developed elsewhere in the book, but nowhere else do we get such a powerful statement of his unknowability to himself, the mystery his body always proposes. If there is a yearning here, it is for some kind of knowable essence—not the sender of *The Post Card*'s cry for a body and world, but Barthes's desire for a pre-Lacanian integrity and self-possession. Barthes wants to look at himself in the way that Elizabeth Bennet wants to look at and into Darcy.

This is a theme Barthes develops more completely in *Camera Lucida*, which I want to quote at length here in order to frame the section of *Roland Barthes* Barthes calls *"Le livre du Moi*—The book of the Self."

I lend myself to the social game, I pose, I know I am posing, I want you to know that I am posing, but (to square the circle) this additional message must in no way alter the precious essence of my individuality: what I am, apart from any effigy. What I want, in short, is that my (mobile) image, buffeted among a thousand shifting photographs, altering with situation and age, should always coincide with my (profound) "self"; but it is the contrary that must be said: "myself" never coincides with my image; for it is the image which is heavy, motionless, stubborn (which is why society sustains it), and "myself" which is light, divided, dispersed; like a bottle-imp, "myself" doesn't hold still, giggling in my jar: if only Photography could give me a neutral, anatomic body, a body which signifies nothing! Alas, I am doomed by (well-meaning) Photography always to have an expression: my body never gains its zero degree, no one can give it to me (perhaps only my mother? For it is not indifference which erases the weight of the image—the Photomat always turns you into a criminal type, wanted by the police—but love, extreme love).[33]

32. *Ibid.*, 5, 42, 36.
33. Barthes, *Camera Lucida*, 11–12.

This is a fairly extraordinary statement: not only does Barthes say he has an essence, however ironic his tone, he says that only "extreme love" can reveal it to him. Now listen to Barthes in "The book of the Self":

> His "ideas" have some relation to modernity, i.e., with what is called the avant-garde (the subject, history, sex, language); but he resists his ideas: his "self" or ego, a rational concretion, ceaselessly resists them. Although consisting apparently of a series of "ideas," this book is not the book of his ideas; it is the book of the Self, the book of my resistances to my own ideas; it is a *recessive* book (which falls back, but which may also gain perspective thereby).
>
> All this must be considered as if spoken by a character in a novel—or rather by several characters. For the image-repertoire, fatal substance of the novel, and the labyrinth of levels in which anyone who speaks about himself gets lost—the image-repertoire is taken over by several masks *(personae),* distributed according to the depth of the stage (and yet *no one—personne,* as we say in French— is behind them). The book does not choose, it functions by alterna- tion, it proceeds by impulses of the image-system pure and simple and by critical approaches, but these very approaches are never anything but effects of resonance: nothing is more a matter of the image system, of the imaginary, than (self-) criticism. The substance of this book, ultimately, is therefore totally fictive. The intrusion, into the discourse of the essay, of a third person who nonetheless refers to no fictive creature, marks the necessity of remodeling the genres: let the essay avow itself *almost* a novel: a novel without proper names.

This is quite different. In the medium of language alone, Barthes is comfortable saying that *"no one . . .* is behind them." This denial of individuating substance is central to poststructuralist thought and to any system of language's ontology. There is no "versionless version" of the self, no single Flaubert in the texts he produced, not even a single parrot. Barthes in this passage, like Joyce in conversation with Arthur Power, can pose himself in this writing against what he has written, resist the abstractions that can be made of him from his previous works, distribute himself as though into several different characters in a novel, depersonalize this book's process of growth, poise himself for the desire he recognizes on the final page to write perhaps a book resisting this, and develop the definition of a new genre—the essay that is *almost* a novel, "the novel without proper names." Without proper names, there are no characters, however, nothing to enable "the person to exist outside the semes," as Barthes puts it in *S/Z*. But as the photographs testify, there are characters in this book. They are named Roland Barthes. And this is the kind of contradiction a book arranged in alphabetized fragments fosters in resisting linear order, conventional structure, and the "descent of discourse toward a destiny of the subject."[34]

There are two other passages in *Roland Barthes* at least as important to my mind as the ones I have quoted. The first is *"Mot-mana—Mana-word"*:

> In an author's lexicon, will there not always be a word-as-mana, a word whose ardent, complex, ineffable, and somehow sacred signification gives the illusion that by this word one might answer for everything? Such a word is neither eccentric nor central; it is motionless and carried, floating, never *pigeonholed*, always atopic (escaping any topic), at once remainder and supplement, a signifier taking up the place of every signified. This word has gradually appeared in his work; at first it was masked by the instance of Truth (that of history), then by that of Validity (that of systems and structures); now it blossoms, it flourishes; this word-as-mana is the word "body."

As I said at the beginning of this chapter, Barthes in *Roland Barthes* aspires to the novel's values without in any way imitating a novel's manner, so when he comes to explicate what the word "body" means, he does it in the lists Braithwaite makes fun of in *Flaubert's Parrot:*

> *J'aime, je n'aime pas* ~ I like, I don't like
> *I like:* salad, cinnamon, cheese, pimento, marzipan, the smell of new-cut hay (why doesn't someone with a "nose" make such a perfume), roses, peonies, lavender, champagne, loosely held political convictions, Glenn Gould, too-cold beer, flat pillows, toast, Havana cigars, Handel, slow walks, pears, white peaches, cherries, colors, watches, all kinds of writing pens, desserts, unrefined salt, realistic novels, the piano, coffee, Pollock, Twombly, all romantic music, Sartre, Brecht, Verne, Fourier, Eisenstein, trains, Médoc wine, hav-

---

34. Barthes, *Roland Barthes*, 110–20, 147–48. On alphabetical order, see Roger Shattuck, *The Innocent Eye: On Modern Literature and the Arts* (New York, 1986), 38–47. Barthes's own thoughts on this are in *Critical Essays*, trans. Richard Howard (Evanston, 1972), 171–84.

ing change, *Bouvard and Pécuchet,* walking in sandals on the lanes of southwest France, the bend of the Adour seen from Doctor L.'s house, the Marx Brothers, the mountains at seven in the morning leaving Salamanca, etc.

I don't like: white Pomeranians, women in slacks, geraniums, strawberries, the harpsichord, Miró, tautologies, animated cartoons, Arthur Rubinstein, villas, the afternoon, Satie, Bartók, Vivaldi, telephoning, children's choruses, Chopin's concertos, Burgundian branles and Renaissance dances, the organ, Marc-Antoine Charpentier, his trumpets and kettle drums, the politico-sexual, scenes, initiatives, fidelity, spontaneity, evenings with people I don't know, etc.

There is a lot to conjure with in these lists: historical characters in their similarity-and-difference—the painters Pollock and Twombly; the musicians Glenn Gould and Harpo Marx; important themes and their unexpected exemplification—all Romantic music, but not Chopin's concertos; realistic novels and *Bouvard and Pécuchet,* which is not realistic in the traditional sense that *Madame Bovary* and *Flaubert's Parrot* are, but does resemble, in its topical organization, *Roland Barthes.* Far more important, however, than any of these items, and the limitless permutability of their combination, is what Barthes himself makes of these lists in the comment that follows:

I like, I don't like: this is of no importance to anyone; this, apparently, has no meaning. And yet all this means: *my body is not the same as yours.* Hence, in this anarchic foam of tastes and distastes, a kind of listless blur, gradually appears the figure of a bodily enigma, requiring complicity or irritation. Here begins the intimidation of the body, which obliges others to endure me *liberally,* to remain silent and polite confronted by pleasures or rejections which they do not share.

(A fly bothers me, I kill it: you kill what bothers you. If I had not killed the fly, it would have been *out of pure liberalism:* I am liberal in order not to be a killer.)

There is hardly a more succinct refutation of an ontology of language than the statement "this, apparently, has no meaning." And there can hardly be a more succinct defense of the novel in all its materialist and social grounding than *"my body is not the same as yours."*[35] And here, in this sentence, is the reason Barthes begins and ends his version of an autobiography with pictures of his handwriting. Don Quixote wanted to speak as though he were a character in a novel—without quite knowing what he meant; and throughout the novel's history, being in a novel has often been like being famous now for fifteen minutes. So speaking like a character in a novel does not distinguish Barthes as *un homme moyen sensual*, a writer, a thinker, a Frenchman, a homosexual, or someone who likes peonies but not geraniums. His handwriting, however, does. What follows in the passage I have quoted, the conclusion that begins with "Hence," someone else could have written. It's professional ideology, and the snappy thuggishness is a mannerism (like the gesture he uses to light his cigarette) which makes him sound like Sartre: "I am liberal in order not to be a killer." His handwriting, however, is more like Barthes, at the age of eight, clinging to his mother. This image, like Caddy Compsons's muddy drawers, could have sponsored a much different kind of narrative, of a more traditional and sentimental education, like an autobiographical novel in which there is a mixture of the writer and the conventions of meaning available to his life that *Roland Barthes by Roland Barthes* is anyhow. Without in any way following its traditional practices, Barthes uses the novel's license to write an autobiography out of theorized materials that argue the illegitimacy of the intention and the impossibility of fulfilling it. This is an exemplary postmodern device and, unlike so much other officially postmodern writing, it's charming.

It is not, however, *totally* charming or completely representative of the recent novel, which I want to turn to now by returning to the four-term diagram I offered earlier and placing it in an historical context. For the sake of the argument's neatness, I'll say that literary postmodernism begins with the end of World War II, because it is not unreasonable to argue that modernism is under full sail with the beginning of World War I.[36] By 1915, Joyce had published *Dubliners* and *A Portrait of the Artist* and had begun *Ulysses;* Woolf had published *The Voyage Out;* Lawrence had issued *The Rainbow;* Frost had published *North of Boston,* and Yeats *Responsibilities.* Eliot had finished "Prufrock," Pound had begun

---

35. Barthes, *Roland Barthes*, 129–30, 116–17. Of importance, too, are *"Le corps pluriel—* The plural body," 60–61, and *"Le vaisseau Argo—*The ship *Argo,"* 46.

36. For an indispensable discussion of modernism, see Monroe K. Spears, *Dionysius and the City: Modernism in Twentieth-Century Poetry* (New York, 1970). For two complementary accounts, see Roger Shattuck, *The Banquet Years: The Origins of the Avant Garde in France: 1885 to World War I* (Rev. ed., New York, 1968), especially chapter 11; and Perry Meisel, *The Myth of the Modern: A Study in British Literature and Criticism after 1850* (New Haven, 1987). Meisel is good on Eliot's desire for wholes and Joyce's subversion of them.

Cantos, Stevens had published his great breakthrough poem "Sunday Morning." By the end of World War II, most of the great modernists were dead or, with some important exceptions, their major work was behind them. Hemingway, Eliot, and Faulkner wrote nothing after 1945 to equal their earlier work, although Williams and Stevens did; and Mann, who had stopped writing a story called "Felix Krull" in 1911, picked it up and finished it in 1954 as the novel *Confessions of Felix Krull.*

There are always anomalies in any attempt at making literary periods; but some of these are created by novelists such as Mann, while others are the work of critics. Ihab Hassan gathers into *The Dismemberment of Orpheus: Toward a Postmodern Literature* two writers from the modernist generation, Kafka and Hemingway, born in 1883 and 1899, with two slightly later writers, Beckett and Genet, born in 1906 and 1910, and joins them to the Marquis de Sade, who was born in 1740. Jean-François Lyotard creates another kind of problem when he argues that the postmodern is "undoubtedly part of the modern. . . . A work can become modern only if it is first postmodern. Postmodernism thus understood is not modernism at its end but in the nascent state, and this state is constant."[37] Although Lyotard's idea of the postmodern is more persuasive to me and more encompassing than Hassan's, it is still a reader's version of the writers. Postmodernism has not had a figure like Pound, who was a poet first and a polemicist second, to organize the troops and define the battle.

Dating postmodernism from the end of World War II also allows us to frame the writing of the last fifty years as responses to two different questions. The first is moral and historical: what do we do *now,* now that the sheer number of people on the planet is greater than the sum of all previous populations and this number has fostered unprecedented means of total control and the technology to annihilate the entire race? The second is aesthetic: how do we follow the previous generation? What, after Kafka and Joyce, "Metamorphosis" and *Finnegans Wake,* do we do next?[38] "Nothing to be done," the opening line of *Waiting for Godot,* is an answer to both questions and *the* quintessential minimalist gesture; but Minimalism is only one strategy, and the diagram I have proposed earlier places it into at least three different relationships.

37. Jean-François Lyotard, *The Post-Modern Condition: A Report on Knowledge,* trans. Geoff Bennington and Brian Massumi (Minneapolis, 1984), 79.

38. The "classic" formulation of this comes from John Barth, "The Literature of Exhaustion," in *The Friday Book; Essays and Other Non-Fiction* (New York, 1984), 62–76. What Barth himself calls its "companion and corrective" is "The Literature of Replenishment," a smart survey of the issues. See 193–206.

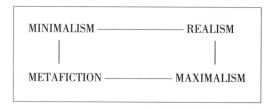

This figure looks like the old logical square of oppositions, and its terminology, which is graceless but efficient, suggests categorical differences between Minimalism and Maximalism, Realism and Metafiction. But this is not exactly the case. For these terms are finally literary strategies more than they are irreconcilable ontological positions, and Maximalist novels have absorbed and put to use both Minimalist modes of characterization and Metafictional assumptions about narrative. Moreover, along the perimeters of this square, the terms are not incompatible. The short flat stories of Raymond Carver are traditionally realistic in their subject matter and Minimalist (in the fashionable American sense that lacks, perhaps, all of Beckett's rigor) in their style. Minimalism and Metafiction can be met in some of John Barth's very short experimental pieces in *Lost in the Funhouse;* and Realism can develop into Maximalism by means of an expanded context for autobiography. Filled out with the names of the exemplary figures I'll be considering, a more complete version of the diagram looks like this:

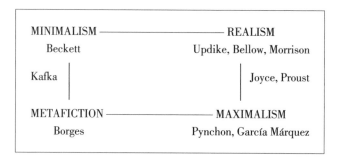

Kafka is the modernist figure who can be seen to supervise Minimalist and Metafictional practice; Joyce and Proust, the move from traditional Realism into Maximalism. Because the diagram is already cluttered, I'll discuss other transitional figures as we go along.[39]

39. A congruent paradigm of postmodern autobiographies would be:

The Words	*Malcolm X*
Roland Barthes	*The Postcard*

Minimalism responds to the historical pressure of totalitarianism and the memory of war by stripping human beings of everything but language and biology in order, apparently, to begin over. "Nothing to be done" is, as I've noted, the opening line of *Waiting for Godot,* and it makes little difference who speaks it. Vladimir and Estragon are vaudevillian stick-figures who have so little to distinguish them that they sometimes can't tell the difference between themselves. It is worth remarking, however, the line's passive voice and the way it broaches the theme of nihilism at the same time that it stipulates the challenge to Minimalist aesthetics: what to do, literally, with nothing—or with as little as it is still possible to constitute and recognize as art: "One would have thought I ate to live! Similarly I would engulf five or six mugs of beer with one swig, then drink nothing for a week. What do you expect, one is what one is, partly at least. Nothing or little to be done." This is *Molloy*'s version of *Godot*'s formula and important for its self-canceling qualifications. *Nothing* to be done leads to empty parodies of narrative activity such as Molloy's routine with the sucking-stones, which presents no real behavioral or existential dilemma, only a specious logical problem. *Little* to be done fosters narrative mottoes such as: "Not to want to say, not to know what you want to say, not to be able to say what you think you want to say, and never to stop saying, or hardly ever, that is the thing to keep in mind, even in the heat of composition." No desire, no self-knowledge, no intention to begin an end, no competence either, nothing but the inertia of language itself that keeps developing sentences such as this toward foreseeable accidents. "To restore silence is the role of objects," Molloy writes.[40] However, there are no objects in the world to resist his language and stop him.

At its best, Minimalism such as Beckett's may be an attempt to renew literature by purification and to fit it to an absurd universe in which each individual has to create the meaning of life in the absence of any transcendent principle or of any certitude but death. To me, however, Minimalism often seems more reductive than purifying, more didactic than tragic, and Beckett's work seems finally Cartesian rather than existentialist because it always favors meaning over experience. D. H. Lawrence complained of Hemingway's *In Our Time*

Sartre's Minimalism is defined, in different ways, as *what is missing* from his autobiography by both Phillipe Lejeune, *On Autobiography,* ed. Paul John Eakin, trans. Katherine Leary (Minneapolis, 1989), 76–77; and Jeffrey Mehlman, *A Structural Study of Autobiography: Proust, Leiris, Sartre, Lévi-Strauss* (Ithaca, 1974), 151–67. Susan Sontag's comparison of Sartre to Barthes is also germane, in *A Barthes Reader,* xxi. I treat Malcolm X's *Autobiography* in *Confession and Community in the Novel* (Baton Rouge, 1980), 193–96.

40. Samuel Beckett, *Molloy,* trans. Patrick Bowles and the author, in *Three Novels* (New York, 1958), 54, 69–71, 28, 13.

that "Nothing matters. Everything happens."[41] Of Beckett I'd say: Nothing happens. Therefore, everything matters—at least as much as anything else matters. It all matters because there's no principle other than the writing to challenge the writing's authority, no objects to restore silence, no other character to open the narrator's version to question. Beyond sheer endurance, therefore, or an exhaustion that isn't exhaustive, Beckett's Minimalism warrants only death as the truly authentic experience.

The prose of Donald Barthelme points to another aspect of Minimalism that his stories share with the novels of Alain Robbe-Grillet. By both these writers, language is pushed to the edge of nonsense or is so removed from the usual conventions of intention and communication that it is liberated from character and therefore calls attention to itself first *as language*. In Robbe-Grillet's *Jealousy*, this reification gives the narrator a discomfiting strangeness. In Barthelme, however, the impersonality can also be funny. Barthelme has heard all of this language, you feel sure, and all of the attitude it holds; he has simply shuffled the contexts to get these voices talking in prose and exposing, therefore, the rules and limits of sense, speech, and writing.

Behind Minimalism we can place Kafka, whom Auden calls the essential artist of the twentieth century: "Sometimes in real life one meets a character and thinks, 'This man comes straight out of Shakespeare or Dickens,' but nobody ever met a Kafka character. On the other hand, one can have experiences which one recognizes as Kafkaesque, while one would never call an experience of one's own Dickensian or Shakespearean."[42] Nobody every met a Kafka character because a Kafka character is *the subject* and is subject, therefore, to the kind of experience in which it has no independent power to make its own interpretation, to characterize the circumstances with a personal meaning. Because some of the shorter pieces in particular, such as "Before the Law" and "The Imperial Message," seem so spare and abstract, it is easy to read them as being about themselves and the condition of their own being. At this point, Minimalism edges toward Metafiction. At this point also, some readers are tempted to make these Minimalist works allegories, to place them as part of a larger whole that is an already interpreted context. The real spirit of Minimalism, however, is opposed to this easy conversion.

Although the relationship between Minimalism and Metafiction is neither causal nor evolutionary, but often one of different perspectives on the same text,

---

41. D. H. Lawrence, *"In Our Time: A Review,"* in *Hemingway: A Collection of Critical Essays,* ed. Robert P. Weeks (Englewood Cliffs, N.J., 1962), 93.

42. W. H. Auden, *The Dyer's Hand and Other Essays* (New York, 1968), 160.

the difference between them can feel like the difference between renewal and refinement, between experience purified and the aesthetic forms that give experience meaning. An instance of this shift from one realm to the other, as Brian McHale points out, happens when we read in *Malone Dies* that he, Malone, not Molloy or Moran, is the author of *Molloy,* a revelation that alters the reader's sense of the earlier novel's form and ontology.[43] It is no longer simply the narrator's autobiography, and Moran's merger with Molloy is no longer inexplicable. Molloy and Moran are only Malone's words, so their story is now also about their story's status and credibility, which makes it a Metafiction. Because they refer to no ontological order outside the language they are in, they are radically different from the traditionally realistic characterization of Braithwaite, whose story refers not only to the historical Flaubert but also to the unwritten "reality" of his own life. They are all fictions, of course, constituted only in writing on the page, but the page itself can also serve as a barrier to anything beyond the language. This is Donald Barthelme in *Snow White:* "We like books that have a lot of *dreck* in them, matter which presents itself as not wholly relevant (or indeed, at all relevant) but which, carefully attended to, can supply a kind of 'sense' of what is going on. This 'sense' is not to be obtained by reading between the lines (for there is nothing there, in those white spaces) but by reading the lines themselves—looking at them and so arriving at a feeling not of satisfaction exactly, that is too much to expect, but of having read them, of having 'completed' them."[44] Reading between the lines for the sense of the world visible through the white spaces in prose is one way of characterizing a naive realism. When those spaces, however, are empty, and the page itself is opaque, we face the difference and incommensurability of the verbal text and the physical book. We still read the words, but now for their own internal play and our renewed self-consciousness.

Metafiction's most representative figure is not Beckett, although he could be made to serve, but Borges, who is very open about his debt to Kafka in "Kafka and His Precursors" and whose *ficcione* "The Library of Babel" epitomizes the attitudes toward experience and language that characterize not only recent

43. Brian McHale, *Postmodernist Fiction* (London, 1991), 12–13. McHale's whole argument is that modernist poetics is dominated by epistemological questions, postmodernist poetics by ontological ones. "All the rest is merely a matter of dotting i's and crossing t's" (xii). By ontological, McHale usually means either the suspension of physical laws, according to a science-fiction model that also alludes to "magic realism," or the structure of embedding that he exemplifies with Beckett. He does not mention Todorov's concept of embedding; he's interested, rather, in Todorov's "fantastic."

44. Donald Barthelme, *Snow White* (New York, 1968), 106.

experimental fictions but also the literary criticism that bases itself on the ontology of language. Borges writes:

> These examples made it possible for a librarian of genius to dis-
> cover the fundamental law of the Library. This thinker observed
> that all the books, no matter how diverse they might be are made
> up of the same elements: the space, the period, the comma, the
> twenty-two letters of the alphabet. He also alleged a fact which
> travelers have confirmed: *In the vast Library there are no two iden-*
> *tical books.* From these two incontrovertible premises he deduced
> that the Library is total and that its shelves register all the possible
> combinations of the twenty-odd orthographical symbols (a number
> which, although extremely vast, is not infinite): in other words, all
> that is given to express, in all languages. Everything: the minutely
> detailed history of the future, the archangels' autobiographies, the
> faithful catalogue of the Library, thousands and thousands of false
> catalogues, the demonstration of the fallacy of those catalogues,
> the demonstration of the fallacy of the true catalogue, the Gnostic
> gospel of Basilides, the commentary on that gospel, the commen-
> tary on the commentary of that gospel, the true story of your death,
> the translation of every book in all languages, the interpolations of
> every book in all books.
>
> When it was proclaimed that the Library contained all books,
> the first impression was one of extravagant happiness. All men felt
> themselves to be the masters of an intact and secret treasure.
> There was no personal or world problem whose eloquent solution
> did not exist in some hexagon. The universe was justified. . . .
>
> As was natural, this inordinate hope was followed by an exces-
> sive depression. The certitude that some shelf in some hexagon
> held precious books and that these precious books were inacces-
> sible, seemed almost intolerable.[45]

The closed system of the Library precludes referentiality and any mimesis. Metafiction is realized not by the traditional functions of realistic characters but by self-generating play. When Kublai Khan says to Marco Polo, in Italo Calvino's

---

45. Jorge Luis Borges, *Labyrinths: Selected Stories and Other Writings*, ed. Donald A. Yates and James E. Irby (New York, 1964), 54–55.

Invisible Cities, "There is still one of which you never speak . . . Venice," Polo answers, "What else do you believe I have been talking to you about? . . . Every time I describe a city I am saying something about Venice. . . . To distinguish the other cities' qualities, I must speak of a first city that remains implicit. For me it is Venice." And for the text of cities, therefore, Venice is not important as a historical actuality, but as a model and matrix, a virtuality out of which variations on the city can be developed and set against each other as possibilities in the language of their exchange.

> "From now on, I'll describe the cities to you," the Khan had said, "in your journeys you will see if they exist."
>
> But the cities visited by Marco Polo were always different from those thought of by the emperor.
>
> "And yet I have constructed in my mind a model city from which all possible cities can be deduced," Kublai said. "It contains every-thing corresponding to the norm. Since the cites that exist diverge in varying degree from the norm, I need only foresee the exceptions to the norm and calculate the most probable combinations."
>
> "I have also thought of a model city from which I deduce all the others," Marco answered. "It is a city made only of exceptions, exclusions, incongruities, contradictions. If such a city is the most improbable, by reducing the number of abnormal elements, we in-crease the probability that the city really exists. So I have only to subtract exceptions from my model, and in whatever direction I proceed, I will arrive at one of the cities which, always as an excep-tion, exist. But I cannot force my operation beyond a certain limit: I would achieve cities too probable to be real."

"Cities too probable to be real" are invisible, but not illegible, and Kublai Khan and Marco Polo themselves realize even their own nonexistence is a possibility in the kind of game they are playing:

> POLO: . . . Perhaps the terraces of this garden overlook only the lake of our mind. . . .
>
> KUBLAI: . . . and however far our troubled enterprises as warriors and merchants may take us, we both harbor within ourselves this silent shade, this conversation of pauses, this evening that is always the same.
>
> POLO: Unless the opposite hypothesis is correct: that those who strive

in camps and ports exist only because we two think of them, here, enclosed among these bamboo hedges, motionless since time began.

KUBLAI: Unless toil, shouts, sores, stink do not exist; and only this azalea bush.

POLO: Unless porters, stonecutters, rubbish collectors, cooks cleaning the lights of chickens, washerwomen bent over stones, mothers stirring rice as they nurse their infants, exist only because we think them.

KUBLAI: To tell the truth, I never think them.

POLO: Then they do not exist.

KUBLAI: To me this conjecture does not seem to suit our purposes. Without them we could never remain here swaying, cocooned in our hammocks.

POLO: Then the hypothesis must be rejected. So the other hypothesis is true: they exist and we do not.

KUBLAI: We have proved that if we were here, we would not be.

POLO: And here, in fact, we are.[46]

There is obviously nothing so extreme in *Flaubert's Parrot* as this linguistic nihilism, which is very elegant, but merely logical, and not quite complete. For in the equality of their discursive roles, there is no possibility that either one of these talking names will subsume the other and reduce him to a different ontological level, as Malone does to Molloy and Moran, as Kinbote does to John Shade in *Pale Fire*. Nabokov's novel is a prophecy and demonstration of a critical practice that does not acknowledge the integrity or priority of the work it addresses. Shade's poem, in Kinbote's notes and critical apparatus, becomes Kinbote's life because Kinbote's theory is his autobiography; and implicit in this hostile takeover are many of the features of the kind of criticism embedded in metafictional principles. Shade's poem "Pale Fire" is not protected by any idea of its separate existence or his originating intention. It is, rather, a set of signifiers for which Kinbote supplies a wholly unanticipated signified, an absence he fills with his own desire. This reduces the poem to the status of a part in another whole that is also its supplement, so "Pale Fire" becomes merely the pretext for its own interpretation. And these components, however they are

46. Italo Calvino, *Invisible Cities*, trans. William Weaver (San Diego, 1974), 86, 69, 117–18.

named, exist in an uneasy disequilibrium that will never settle. For an important difference between *Invisible Cities* and *Pale Fire* is in the difference between the hypothetical nonexistence of Kublai Khan and Marco Polo and Shade's murder. Nabokov has claimed that "one of the functions of all my novels is to prove that the novel in general does not exist. . . . I have no purpose at all when composing the stuff except to compose it. I work hard, I work long, on a body of words until it grants me complete possession and pleasure."[47] It is possible to agree with Nabokov that "the novel in general does not exist"—and that each individual novel, as Flaubert says, has to have "its own inherent poetics"—and still to refuse the implications of his formalism that the body of words exists only in the vacuum of his "complete possession and pleasure." Novels and their language refer to a shared world in which Shade's death is more than a "discursive construct" or a satisfaction of the author's narcissism. In this sense, therefore, there is more at stake in the content of *Pale Fire* than there is in the conversations of *Invisible Cities,* and Kinbote's appropriation of Shade offers a demonstration that the boundlessness of textuality does not have a correlative freedom in the material world off the page. The annihilation of a character is a moral issue that cannot always be resolved in the manner in which Beckett alters the ontology of Molloy.

Metafiction and Realism seem categorically opposed at this point of life and death at which it is no longer possible to read a narrative simply as a sentence, merely in terms of its linguistic and structural relationships: *Invisible Cities* in this respect is "purer" than *Pale Fire,* but it can also seem more simply irrelevant. Not because it never refers to or represents the world, but because, in Walter Reed's formulations, it doesn't confront other conventions or paradigms, "the fictions, more truthful historically or merely more familiar, by which we lead our daily lives."[48] Reed's formula favors neither the novel nor the world, but puts them into a lateral relationship in which they inform and confront each other. Thinking of Realism in this way obviates the arguments between a passive, transparent, dependent mimesis and an active, politicized representation, by allowing us to see again that the novel is both realistically mimetic *and* representational. This realization, therefore, also allows us to grant to historical content its full force, of novelty, immediacy, and illumination.

> To help them see when darkness comes, Janice turns on the television
> set without sound, and by the bluish flicker of module models pan-

47. Quoted in Tony Tanner, *City of Words: American Fiction, 1950–1970* (New York, 1971), 33.

48. Walter L. Reed, *An Exemplary History of the Novel: The Quixotic Versus the Picaresque* (Chicago, 1981), 5.

tomiming flight, of riot troops standing before smashed supermarkets, of a rowboat landing in Florida having crossed the Atlantic, of situation comedies and Western melodramas, of great gray momentary faces unstable as quicksilver, they make love again, her body a stretch of powdery sand, her mouth a loose black hole, her eyes holes with sparks in them, his own body a barren landscape lit by bombardment, silently exploding images no gentler than Janice's playful ghostly touches, that pass through him and do him no harm. She inverts herself and pours out upon him the months of her new knowledge; her appetite frightens him, knowing he cannot fill it anymore than Earth's appetite for death can be satisfied.[49]

This passage is from Updike's *Rabbit Redux,* a traditionally realistic novel that confronts the narrative and representational conventions of television and poses sexual love against the violence of the '60s living-room wars, its forms of intimacy against the exploration of space. Updike, in my paradigm, stands for the kind of Realism that characterizes the nineteenth-century novel and still informs the practice of many important writers. Like Minimalism, it is a strategy for winning renewal, but it does not strip so much away from individual character as Minimalism does because it doesn't prefer meaning to experience or the epistemological to more common familial and psychosexual routines of a time and place. The continuing importance of this kind of traditional Realism is more obvious in its political dimensions. For characters such as Updike's Janice and Rabbit are diminished by the global politics and scientific scope of the images cast across their bodies, and the new ratio of their individuality, of individual integrity and power, is always at stake in the resistance that realistic writers now have to offer to the historical forces that seem also to be nature's. The great oppressive systems of *Bleak House* seem shrunken within the contexts of global war and outer space, and Hardy's Wessex fatalism seems very local compared to the plate tectonics that ground human helplessness in the earth's own structural relations in Russell Banks's *Continental Drift.*

Nature metaphors, figures of naturalistic diminution, also grow from Saul Bellow's catalogue of the cultural forces, the abstraction into categories, that his individual characters have to withstand to preserve their sanity and performance. Here is Herzog as he awaits Ramona's dispensation of her healing sexual wisdom:

49. John Updike, *Rabbit Redux* (Greenwich, Conn., 1972), 68.

In substance, however, he understood that she was trying to teach him something and he was trying (the habit of obedience to teaching being so strong in him) to learn from her. But how was he to describe this lesson? The description might begin with his wild internal disorder, or even with the fact that he was quivering. And why? Because he let the entire world press upon him. For instance? Well, for instance, what it means to be a man. In a city. In a century. In transition. In a mass. Transformed by science. Under organized power. Subject to tremendous controls. In a condition caused by mechanization. After the late failure of radical hopes. In a society that was no community and devalued the person. Owing to the multiplied power of numbers which made the self negligible. Which spent military billions against foreign enemies but would not pay for order at home. Which permitted savagery and barbarism in its own great cities. At the same time, the pressure of human millions who have discovered what concerted efforts and thoughts can do. As megatons of water shape organisms on the ocean floor. As tides polish stones. As winds hollow cliffs. The beautiful supermachinery opening a new life for innumerable mankind. Would you deny them the right to exist? Would you ask them to labor and go hungry while you enjoyed delicious old-fashioned Values? You—you yourself are a child of this mass and a brother to all the rest. Or else an ingrate, dilettante, idiot. There, Herzog, thought Herzog, since you ask for the instance, is the way it runs.[50]

It is not unimportant that the characters' bodies and physical experience itself, in both these writers, are resorts to restoration, to equilibrium. But Bellow, in my paradigm of postmodernist writing, is also important as a Jew. The 1976 Nobel laureate for literature was not so long ago (it seems amazing to say) a "minority writer" who used the open, democratic, liberal, and progressive program of Realism to write himself, and his community, into the mainstream. *The Adventures of Augie March*, as Norman Podhoretz recounts it, made Bellow a hero to the community of New York Jewish intellectuals who saw it as a great breakthrough. Podhoretz's formulation of the moment is important:

Bellow, in his third novel, boldly hit upon the idea of following the example of a book which had found the solution to the problem of literary pluralism at a time when regional cultures stood in the same

50. Saul Bellow, *Herzog* (New York, 1964), 200–201.

"colonial" relation to the genteel tradition of the East as ethnic cultures later came to do. Mark Twain in *Huckleberry Finn* had crossed the regnant "high" literary language with the "low" frontier vulgate, and Bellow now similarly crossed it with American-Jewish colloquial, thus asserting in the idiom of the novel itself what its opening sentence, in full awareness of what it is saying, makes altogether explicit: "I am an American, Chicago-born."[51]

Bellow, who was born in Lachine, Quebec, actually, announces with Augie's autobiography his own arrival, assimilation, and credentials; and in doing so he gives a certain generation of Jewish readers their place in the mainstream of the culture. Podhoretz's recognition that it is Bellow's language, his combination of the demotic and the mandarin, not just his ethnic types and neighborhoods, that creates a new narrative reality is also important and points to some of the additions to the novel that Toni Morrison represents.

Morrison has said she wrote her first novel, *The Bluest Eye*, for two reasons. One is her version of the epistemological motive behind all realistic narrative— her need to understand the world, to make it meaningful: "I was writing for some clear, single person—I would say myself, because I was quite content to be the only reader. . . . I am not being facetious when I say I wrote *The Bluest Eye* in order to read it. And I think that is what makes the difference, because I could look at it as a reader, really as a reader, and not as my own work."[52] *The Bluest Eye* supplies an interpretation and puts it into play with everything else Morrison has read. Her novel constitutes not so much what she has to express, as what she has to understand, "not as my own work," but as all of the world that the act of reading brings to her. In Morrison's purpose, it seems to me, is the real operation of desire in writing, and the practical possibility of its fulfillment. In it is also the deepest and most constant aspect of autobiography that is always present in writing of any kind: not the representational record or redaction of the author's past and experience, but the unfolding record of questions, desires, choices, and decisions made in the construction of any sentence. Not all of these are evident to any other reader in the published version, but they are to the writer, writing, life itself.

Morrison's other reason for beginning to write is equally classic for its realistic

---

51. Norman Podhoretz, *Making It* (New York, 1967), 162–63.

52. Kathy Neustadt, "The Visits of Writers Toni Morrison and Eudora Welty" in *Conversations with Toni Morrison,* ed. Danielle Taylor-Guthrie (Jackson, Miss., 1994), 89. For writer as first reader, see Brook Thomas, *James Joyce's Ulysses: A Book of Many Happy Returns* (Baton Rouge, 1982), chapter 5.

politics: "The impetus for writing *The Bluest Eye* in the first place was to write a book about a kind of person that was never in literature anywhere, never taken seriously by anybody—all those peripheral little girls."[53] This novelty of content, this inclusion of the unincluded, especially when they are not simply peripheral but brutalized as well, is a way in which Realism extends and renews itself in every generation, in different local colors, with the same gesture by which it also recognizes and addresses another previously unattended readership, for whom the moral content of the story is often much more important than any aesthetic finish, for whom aesthetic standards have often functioned as forms of exclusion or censorship.

An African American woman brings to the table different offerings than a WASP such as Updike or a Jewish immigrant such as Bellow. The most important thing in Morrison may be the historical matrix of values she identifies with the "village"—or, in *Jazz*, its urban equivalent the neighborhood. The culture of her village is first of all oral; it is traditional rather than modernist, but its traditions include the unorthodox spirituality of magic and the social arrangements of a casual matriarchy; its tolerance of eccentricity and moral difference is very broad; and alienation is never quite the advantage or distinction it is in Modernism. These values supply Morrison with a number of narrative resources that do not come to her otherwise from the legacy of Woolf and Faulkner, who were the subjects of her master's essay at Cornell. They place her, moreover, *prima inter pares*, with a number of other writers—such as Leslie Marmon Silko, Maxine Hong Kingston, and Sandra Cisneros—who are also working in very different traditions themselves to include the unincluded of their communities, with storytelling protocols a realist such as Updike has no natural access to. And this new kind of realism, this realism renewed by its incorporation of fictions operative outside the conventions of fiction, allows us to distinguish in Maximalism its most important differences. In Leslie Marmon Silko's *Ceremony*, there is a basis from which we can make the distinctions and transition.

Ceremony begins with the narrator's invocation of the muse:

> Ts'its'tsi'nako, Thought-Woman
> is sitting in her room
> and whatever she thinks about
> appears.
> . . . .
> I'm telling you the story
> she is thinking.

53. Morrison quoted in Neustadt, *Conversations*, 88–89.

This invocation implies the creative principle itself is female; it establishes narrative authority in an oral-visionary mode not grounded in the narrator's experience as an individual; and, in fact, it constitutes "individuality" itself as a mode of consciousness entirely permeable by another consciousness. In *Ceremony*, however, this is normative, not extraordinary, so the narrator's performance here is not like Pökler's dream of Kekulé's dream of the benzene ring in *Gravity's Rainbow*, nor is it necessary to narrate her in the indirect discourse Woolf has to use as Mrs. Ramsay becomes the wedge of darkness. Moreover, this kind of characterization also has important ramifications in the story's moral order and in its attitude toward language itself.

Tayo, the protagonist, is an illegitimate half-breed whose mother has become alienated, and to some extent ostracized, from her family and the Laguna Pueblo community for her drunkenness and promiscuity.

> She hated the people at home when white people talked about their peculiarities; but she always hated herself more because she still thought about them, because she knew their pain at what she was doing with her life. The feelings of shame, at her own people and at the white people, grew inside her, side by side like monstrous twins that would have to be left in the hills to die. The people wanted her back. Her older sister must bring her back. For the people, it was that simple, and when they failed, the humiliation fell on all of them; what happened to the girl did not happen to her alone, it happened to all of them.

Tayo, like Morrison's Pecola in *The Bluest Eye*, is a victim of many things—his mother's behavior, his mixed blood and its guilt, his Auntie's cruelty, white racism, and the unforgettable horror of his heroic older "brother's" death at the hands of the Japanese who took them prisoner during World War II. His mind is broken, and the fragments of narrative that juxtapose several levels of his memory and experience align *Ceremony* with *Sula, The Death of Artemio Cruz*, and all the other novels that could have acquired their tactics of manipulation and delay from *As I Lay Dying* and *Jacob's Room*. Tayo's hallucinations, and the difficulty the reader often has in discriminating one level of reality from another, also align *Ceremony* with Tim O'Brien's *Going After Cacciato*, a novel about the war in Vietnam that has also found a way to represent broken minds and narrate the almost unspeakable. O'Brien's characters do not have a way to heal in a community, however, where the healing itself is dependent on the language of the healer and the ceremonies of his speech. When Tayo is first treated by the medicine man, old Ku'oosh "spoke softly, using the old dialect full of sentences that were involuted with explanations of their own origins, as if nothing the old man said were his own but all had been said before and he was only there to repeat it."

> "But you know, grandson, this world is fragile." The word he chose to express "fragile" was filled with the intricacies of a continuing process, and with a strength inherent in spider webs woven across paths through sand hills where early in the morning the sun becomes entangled in each filament of web. It took a long time to explain the fragility and intricacy because no word exists alone, and the reason for choosing each word had to be explained with a story about why it must be said this certain way. That was the responsibility that went with being human, old Ku'oosh said, the story behind each word must be told so there could be no mistake in the meaning of what had been said; and this demanded great patience and love.[54]

In the examples of Maximalism I want to discuss, there is no communal consciousness or practice to normalize the extraordinary, nothing to make the unrealistic anthropologically correct, no "folk" to the magic. The alternative logic of Maximalism is this: if the laws of physical nature can be suspended, so, too, can moral laws and their historical probability. If, in other words, Gibreel Farishta can fall from a plane at twenty-nine thousand feet and survive, it's not much of a trick for him to dream himself the archangel Gabriel and rethink the origins of Islam in *The Satanic Verses*. Gibreel is, after all, an actor, famous for playing metamorphic gods in the movies, and we know how movies alter ontology. And if Remedios the Beauty can ascend into heaven as she is hanging out the laundry (an easy cinematic effect), if Petra Cotes's sexuality can sponsor a plague of fertility in Macondo, then the massacre of the striking banana workers can be erased from the historical record in *One Hundred Years of Solitude*. And if Oskar Matzerath, the narrator and little drummer boy of *The Tin Drum*, can deliberately stop his physical growth at the height of three feet, then Hitler's rise and the Holocaust, however "unthinkable," are possible, too. Oskar, who narrates his extraordinary autobiography through the peephole of his cell in a mental asylum to his keeper Bruno, also articulates an aesthetic for Maximalism that makes explicit the relationship between a narrative license and postwar

---

54. Leslie Marmon Silko, *Ceremony* (New York, 1986), 1, 69, 34, 35–36. *Ceremony* is given a central place but a different accent in Jay Clayton, *The Pleasures of Babel: Contemporary American Literature and Theory* (New York, 1993), which is another version of postmodernist relations between theory and practice.

politics, between the numbers on the planet and the need for new forms, between the physical laws of space and time and the morality of modern solitude:

> You can begin a story in the middle and create confusion by striking out boldly, backward and forward. You can be modern, put aside all mention of time and distance and, when the whole thing is done, proclaim, or let someone else proclaim, that you have finally, at the last moment, solved the space-time problem. Or you can declare at the very start that it's impossible to write a novel nowadays, but then, behind your own back so to speak, give birth to a whopper, a novel to end all novels. I have also been told that it makes a good impression, an impression of modesty so to speak, if you begin by saying that a novel can't have a hero any more because there are no more individualists, because individuality is a thing of the past, because man—each man and all men together—is alone in his loneliness and no one is entitled to individual loneliness, and all men lumped together make up a "lonely mass" without names and without heroes. All this may be true. But as far as I and Bruno my keeper are concerned, I beg leave to say that we are both heroes, very different heroes, he on his side of the peephole, and I on my side; and even when he opens the door, the two of us, with all our friendship and loneliness, are still far from being a nameless, heroless mass.[55]

Not all of the Maximalist "whoppers" I am interested in are so affirmative or communitarian as this opening note on *The Tin Drum,* but they are all categorically opposed to the Minimalism represented in Beckett. They are not reductive books, devoted to meaning; they have exploded, and the range of experiences they contain includes alternative ontologies not limited to the possibilities in language alone, as in *Invisible Cities,* or predicated on the science-fiction model Brian McHale posits. What marks these books is the combination of political history and the marvelous—slavery and the witnessed disappearance of Beloved in Morrison; rocket technology, the Blitz, and the dispersal of Slothrop in Pynchon; German Fascism and Oskar's vocal power; colonial racism, the origins of Islam, and the flights of Gibreel Farishta and Saladin Chamcha in *The Satanic Verses.* In their inclusiveness, these are also "exemplary poststructuralist texts" and they extend the traditional project of the novel into both new and preterite

---

55. Gunter Grass, *The Tin Drum,* trans. Ralph Manheim (New York, 1990), 17.

realms.[56] In doing so, moreover, they recapitulate many of the devices and values of the other categories, such as Minimalist forms of characterization, Metafictional modes of storytelling, Realistic concerns with the family structure and history. By comparing *Gravity's Rainbow* and *One Hundred Years of Solitude*, we can also develop these points and their own important differences.[57]

Both novels are rich in the number of characters they offer and in the different modes in which these characters are constructed. Slothrop's ontology, as we have seen, is not one he shares with every character, but neither is the gypsy Melquíades's, who is the author of the magic book which is the origin of the other book by García Márquez in which Melquíades has his only being. But most of the characters in both books have only the thin, apsychological signing function of Minimalist practice rather than the thicker interiority of even minor characters in novels such as *Middlemarch* or *War and Peace*. In *Gravity's Rainbow*, there are more than three hundred characters, with Dickensian names such as Tantivy Mucker-Maffick, Basher St. Blaise, Nora Dodson-Truck, the Japanese Kamikaze Ensign Morituri, and Tchitcherine's Tonto-figure Dzaqyp Qulan. Even the conventional lovers caught in a war-movie romance are named Mexico and Swanlake. The names in *One Hundred Years of Solitude* are not so many or so funny. All the Buendia males, in fact, are named with variations of José Arcadio or Aureliano: the twins in the fourth generation of the family who have these names switch identities; and all of Colonel Aureliano's seventeen illegitimate sons are named Aureliano, too. Still more distinctive about this novel's characterization is that there is so little dialogue. No one has much to say, about himself or anyone else. Moments of explicit interpretation—such as Ursula's insight into Aureliano and Amaranta in the thirteenth chapter when "for the first time she saw clearly the truths that her busy life in former years had prevented her from seeing"—are very rare; so, too, are moments of characterization in a free indirect discourse that is clearly distinct from the narrative.[58] This silence is an aspect of the Buendias's isolation and solitude; but it

56. See Geoffry H. Hartman, *Beyond Formalism: Literary Essays, 1958–1970* (New Haven, 1970), 61–70, for a parallel account of Realism's relation to Maximalism (which is not a term he uses).

57. Edward Mendelson, "Gravity's Encyclopedia," in *Mindful Pleasures: Essays on Thomas Pynchon*, ed. George Levine and David Leverenz (Boston, 1976), 251–63, describes a "genre" of encyclopedic novels that culminates in *Gravity's Rainbow*. From this excellent but ahistorical version of a kind of "maximalism," he pointedly excludes *One Hundred Years of Solitude*. But Michael Wood, in *Gabriel García Márquez: One Hundred Years of Solitude* (Cambridge, U.K., 1990), answers, without explicitly intending to, Mendelson's reservations.

58. Gabriel García Márquez, *One Hundred Years of Solitude*, trans. Gregory Rabassa (New York, 1971), 233. See Fernanda's outrage on 299–300.

also indicates that García Márquez, like Pynchon, sees his characters' tragedy in the fact that their inner lives are unknown to them and offer no resistance to their helpless participation in sweeping historical plots that produce obsession and fatalism in García Márquez's characters and obsession and paranoia in Pynchon's.

Both novels build these sweeping plots into high paradigms that suggest an organizing, transcendent principle that is never fully articulated or identified. So, in each case, the stories turn in on themselves and onto the nature of both their own causality and its representation, which is a usual inquiry of Metafiction. We may be able to infer what happened to Baby Tyrone in the behavioral experiment at Harvard, but it is still a mystery how the pattern of Slothrop's amorous adventures anticipates, if it does, the pattern of the falling rockets; and this limit to our interpretive authority, this disruption of the usual orders of cause and effect, also call into question, therefore, the narrative's own powers of interpretation and order. In *One Hundred Years,* this issue is framed in the tension or confusion between fiction and history. The massacre of the banana workers actually happened; Melquíades didn't make it up. He is, however, the author of the book of the Buendias's fate, a book we are never allowed to read although it is a "cause" of the book by García Márquez that we do read; and Melquíades's book decomposes in Aureliano Babilonia's hands as he is deciphering the prophetic history of his family's demise, and his own, in the final paragraph of the book that remains in our hands and, by its very presence, seems to vitiate the rhetorical flourish that ends the story: "And that everything written on them was unrepeatable since time immemorial and forever more, because races condemned to one hundred years of solitude did not have a second opportunity on earth."[59]

As we have seen, realists as different as Joyce, Flaubert, and Dostoevsky all refer to an ultimate reality they can approach in their fiction but never quite capture. In Pynchon, this ultimate reality would be, perhaps, an explanation of the relationship between the living and the conventionally "dead"; in García Márquez, it might be the principle of historical causality and meaning. Lyotard calls this unsignifiable ideal the sublime and says its representation has been the central problem of both modernism and postmodernism.[60] We can say that

---

59. Michael Bell, *Gabriel García Márquez: Solitude and Solidarity* (New York, 1993), discusses the interpretive difficulties intrinsic to the novel's conclusion and its play with the demands of both fiction and history. For a reading of its ending as deliberate closure, see Lois Parkinson Zamora, *Writing the Apocalypse: Historical Vision in Contemporary U.S. and Latin American Fiction* (Cambridge, 1993), 25–51.

60. Lyotard, *Post-Modern Condition,* 77–78.

since Cervantes, this ideal, the ideal of realism, has been central to the novel in every era, not only in theory, but in its generic ambition and practice. However, it is possible to make a further distinction between Joyce and Pynchon, which addresses the difference between modernism and postmodernism and is symmetrical with Brian McHale's claim that the difference between them is the difference between the epistemological and the ontological. Modernism questions the ways we know; postmodernism asks what are we.

When Joyce says he has approached reality in the Mabbot Street scene and Penelope, he implies that he knows what that reality is but lacks the words, the technique to get it. Although Joyce's modesty should be heartening to us all, it probably does not move us to feel that *Ulysses* is lacking anything. It feels whole; it feels, in fact, so complete that, as Derrida says, it seems to anticipate anything that can be said about it. *Gravity's Rainbow* does not feel whole; and so much is left unexplained, at so fundamental a level, that it is hard to imagine what could complete it. It feels, rather, like part of another system of being, in which the Earth is animate, death merely another aspect of that animation, conventional individuality of no final significance, and the conventions of realism irrelevant. And if Pynchon were to disclose in an interview exactly what has happened to Slothrop and where he is now, how would you take his explanation? What would it mean? I can't imagine.

However, *Gravity's Rainbow* and *One Hundred Years* have other elements of traditional realism in their makeup. Lieutenant Tyrone Slothrop and Colonel Aureliano Buendia are soldiers from families whose origins suggest the early colonial histories of both North and South America and the destiny of both continents in war. Mathew Winston has sketched for us the real, if faint, autobiographical parallels between Pynchon's own Puritan ancestors and Slothrop's; García Márquez, in countless interviews, has attested to the familial roots of the early stories and novels preceding, and preparing the way for, *One Hundred Years* and even traced his "magic realism" to his grandmother's storytelling habits.[61] If Pynchon's connection to Slothrop is a part of the almost inevitable autobiographical strain in North American writing, García Márquez has an even longer pedigree. Like Cervantes, he has written a character who shares his name into the novel's final episodes. This Gabriel, who certifies the incredible reality of Colonel Aureliano by linking him to his own grandfather Gerineldo Márquez, escapes to Paris with his complete edition of Rabelais,[62] so that he can grow up

61. Mathew Winston, "The Quest for Pynchon," in Levine and Leverenz, *Mindful Pleasures*, 251–63; and Gene H. Bell-Villada, *García Márquez: The Man and His Work* (Chapel Hill, 1990), 3–90.

62. García Márquez, *One Hundred Years*, 359, 371.

to write the book we hold, in which he has become a fictional character *after* he has been merely a historical person. He is now immortalized like the Don, memorialized like Cervantes, and the creator of his own "enchanter," Melquíades.

This Gabriel character is also like Stephen Dedalus. One way in which Realism has expanded toward Maximalism is exemplified in Joyce and Proust and is the reason for their supervisory presence, matching Kafka's, on this side of the diagram. In moving his autobiographical figure from the center of *A Portrait of the Artist* into *Ulysses*, Joyce has changed the ratio of that traditional character to the untraditional fictional structures of the larger novel. Stephen is no longer the central character; his individual psychology doesn't matter so much in the prose environments of Circe or Oxen of the Sun; the theory of autobiography he offers in Scylla and Charybdis, however important for him, is not a comprehensive aesthetic for *Ulysses*. The same kind of alteration in scale takes place in Proust's move from *Contre Sainte-Beuve* to *Remembrance of Things Past*. The ground of autobiographical reference remains the same, as does the historical importance of the Dreyfus case, but Proust's thematization of writing itself alters the nature of his narrative absolutely.[63]

Finally, the way in which García Márquez deploys the paradigm of the family tree suggests something else he shares with Pynchon—a skepticism toward totalizing systems that is both traditional and specifically postmodern. As a family chronicle, *One Hundred Years* has roots in the nineteenth century and, in the opening chapters, the prohibition of the incest theme seems very strong. But this is reductive and misleading. Actual incest is rare and finally inconsequential; the family's real tragedy is that they are so isolated from each other, in a silence and lovelessness that many of them can never overcome. In the fullness of the whole story, however, there are enough exceptions to every pattern and typology that the visual order and natural fatality of the tree metaphor become inadequate. Pynchon's systems are less novelistic than the family and less organic than the tree. He speculates that alphabets are structurally related to the interchangeable modules of molecular chains. This textualizes chemistry and links writing to physical law, which links Pynchon himself, at one end, to Balzac's connection between language and the development of paper in *Lost Illusions* and, at the other end, to Primo Levi's faith in matter in *The Periodic Table*.[64] Pynchon also links the calculus to the subtly differentiating individual

63. This same pattern can also be seen in Robert Lowell's development from the autobiographical *Life Studies* (1959) into *History* (1973), and in Derek Walcott's development from *Another Life* (1973) to *Omeros* (1990).

64. Primo Levi, *The Periodic Table*, trans. Raymond Rosenthal (New York, 1984), 52: "Matter was our ally precisely because the spirit, dear to Fascism, was our enemy."

frames of the cinema, which links both of them, therefore, in the history of Western thought, to rocket technology and death. Whereas García Márquez collapses things in upon traditional metaphors—the name, the book—in a centripetal world that has the density of a dark star, Pynchon spins the things of his world off and away from its many accidental "centers" into a series of metonyms that cannot be traced to any single origin. The world of *Gravity's Rainbow* is so centrifugal, so entropic, it Big Bangs—I would've said until I realized that even that metaphor, in counterpoint to García Márquez's dark star, is too reductive, too systematic. And this, in turn, points again to the differences in the way each book ends. The Buendia family chronicle, which is the distillation of a national history, contains an origination myth and a story of the fall; so its Apocalyptic ending is not inappropriate. It is not entirely satisfying, however. There is more magic than realism to it because there is no concomitant political event. The family's dissolution is not the nation's; it is a formality that brings the story to a stop without containing it. More finally satisfying and truer to the anarchy of the Zone and of Maximalism is the ending of *Gravity's Rainbow*. When Slothrop goes out on page 626 in a passage set between ellipses, he is reorganized at the molecular level, and at the ontological level it seems, and at the level of the novel's representational traditions. In the kind of timelessness and silence he achieves, narrative possibility would seem to end. Pynchon's book goes on for another one hundred and thirty-four pages, however, to end with the singing of a song by William Slothrop, "centuries forgotten and out of print," projected on the screen of the movie theater that seems to be the target of the rocket containing Gottfried. It makes no sense.

And if it makes *Gravity's Rainbow* "more" postmodern, it doesn't necessarily make it a better novel. The four categories I have used to organize the writing in the novel since the end of World War II are intended to begin discussion rather than end it. For the categories are soft, and there are a number of important novels I haven't mentioned. In García Márquez's own mind, his masterpiece is *The Autumn of the Patriarch*, which fits every requirement of Maximalism, but is not so neatly apposite to *Gravity's Rainbow*. Cortazar's *Hopscotch* is an exemplary Metafiction and very long; it lacks the political elements of *The Tin Drum*, but it is not "unrealistic" and it does not become allegory like *Giles Goat-Boy*. Philip Roth's *The Ghost Writer* deals with nothing less than the Holocaust, its representation, and the responsibility of the American Jewish writer. It is metafictional and political both, but it is short and very funny. Is it a Big Book nonetheless? Does the tetralogy it initiates make it any bigger? And does the brilliant bad writing in *At Swim-Two-Birds* qualify it for serious consideration as a Metafiction? Is it possible to imagine Borges rewriting *The Ginger Man?*

Roland Barthes by Roland Barthes is important for many reasons. The values it develops as an autobiography demonstrate the limit of any theory in which the subject is merely an effect of language, and this in turn points to the limits of an ontology based solely in linguistic principles. Its aspiration to the status of a novel suggests the ways in which the novel has anticipated the theory now brought to bear on it and the ways it can resist theory's reductions. *Roland Barthes* also illustrates that the core of the novel is not a realism based on mimesis, but a concept of character that keeps interpretation open and unresolved. This resistance to established conventions and their closure is what brings the novel and serious autobiography together in every generation in some combination that renews each of them; and the case can be made that in every generation since Rousseau there has been an autobiography central to the era's sense of itself and entailed in the novel's values at that moment. *Roland Barthes* may be the signal autobiography of this postmodernist generation because it is written by a critic whose work is so important to the definition of postmodernism itself. It is unlikely that *Roland Barthes* will influence any subsequent novels, and it lacks the political dimension of *Gravity's Rainbow, The Tin Drum, The Satanic Verses, One Hundred Years of Solitude,* or Vargas Llosa's *The War of the End of the World.* But it has had a political effect, nonetheless, on a kind of writing that would have been hard to predict twenty years ago. For many academic critics have begun to use an autobiographical mode as a way of escaping the subject's anonymous essentialization. The subject is written; it doesn't write. So it cannot be politically responsible in invisible ink. The five critics I will look at do not all descend from Barthes in a direct line, but they illustrate the variety of the ways his example can be felt.

Jane Gallop's polemical title *Thinking Through the Body* is a phrase she takes from Adrienne Rich's book *Of Woman Born. Thinking Through the Body* is a group of essays written over a ten-year period and then embedded in a matrix of autobiography that gives them a unified purpose and Gallop a historical identity. In adapting Barthes's emphasis on the writer's body to Rich's emphasis on the woman's body, Gallop explains the political advantage to be gained: "Men who do find themselves in some way thinking through the body are more likely to be recognized as serious thinkers and heard. Women first have to prove that we are thinkers, which is easier when we conform to the protocol that deems serious thought separated from an embodied subject in history. Rich is asking women to enter the realm of critical thought and knowledge without becoming disembodied spirit, universal man."[65]

Thinking Through the Body was published in 1988. By the time Helena

---

65. Jane Gallop, *Thinking Through the Body* (New York, 1988), 7.

Michie published *Sorophobia* in 1992, Gallop's breakthrough strategy had become ritualized necessity. Michie explains in her "Introduction":

> My final inter-chapter is a response, in part to those who have asked, when reading the rest of it, where I am, where I stand in this dance of otherness. Entitled "Helena and Elizabeth," an account of one encounter between myself, as a rape-crisis counselor, and a rape survivor, it is intended both as compensation for and a corrective to any moments in the body of my work where I might seem to imply that I have transcended the problem of otherness between women, or that I am in any position to judge other women's struggles to negotiate that otherness. I prefer to tell the story of my fumblings with otherness than to announce my presence at the beginning of this text, or freeze myself into a series of epithets that might explain my interest, my qualifications, or my hesitations about this project. I have delayed as long as possible the obligatory feminist confessional moment by speaking in the sustained first-person only in this final inter-chapter.

"Elizabeth and Helena" itself begins with a paragraph that encapsulates its whole method: "I, like Catharine Stimpson, begin with the rape of another woman: not a colleague, but a prostitute, a heroin addict, a carrier of the HIV virus, a woman whose scarred body was literally marked with the signs of otherness in the form of bruises, gashes, injection sites. I call up the names 'prostitute,' 'heroin addict,' and 'carrier' because these were the terms I heard before I heard her name: it was—perhaps still is, for she might still be alive—Elizabeth." From this point on, Elizabeth is a character rather than the subject of any discourse the paragraph mentions, and in her characterization, she is granted by this first-person narrator an independence and opacity that preserve her. Elizabeth does not apologize for herself, and she is not self-pitying. She is a storyteller whose stories are "full of people," and she is curious about Helena and concerned about how Helena will get home that night. They share a hospital meal, which is better than they both expect. "Elizabeth seemed especially to enjoy dessert; a small square of coffee cake, and a cup of coffee, which she drank slowly with sugar and cream. 'I feel bad,' she said, in a gentle, far-off voice. 'About what?' I asked, wondering if she were going to mention the rape. 'About that coffee. It's the first cup I've had in two months. I'm trying to stay off the caffeine.'"[66]

---

66. Helena Michie, *Sororophobia* (New York, 1992), 13, 199, 201.

The narrator Helena is more knowable and less interesting than Michie's character Elizabeth, who resists and exceeds any easy accommodation, doing in person what "the body" is always supposed to do in principle. But whatever name we give the distance between them—respect, reserve on Helena's part, bewilderment at the difficulty in reading Elizabeth's character—it is this distance that also constitutes the impersonality of novelistic realism, the distance that gives any description both its values and its limits. There is nothing like this in Barthes because he is always writing only about himself; *Roland Barthes* aspires to the values of the novel, but he doesn't do other characters. Used this way, at a juncture of theory and autobiography as a means of refusing the kind of appropriation common to them both, Michie's solution seems necessary, just, and quite moving.

Wayne Kostenbaum mentions Barthes twice, but not as an influence. It is, however, hard to read Kostenbaum's hybrid of autobiography and cultural criticism without thinking of the license Barthes has granted. *The Queen's Throat: Opera, Homosexuality, and the Mystery of Desire* is not a chronological narrative, but a catalogue of topics from diva lore and Kostenbaum's own sentimental education that reads like an exploded, erudite, and eccentric version of Barthes's lists "I like"/"I don't like." Its method is not so novelistic as Michie's is in the story of "Elizabeth and Helena," but *The Queen's Throat* is an entirely self-defining demonstration of its own singularity and capaciousness. And to complement this formal courage, the book's end has a very touching moment of anxiety and need.

> I, who possess no special knowledge of music, have blurted out, in public, my experience of living inside a modern queer identity— just my own experience, not everyone's; I've dared to narrow the commonwealth down to my own body, and I've pinned these private nonuniversal intimations of "queerness" onto opera arias that put me in a trance.
>
> Isolde sings, "Do I alone hear this melody?" and I want to say to you, "Do you hear what I hear? When you listen to opera, do you hear your least sanctioned desires speak?"[67]

"To narrow the commonwealth down to my own body" is a wonderful epitome of the autobiographer who writes as an outsider looking in toward a community he wants to belong to. The opposite autobiographical motive, that of the insider

---

67. Wayne Kostenbaum, *The Queen's Throat: Opera, Homosexuality, and the Mystery of Desire* (New York, 1994), 240.

who wants out, is Frank Lentricchia's in *The Edge of Night*. "I live in the literary academy," Lentricchia writes, "the Imperial Palace of Explanation, among those-who-always-already-know, among the Princes and Princesses of Pre-reading, the executioners of mystery." The dustjacket subtitles *The Edge of Night* a confession; the title page doesn't use the word; and this indecision is enacted on every page as Lentricchia writes against the confession's convention of self-discovery and self-disclosure. He resembles Augustine insofar as he writes from a deep personal and professional crisis that results in a spiritual impasse; but he also resembles Dostoevsky's Underground Man who resists the community Augustine seeks and wants to dominate the reader in order to preclude any independent interpretation: as Derrida's sender does in *The Post Card*, as Sartre does in *The Words*. For Lentricchia, the *act* of writing is therapeutic, but its content isn't necessarily important:

> I'll tell you what I like about writing. When I'm doing it, there's only the doing, the movement of my pen across the paper, the shaping of rhythms as I go, myself the rhythm, the surprises that jump out of the words, from heaven, and I am doing this, and I *am* this doing, there is no other "I am" except for this doing across the paper, and I never existed except in this doing.
>
> I'll tell you what I hate about writing. Finishing it. It comes to an end. You can't come forever. When I'm finished, I can't remember what it was like inside the doing. I can't remember. When I am not writing, I want to become the man with the brutal face.

This man with the brutal face is a figure whom Lentricchia has seen in New York City near the East Village. He is "elegantly dressed, . . . utterly manicured, a shave every four hours, a haircut every five days, who would occasionally walk outside to talk to youngish guys built like bulls in flowered shirts, with envelopes in their hands who kissed him on the cheek when they left. It was a movie, post-*Godfather*. They knew they were in a movie; they were enjoying themselves in the movie." And Lentricchia is enjoying himself, too, in identifying with this type who represents impermeable authority and silence. The man with the brutal face wouldn't hear "those-who-always-already-know" as a Derridean joke and an insult to us all, and he wouldn't care. He would understand Lentricchia's reluctance to confess.

The *intransitivity* of Lentricchia's writing, however, is not constant. In order to resolve his essay into some kind of narrative closure, he has to discuss his inability to finish a book on modern poetry which he had been working on for some time (apparently *Modernist Quartet*, 1994) and the failure of his marriage.

He does not say a lot about either. When Braithwaite cannot face himself, he writes about Flaubert; Lentricchia, in roughly the same circumstances, writes about writing. In doing so, he makes clear that the elaboration of autobiographical protocols is no guarantee of revealing personal truth:

> In early September, when the actual physical separation took place, I was launched into the writing that would become the opening section of this book, this writing is unleashed, and the passive voice is right, because I can't claim to be the unleasher, I am the unleashee, it's some Higher Power, and it pours forth, the best time I've ever had as a writer. I became a surfer of infinite finesse, carried by a wave of inexhaustible power, the Higher Power of the Wave God of Writing. . . .
>
> In fact, one thing alone is good for me. Everything else is bad only when this is not happening. You know "this"? When this is happening nothing is bad, I can stand anything, I can take their best shot, they nail me with their best shot and I don't go down, I feel no pain, I'm anesthetized. I like my disease very much. God of Writing, let me embrace it. God of Writing, let me not call it a disease. Is it true? Never friends? Eighteen years?[68]

But it is not the whole truth we feel we get from *Roland Barthes* either; it is not the whole truth we expect from a writer who is always writing for writing's sake:

> I have often asked myself why I enjoy writing (manually, that is), to such an extent that on occasion the vain effort of intellectual work is redeemed in my eyes by the pleasure of having in front of me (like some do-it-yourself workbench) a beautiful sheet of paper and a good pen: while thinking about what I should write (as is the case at the very moment) I feel my hand move, turn, join, dive, and lift . . . constructing from the apparently functional lines of the letters a space that is quite simply that of a work of art. I am an artist, not because I am representing an object, but, in a more basic sense, because in writing my body knows the joy of drawing on and rhythmically incising a virgin surface (its virginity representing the infinitely possible). . . .

68. Frank Lentricchia, *The Edge of Night* (New York, 1994), 121, 7, 6, 175–76.

. . . Writing is not only a technical process; it is also a joyous physical experience.

If I give this aspect a position of primary importance, it is because it is normally denied.[69]

This is a remarkably selfless originality in Barthes. And while it distinguishes his writing from the truculence and opera of Lentricchia's autobiography, it defines their common ground in writing's enclosure: not its prison house, but its redoubt.

This is not the destination of every recent academic autobiography, however, and I would like to mention one more, Henry Louis Gates Jr.'s *Colored People*. This is a communal book, addressed in the preface to his daughters, Maggie and Liza, and "written to you because a world into which I was born, a world that nurtured and sustained me, has mysteriously disappeared." In explaining the time, region, and community he came from in order to explain to his children certain aspects of his character, Gates explores the contradictions created by racism in America. He has stopped, for instance, "trying to tell other Negroes how to be black" and looks for those "unselfconscious moments of a shared cultural intimacy, whatever form they take, when no one else is watching, when no white people are around." But he goes on to say: "I rebel at the notion that I can't be part of other groups, that I can't construct identities through elective affinities, that race must be the most important thing about me. Is that what I want on my gravestone: Here lies an African American? So I'm divided. I want to be black . . . but to do so in order to come out the other side, to experience a humanity that is neither colorless nor reducible to color."

In this self-division, there is the opportunity and precedent for a very different kind of book from the one he writes. But *Colored People* is a memoir rather than a confession, and in it Gates is only part of a more important whole that he describes as "artlessly and honestly as I can . . . a colored world of the fifties, a Negro world of the early sixties, and the advent of a black world of the later sixties, from the point of view of the boy I was." His artlessness is not a pose, it is a tone you take with your children. It is, also, of course, the political strategy of the book's address to its other readers, and it counts for its power on the possibility that even today there can be something more important about a book than its *writing*.[70]

Colored People is as exemplary in its way as *Roland Barthes* is, and as

69. Quoted in Georges Jean, *Writing: The Story of Alphabets and Scripts*, trans. Jenny Oates (New York, 1992), 196–97.

70. Henry Louis Gates Jr., *Colored People* (New York, 1994), xi, xiv, xv, xvi.

Gravity's Rainbow is, although none of them sums up or represents either postmodernism, the recent novel, or theoretical autobiographies. No one book or writer can do this. My argument, however, and its novelistic values, both formal and moral, can be epitomized in a passage from Nadine Gordimer's *A Sport of Nature*. Like Bellow a Jew with Eastern European roots; like Morrison a woman who writes on race (and whom Morrison admires), Gordimer is a South African who has always written in English and is therefore both a colonial and a minority writer. A Nobel laureate, Gordimer is a traditional realist. Her protagonist is a self-inventing white South African woman, whose adopted name Hillela emphasizes her Jewishness and whose instinct and sexuality are both anarchic and utopian. Hillela marries two important black African leaders; the first is assassinated, the second becomes the first black president of an unnamed African nation, in the book's happy, convincing, and prophetic ending. (It was published in 1987, seven years before the election of Nelson Mandela.) And although Gordimer's narrator is engaged, worldly, and knowing, she is not omniscient about Hillela, who slips out of the historical record every once in a while and who as a *lusus naturae* remains inexplicable, too spontaneous and different for conventional categorization and, therefore, as apt for a novel as Don Quixote. In the passage quoted below, Hillela is with Whaila, the man who becomes her first husband; although they seem primarily conscious of each other, the narrator explains in a shifting mode of direct and indirect discourse all that their consciousness assumes at the moment, the play between their subjection and subjectivity, discursive formation and tactile experience, her writing and their bodies—all of which can almost go without saying into the phrase "the laws made of skin and hair."

> Lying beside him, looking at pale hands, thighs, belly: seeing herself as unfinished, left off, somewhere. She examines his body minutely and without shame, and he wakes to see her at it, and smiles without telling her why: she is the first not to pretend the different colours and textures of their being is not an awesome fascination. How can it be otherwise? The laws that have determined the course of life for them are made of skin and hair, the relative thickness and thinness of lips and the relative height of the bridge of the nose. That is all; that is everything. The Lilliesleaf houseparty is in prison for life because of it. Those with whom she ate pap and cabbage are in Algeria and the Soviet Union learning how to man guns and make bombs because of it. He is outlawed and plotting because of it. Christianity against other gods, the indigenous against the foreign invader, the masses against the ruling class—where he and she come

from all these become interpretative meanings of the differences seen, touched and felt, of skin and hair. The laws made of skin and hair fill the statute books in Pretoria; their gaudy savagery paints the bodies of Afrikaner diplomats under three-piece American suits and Italian silk ties. The stinking fetish made of contrasting bits of skin and hair, the scalping of millions of lives, dangles on the cross in place of Christ. Skin and hair. It has mattered more than anything else in the world.[71]

Roland Barthes by Roland Barthes, important as it is, can't touch this.

71. Nadine Gordimer, *A Sport of Nature* (New York, 1988), 184.

6

AND NOW FOR
SOMETHING COMPLETELY
SIMILAR-AND-DIFFERENT

The book is the only thing that matters, the book as it is, far from genres,
outside of the categorical subdivisions—prose, poetry, novel, document—
in which it refuses to lodge and to which it denies the power of establishing
its place and determining its form. A book no longer belongs to a genre;
every book stems from literature alone, as if literature held in advance,
in their generality, the secrets and formulas that alone make it possible
to give to what is written the reality of a book.
—MAURICE BLANCHOT, *Le Livre à venir*

The truth was that he dreamed of writing a book. . . . It would be a large,
bound volume about the size and shape of the Holy Qur'an, and, like the
Qur'an, its pages would have margins filled with notes and commentaries.
But what would he write about? The Qur'an embraced everything,
did it not? There was no cause for him to despair. He would find
his subject one day. It was enough for him to know the size, shape,
and style of annotation for the book.
—NAGUIB MAHFOUZ, *Palace of Desire*

CHARACTER IS THE principle form of mediation in the novel. Characters read other characters for their meaning, for the meaning of themselves, and for the meaning of the world; and we read characters, graphic marks printed on the page, as the figures the narrative lines raise into the play of meaning in paradigms of similarity-and-difference. Since a character is a sign, it is a structure of meaning, a form for interpretive use, before it is anything else; and its structure has been and can be filled out in many different ways, by different interpretive principles—psychological, phenomenological, or psychoanalytic, for instance—within the frames of many other kinds of differentiation. Historical, national, racial, sexual, and class *characteristics* all influence and particularize the realistic epistemology of human figures in a novel. What Don Quixote knows of Sancho Panza and how he knows it are very different, in many ways, from what Molly Bloom knows and reads in Poldy, who has so much more about him to know that Molly can do nothing like the reader's reading of him. Yet none of these four characters is simply a zone of legibility, for character in the novel is never so completely vulnerable to another character's reading as Goethe's Eduard believes himself to be as he is reading in *Elective Affinities.* As Tristram Shandy writes: "our minds shine not through the body, but are wrapt up here in a dark covering of uncrystallized flesh and blood; so that if we would come to the specific characters of them, we must go some other way to work."[1]

"The body" has become a specific category of discourse lately in order to correct the etherealizations of matter that structuralist theory promoted as it made "the subject" the term of choice and simplified everything into an ontology of language. "The body" now brings "the subject" back to earth; and in a correlative turn, exemplified by *Roland Barthes by Roland Barthes,* academic critics have begun to write about themselves in criticism that is explicitly autobiographical, as though we are all again speaking like characters in a novel, embodied in matter and its forms of presence that language can refer to but never fully represent, but placed in history and in politics that language can reflect, discover, and confront. This is the kind of being that characters in the novel have always had, as marks on the page to begin with, print before they became *écriture,* in books that are less like the texts they contain than they are like the furniture in the library. "The body," however, does not exist in the novel. Bodies do; they figure in novels in ways that reveal the inadequacies of treating them as a single category. So I would like to look at six characters in four novels to reprise, in this final chapter, the high notes of my argument and some of the various relationships that consciousness can have to matter in the human figures held in books.

The first pair of characters I want to contrast are Austen's Mr. Collins in *Pride and Prejudice* and the punkah wallah in E. M. Forster's *A Passage to India.* In her description of Mr. Collins, Austen does not have to mention his physical qualities; they are not prepossessing, nor are they as important as his character, the moral qualities Elizabeth and her father can readily read in him, which are the qualities he reads them with.

> Mr. Collins was not a sensible man, and the deficiency of nature had been but little assisted by education or society; the greatest part of his life having been spent under the guidance of an illiterate and miserly father; and though he belonged to one of the universities, he

---

1. Laurence Sterne, *The Life and Opinions of Tristram Shandy* (Harmondsworth, 1967), 97.

had merely kept the necessary terms, without forming at it any useful acquaintance. The subjection in which his father had brought him up, had given him originally great humility of manner, but it was now a good deal counteracted by the self-conceit of a weak head, living in retirement, and the consequential feelings of early and unexpected prosperity. A fortunate chance had recommended him to Lady Catherine de Bourgh when the living of Hunsford was vacant; and the respect which he felt for her high rank, and his veneration for her as his patroness, mingling with a very good opinion of himself, of his authority as a clergyman, and his rights as a rector, made him altogether a mixture of pride and obsequiousness, self-importance and humility.

What is important here is the access to compassion for Mr. Collins that Austen gives us (although she is not interested in doing much more with it herself). Collins is a fool partly because there is no fulcrum for his pride and humility, no point on which to poise the difference between his "subjection" to his miserly and illiterate father and his subsequent good fortune under Lady Catherine. He is all extremes, so he has never developed the sense of proportion, of *ratio,* so important to Austen's world. He thinks of his intention to marry one of the Bennet girls as his "plan of amends—of atonement—for inheriting their father's estate," and he thinks of himself as "generous and disinterested" as well. And he is disinterested—for a woman who is interested in her estate rather than in her romantic happiness. But the word to conjure with is "atonement," which signals the guilt Mr. Collins feels for being simply his father's son. Collins is Darcy's foil in the novel's paradigm of eligible male characters, for he is every-thing that Darcy isn't, and both of them are played off Wickham, who looks right for the part but is neither as guilt-ridden as Collins nor as *measured* as Darcy. In another paradigm, however, governed by father figures rather than eligibility, Collins is much closer to Elizabeth and reveals something important about her. There is never any hint that Mr. Bennet has brutalized her, but their relation-ship, and the exaggerated sense of her own merit that it has given her, are im-pediments when she first meets Darcy and the point on which her recognition scene turns: "How despicably have I acted! . . . I, who have prided myself on my discernment!—I, who have valued myself on my abilities! who have often disdained the generous candor of my sister, and gratified my vanity in useless or blameable distrust. —How humiliating is this discovery!—Yet, how just a humiliation!—Had I been in love I could not have been more wretchedly blind. But vanity, not love, has been my folly. . . . Till this moment, I never knew myself."[2]

Collins never has the advantage of such a scene, but it is not Mr. Bennet who provides Elizabeth with this insight and Lydia with the money that saves her. It is Darcy, who has had the best father in the book, a fact which characterizes him both thematically and socially and gives his status its full force. And Wickham's wickedness is measured by his abuse of what Darcy's father has also done for Wickham himself. In a less patriarchal world, in a more open novel, Mr. Collins's disadvantages could have been developed differently, and he could have been given another opportunity or a different interpretation. As he is, however, we can still read-with him in order to imagine his reading of Elizabeth's presumption and his sense of the motives in Charlotte Lucas that Elizabeth cannot bring herself to understand. Collins remains flat and funny, but Austen has given us more than her comedy seems to need by allowing in Mr. Collins an excess that begins to constitute a character's independence.

Forster's punkah wallah has no such excess or independence. He is a human figure, but he is not a character in the sense that we can read-with him an interpretation of the world. He is rather an abject body and a blank screen onto which Adela Quested and Forster project a reading that is themselves and their needs.

> The Court was crowded and of course very hot, and the first person Adela noticed in it was the humblest of all who were present, a person who had not bearing officially upon the trial: the man who pulled the punkah. Almost naked, and splendidly formed, he sat on a raised platform near the back, in the middle of the central gangway, and he caught her attention as she came in, and he seemed to control the proceedings. He had the strength and beauty that sometimes come to flower in Indians of low birth. When that strange race nears the dust and is condemned as untouchable, then nature remembers the physical perfection that she accomplished elsewhere, and throws out a god—not many, but one here and there, to prove to society how little its categories impress her. This man would have been notable anywhere: among the thin-hammed, flat-chested mediocrities of Chandrapore he stood out as divine, yet he was of the city, its garbage had nourished him, he would end on its rubbish heaps. Pulling the rope towards him, relaxing it rhythmically, sending swirls of air over

2. Jane Austen, *Pride and Prejudice* (Harmondsworth, 1972), 114, 236–37.

others, receiving none himself, he seemed apart from human des-
tinies, a male fate, a winnower of souls. Opposite him, also on
a platform, sat the little assistant magistrate, cultivated, self-
conscious, and conscientious. The punkah wallah was none of these
things: he scarcely knew that he existed and did not understand why
the Court was fuller than usual, indeed he did not know that it was
fuller than usual, didn't even know he worked a fan, though he
thought he pulled a rope.[3]

This is condescending and sentimental in every way, a perfect example of the
values in modernism that make the primitive sacred: wholly other, entirely
unconscious, erotically beautiful, and so exclusively present to itself that its
body is its mind. The punkah wallah is less like Rilke's figure of Apollo, whose
presence is radiant and imperative, than he is like one of Braithwaite's parrots.
We know from this passage *what* he is, what he has been read as and made to
mean, but not who he is to himself and how he would read the world. "He
scarcely knew that he existed" indicts Adela and Forster, but says nothing
whatsoever of him and gives us no access through him to anything else. By
contrast, Mr. Collins is richly developed, and the fact that Austen makes so
little of him physically indicates how completely entailed Mr. Collins and his
character are in the real estate, furniture, and properties of that world. They go
without saying.[4]

But the Rekha who had been pursuing him ever since he fell from
the *Bostan* was, Gibreel knew, not real in any objective, psychologically or corporeally consistent manner. —What, then, was she?

Psychological consistency is what we mean, in part, by the term identity; it is
not only an internal continuity, but also a continuity between what a person
feels herself to be and the ways in which she is perceived by others. Mrs.
Ramsay, for instance, is a wife and mother, a great social beauty, and a Madonna
figure as she sits for Lily's painting, and none of these roles creates an inconsistency in her that is any problem. She may also feel the kind of need and
devotion Lily has for her without knowing that Lily construes her as a tabernac-
ular enclosure of sacred secrets—but even knowledge of this metaphor would

3. E. M. Forster, *A Passage to India* (New York, 1952), 217–18.

4. See D. A. Miller, *Narrative and Its Discontents: Problems of Closure in the Traditional
Novel* (Princeton, 1981), 3–5, for a discussion of the elements such as this he calls the "unnar-
ratable."

not create the kind of discontinuity she relishes in feeling herself sink into the wedge of darkness. This state can be used to challenge conventional notions of identity, of persistent sameness, and it also calls into play the way in which I have used individuality to indicate the *physical* distinction between one person and another established by their bodies. Neither identity nor individuality is the same thing as character, although all three are closely related and clearly involved in Gibreel Farishta's question about the Rekha in *The Satanic Verses*. *What* was she? "Not *real*" is clearly one answer, but this only begs the fundamental question that recent novels have been asking about the construction of the human natures within them. Slothrop asks the question himself, as we have seen, and Rushdie's book is indebted in many ways to *Gravity's Rainbow*: it echoes the opening scream across the sky; and it develops in Gibreel a character who resembles Pirate Prentice, Franz Pökler, and Slothrop himself.[5] For Gibreel dreams the dreams of others, apparently, and is unable to decide either who he is or what he is because he seems inhabited at his core by someone else.

This is not the case with Saladin Chamcha, who also falls from 29,000 feet when the *Bostan* explodes and lives to suffer his survival. He is transformed into a goatlike figure of the devil; this causes him great anguish, but does not alter the nature of his consciousness. His metamorphosis is more political, finally, than ontological because Chamcha is "really" transformed by the racism he encounters in England. After he has been arrested, he asks another prisoner, a manticore, a human body with the head of a tiger:

> "But how do they do it?"
> "They describe us," the other whispered solemnly. "That's all. They have the power of description, and we succumb to the pictures they construct."

Even Braithwaite has realized that "words give birth to things as much as things give birth to words," and therefore the punkah wallah is born a god, Chamcha is born a devil, and Dudkin is simply born from the fearful, shadowy consciousness of Apollon Apollonovich Ableukhov in *Petersburg*. The punkah wallah and Chamcha at this point are not so much imitated characters, if we can make this distinction, as they are representative of an ulterior discourse that has nothing to do with their own consciousness, their self-consciousness, or any experience they may have of their integrity and internally generated difference. The punkah wallah is a signified, without being a signifier to himself; he is a sign only of someone else's reading. Chamcha, on the other hand, does have a consciousness

5. Salman Rushdie, *The Satanic Verses* (New York, 1989), 323–24, 8.

with which he can resist what his physical metamorphosis represents, and those who are sympathetic to him can recognize and theorize his plight. Jumpy Joshi says:

> "Objectively, . . . what has happened here? A: Wrongful arrest, intimidation, violence. Two: Illegal detention, unknown medical experimentation in hospital,"—murmurs of assent here, as memories of intra-vaginal inspections, Depo-Provera scandals, unauthorized post-partum sterilizations, and further back, the knowledge of Third World drug-dumping arose in every person present to give substance to the speaker's insinuations,—because what you believe depends on what you've seen,—not only what is visible, but what you are prepared to look in the face,—and anyhow, something had to explain horns and hoofs; in those policed medical wards, anything could happen—"And thirdly," Jumpy continued, "psychological breakdown, loss of sense of self, inability to cope. We've seen it all before."

This makes a cliché of Chamcha, but it eventually saves him; and as an aspect of his salvation, he becomes a public figure, not simply as a victim, but as a kind of hero: "What was happening, although nobody admitted it or even, at first, understood, was that everyone, black white brown white, had started thinking of the dream-figure as *real,* as a being who had crossed the frontier, evading the normal controls, and was now roaming loose about the city. Illegal migrant, outlaw king, foul criminal or race hero, Saladin Chamcha was getting to be true."[6] This is another definition of *real,* which has nothing to do with the psychological or bodily consistency Gibreel Farishta posits, and everything to do with the "truth" established by representational systems and social and political consensus. Gibreel's own crisis has no such resolution because it is not bodily and public. At the beginning of the novel's second section, "Mahound," he dreams the history of the origins of Islam, first from a perspective that makes him feel like the archangel Gabriel as both a camera and a spectator, but then from *within* Mahound, where he is not only the businessman about to become Muhammad himself but the archangel interiorized within Mahound as voice or psychological projection. This is not only confusing to him because of the multiplicity of simultaneous roles—as himself, as the archangel Gabriel, as Mahound-Muhammad, as the archangel-as-Muhammad—with their different ontologies; this is heretical. It means that Muhammad was not the passive

6. *Ibid.,* 168, 252–53, 288.

Messenger of Allah, but the *author* himself of the words of God, and Gibreel's helpless possession by these dreams and their culpability drives him mad.

Chamcha's bodily transformation does not alter his consciousness, and he continues to speak in dialogue as himself. Gibreel's alteration in consciousness does not alter him physically, but he must be spoken for by the narrator in a slippery and complex indirect discourse. Chamcha could be a character from out of folklore and horror movies; but Gibreel, in a way like Pirate Prentice, represents all that is entailed in Rushdie's *writing:* all the levels of history and fiction, social truth and visionary experience, dreaming and being dreamed, actual agency and intertextual determination. Gibreel is a much more important, more interesting, and more fully novelistic character than Chamcha, and his political significance is much more complex. Yet when Rushdie summarizes their paradigmatic similarity-and-difference, his argument takes a surprising moral turn:

> For are they not conjoined opposites, these two, each man the other's shadow?—One seeking to be transformed into the foreignness he admires, the other preferring, contemptuously, to transform; one, a hapless fellow who seems to be continually punished for uncommitted crimes, the other, called angelic by one and all, the type of man who gets away with everything.—We may describe Chamcha as being somewhat less than life-size; but loud, vulgar Gibreel is, without question, a good deal larger than life, a disparity which might easily inspire neo-Procrustean lusts in Chamcha: to stretch himself by cutting Farishta down to size.
> What is unforgivable?

The apparent answer is, the unforgivable is Chamcha's desire to Anglicize himself and become assimilated into the culture that has been punishing him for his difference. "Saladin Chamcha is a creature of *selected* discontinuities, a *willing* re-invention; his *preferred* revolt against history being what makes him, in our chosen idiom, 'false.'" On the other hand, Gibreel, for all his faults, has always wanted to remain completely Indian, "at bottom an untranslated man."[7] This is not, however, how it all turns out.

---

7. *Ibid.,* 426, 427. See also Salman Rushdie, *Midnight's Children* (New York, 1991), 283: "O eternal opposition of inside and outside! Because a human being, inside himself, is anything but a whole, anything but homogeneous; all kinds of everywhichthing are jumbled up inside him, and he is one person one minute and another the next. The body, on the other hand, is homogeneous as anything. Indivisible, a one-piece suit, a sacred temple, if you will. . . . Uncork the body, and

Rushdie has gone to great lengths to give these two characters great psychic mobility. Chamcha is a radio actor capable of many hundreds of different voices, and Gibreel has been a movie star who specializes in portraying the metamorphic gods of the Hindu tradition. (In the movie version of this novel, they can both be played by Peter Sellers, who will fall back to life on earth to do it.) And their survival of the fall frees them not only from the physical laws the rest of us are subject to, but also, according to the principles of Maximalism, from the usual moral laws and rules of consciousness. Yet what is finally most important about Gibreel is his desire for authenticity, and what is most striking about his madness and suicide is that this death is actually his punishment. This is a very nineteenth-century moral fate to befall so completely contemporary a character. It means that Rushdie repudiates everything his *writing* represents because he cannot allow Gibreel to get away with what the prose permits. This is a writing turned against itself in the name of a morality which approves Chamcha's return to India, his reconciliation with his father, and his repudiation of his desire to be different. In other words, none of the experiments with identity, with consciousness, with the relation of the physical states of these two characters to their mental states, with the connection between the "real" and the merely "true," finally matters. And by this measure, Slothrop's dispersal seems not only still radical, but ultimately moral as well, and now even simply honest.

Because the other who is palpable and unique between one's arms
is—at least for a few instants—exclusively desired, she or he
represents, without qualification or discrimination, life itself.
The experience = I + life.
But how to write about his? The equation is inexpressible in the
third person and in narrative form. The third person and the
narrative form are clauses in a contract agreed between writer and
reader, on the basis that the two of them can understand the third
person more fully than he can understand himself;
and this destroys the very terms of the equation.
—John Berger, *G.*

God knows what you permit to come tumbling out. Suddenly you are forever other than you were; and the world becomes such that parents can cease to be parents, and love can turn to hate." The moral version of this inside-and-outside, form-and-matter discrepancy, Rushdie offers in his own interpretation of *The Satanic Verses*. See "In Good Faith" in *Imaginary Homelands: Essays and Criticism, 1981–1991* (New York, 1991), 393–414. This conflict in Rushdie is also discussed in W. J. Weatherby, *Salman Rushdie: Sentenced to Death* (New York, 1990), 43.

This passage from John Berger's *G.* sets up what I want to discuss, finally, in Toni Morrison's *Jazz*, in which there is none of Rushdie's recidivist morality. Joe Trace murders his teen-aged lover Dorcas; his wife Violet, who is mentally disturbed already, attacks the girl's corpse in the funeral parlor. Joe and Violet, nonetheless, end the book in each other's arms, happy in bed, in intimate talk, a state the narrator calls "ecstasy."[8] What I want to explore is the relationship between this narrator and Violet, because the narrator's ultimate words, in direct address to the reader, develop not only the principles in the passage from Berger, but also the principles I have been developing throughout this argument: that a character, unlike the subject, is a sign that always entails the physical relationship between the printed marking on the page and the writer's and reader's bodies; that an ontology of language is ultimately exclusionary and delimiting; and that the novel is a text which has always been, necessarily, a book, too, a physical object which takes its place among other things.

The importance of free indirect discourse, moreover, keeps this argument from slipping into any nostalgic simplicities. Characters in a novel, the narrator included, are *written*. And, although some of them can be imagined off the page, outside the book, the relationship between a narrator and character in free indirect discourse can take place only in the language that constitutes them. The fact that neither is enclosed within a physical boundary, as living people are, emphasizes the importance of those physical distinctions and the politics that begin at the surface of the skin, in the world that is always more than the language that represents its meaning at the moment—the changing names, Robbe-Grillet might say, for the things that remain themselves.

Morrison's narrator is an unnamed voice, who begins her story in a tone of immediate intimacy—"Sth, I know that woman. She used to live with a flock of birds on Lenox Avenue. Know her husband, too. He fell for an eighteen-year-old girl with one of those deepdown, spooky loves that made him so sad and happy he shot her just to keep the feeling going." She also operates in a much broader mode; and as Morrison's allusion to Ellison's *Invisible Man*, this invisible woman tries to develop an epistemology of the city that both protects her isolation and expands her vision.[9] A great deal is permitted to this mobile point of view, including a knowledge of the deep past whose effects even the advent of the New Negro cannot overcome. And the narrator has access to Violet's mind when Violet, at her most disturbed, her most divided, does not. The novel's fourth section is important, because in it Violet emerges from the silences of her self-division into a possession of herself and the ability to say "I" and, in

8. Toni Morrison, *Jazz* (New York, 1993), 229.
9. *Ibid.*, 3; see 7–9, 120.

doing so, begins to turn her life toward the climax that leaves her happy and the narrator bereft. For the narrator realizes completely the failures of her strategy of deliberate isolation and the insuperable limits of her existence in language alone. She is, in other words, a text, merely, who charges the reader to give her body and life out of a freedom that she herself does not have. Like the sender of *The Post Card*, the narrator of *Jazz* has no other ontology. But Morrison, unlike Rushdie, does not punish her characters for the limitations of her writing or for writing's own limits. In the last pages of *Ulysses*, Joyce tries, it seems, to take his book away from all its art and give it back to life in Molly's proposition of a future with Poldy that is unknowable to the reader. Morrison also tries, it seems, to give her book to life, but she does it by placing its future physically, literally, in the reader's hands.

The long, four-page paragraph in which Violet regains her own voice begins with this:

> She had meant to bring a package of Dr. Dee's Nerve and Flesh Builder to stir into the malted milkshake, because the milkshakes alone didn't seem to be doing any good. The hips she came here with were gone, too, just like the power in her back and arms. Maybe *that* Violet, the one who knew where the butcher knife was and was strong enough to use it, had the hips she had lost. But if *that* Violet was strong and had hips, why was she proud of trying to kill a dead girl, and she was proud. Whenever she thought about *that* Violet, and what *that* Violet saw through her own eyes, she knew there was no shame there, no disgust. That was hers alone, so she is behind the rack at one of Duggie's little illegal tables and played with the straw in a chocolate malt. She could have been eighteen herself, just like the girl at the magazine rack, reading *Collier's* and playing for time in the drugstore. Did Dorcas, when she was alive, like *Collier's*? *Liberty Magazine?* Did the blonde ladies with shingled hair capture her?

Within a page-and-a-half, this free indirect discourse gathers Violet's anger to the liberating point at which she emerges into articulate independence and can say "I":

> so it looked like soda pop, which a girl like her ought to have ordered instead of liquor she could sip from the edge of a glass wider at the mouth than at its base, with a tiny stem like a flower in between while her hand, the one that wasn't holding the glass shaped like a

flower, was under the table drumming out the rhythm on the inside of his thigh, his thigh, his thigh, thigh, thigh, and he bought her underwear with stitching done to look like rosebuds and violets, VIOLETS, don't you know, and she wore it for him thin as it was and too cold for a room that couldn't count on a radiator to work through the afternoon, while I was where? Sliding on ice trying to get to somebody's kitchen to do their hair? Huddled in a doorway out of the wind waiting for the trolley? Wherever it was, it was cold and I was cold and nobody had got into the bed sheets early to warm up a spot for me or reached around my shoulders to pull the quilt up under my neck or even my ears because it got that cold sometimes it did and maybe that is why the butcher knife struck the neckline just by the earlobe. That's why. And that's why it took so much wrestling to get me down, keep me down and out of that coffin where she was the heifer who took what was mine, what I chose, picked out and determined to have and hold on to, NO! *that* Violet is not somebody walking round town, up and down the streets wearing my skin and using my eyes shit no *that* Violet is me! The me that hauled hay in Virginia and handled a four-mule team in the brace. I have stood in cane fields in the middle of the night when the sound of it rustling hid the slither of the snakes and I stood still waiting for him and not stirring a speck in case he was near and I would miss him, and damn the snakes my man was coming for me and who or what was going to keep me from him? . . . do what you will or may he was my Joe Trace. Mine. I picked him out from all the others wasn't nobody like Joe he make anybody stand in cane in the middle of the night; make any woman dream about him in the daytime so hard she miss the rut and have to work hard to get the mules back on the track. Any woman, not just me. Maybe that is what she saw. Not the fifty-year-old man toting a sample case, but my Joe Trace, my Virginia Joe Trace who carried a light inside him, whose shoulders were razor sharp and who looked at me with two-color eyes and never saw anybody else. Could she have looked at him and seen that? Under the table at the Indigo was she drumming on a thigh soft as a baby's but feeling all the while the way it used to be skin so tight it almost split and let the iron muscle through? Did she feel that, know that? That and other things, things I should have known and didn't? Secret things kept hidden from me or things I didn't notice?[10]

10. *Ibid.*, 93–94, 95–96. For another discussion of free indirect discourse, see Henry Louis

One of the secret things Violet comes to understand is how she regained her sanity and control of her life by an act of self-acceptance that dispelled both the inauthentic fictions that controlled her desire and the other within her, *that* Violet, who was the figure of her madness. This following section is narrated by Felice, the young woman who was Dorcas's friend and is now the surrogate "daughter" Violet and Joe have adopted, not so much to replace Dorcas, as to signal their reconciliation and a new familial turn. It is as though Felice is a kind of Stephen Dedalus who stays at 7 Eccles Street:

> I laughed but before I could agree with the hairdressers that she was crazy, she [Violet] said, "What's the world for if you can't make it up the way you want it?"
>
> "The way I want it?"
>
> "Yeah. The way you want it. Don't you want it to be something more than what it is?"
>
> "What's the point? I can't change it."
>
> "That's the point. If you don't, it will change you and it'll be your fault cause you let it. I let it. And messed up my life."
>
> "Messed it up how?"
>
> "Forgot it."
>
> "Forgot?"
>
> "Forgot it was mine. My life. I just ran up and down the streets wishing I was somebody else."
>
> "Who? Who'd you want to be?"
>
> "Not who so much as what. White. Light. Young again."
>
> "Now you don't?"
>
> "Now I want to be the woman my mother didn't stay around long enough to see. That one. The one she would have liked and the one I used to like before. . . . My grandmother fed me stories about a little blond child. He was a boy, but I thought of him as a girl sometimes, as a brother, sometimes as a boyfriend. He lived inside my mind. Quiet as a mole. But I didn't know it till I got here. The two of us. Had to get rid of it."
>
> She talked like that. But I understood what she meant. About having another you inside that isn't anything like you. Dorcas and I used to make up love scenes and describe them to each other. It was

Gates Jr., *The Signifying Monkey: A Theory of African American Literary Criticism* (New York, 1989), 207–16. Gates is especially good on both the pathology and the political dimension that this style can represent.

fun and a little smutty. Something about it bothered me, though. Not the loving stuff, but the picture I had of myself when I did it. Nothing like me. I saw myself as somebody I'd seen in a picture show or a magazine. Then it would work. If I pictured myself the way I am it seemed wrong.

"How did you get rid of her?"

"Killed her. Then I killed the me that killed her."

"Who's left?"

"Me."[11]

There are three things to underscore in this passage. First is Violet's distinction between *who* she is and *what* she wanted to be, a distinction which turns on the difference between a traditional sense of self based on consciousness and intention and the more problematic self that is the construction of another discourse. Violet, I am sure, has not read the passage in *Gravity's Rainbow* where Slothrop wonders *what* we are, but she has experienced, it's clear, the kinds of discrepancies Saladin Chamcha has felt. And before she was possessed by *that* Violet, she was inhabited by the fictions of Golden Gray and the whole history of race relations in the South that being a New Negro in New York cannot erase. The second thing is the way in which this passage works out Walter L. Reed's formula that the novel does not oppose appearance with reality, but contests one set of fictions against another. One value is not replaced by a higher one; two values are put into play with each other. And in *Jazz*, this happens right here, at the level of the characters whose most significant action at this moment is an act of interpretation. It is not unimportant that Joe murdered Dorcas, but more important is that Violet has killed *that* Violet in an act of self-definition that determines nothing less than the meaning of her life. And that she can explain this in conversation, in the community that intimate conversation signifies, is one of the things that distinguishes Violet's character from the narrator's.

The plot in *Jazz* parallel to Violet's is the story of the narrator's effort to understand Violet and Joe in terms of their full past. The opening paragraph of the sixth section discloses her ambition, her attributes—curiosity, information, inventiveness—the superiority she assumes, and the mode of speculation she favors: "Risky, I'd say, trying to figure out anybody's state of mind. But worth the trouble if you're like me—curious, inventive and well-informed. Joe acts like he knew all about what the old folks did to keep on going, but he couldn't have known much about True Belle, for example, because I doubt Violet ever

11. *Ibid.*, 208–209.

talked to him about her grandmother—and never about her mother. So he didn't know. Neither do I, although it's not hard to imagine what it must have been like." Throughout her subsequent narration, there are many signs of her distance, her predilections, and her limits. For instance:

> I like to think of him that way. . . .
> That is what makes me worry about him. How he thinks first of his clothes, and not the woman. . . .
> I know he is a hypocrite; that he [Golden Gray] is shaping a story for himself to tell somebody.

She, however, is not shaping a story to tell somebody. One of the things Morrison dramatizes here is that the simply assumed formal authority of an anonymous, "omniscient" narrator is a very questionable convention: that a narrator who is in effect a function rather than a character, such as the general narrator of *Bleak House,* has important limitations. Her narrator has, as we have seen, the intimacy of the first person, the breadth that accompanies the communal intelligence a third person narrator takes on, and the access to a consciousness the character Violet does not have of herself in the mode of indirect discourse. Morrison's narrator never settles into any one of these narrative roles and, by staying in motion, exposes the advantages and restrictions of each: "What was I thinking of? How could I have imagined him so poorly? Not noticed the hurt that was not linked to the color of his skin, or the blood that beat beneath it. But to some other thing that longed for authenticity, *for a right to be in this place,* effortlessly without needing to acquire a false face, a laughless grin, a talking posture."[12] I have added the italics to indicate the point at which this particular accusation is also more broadly self-defining. Like her version of Golden Gray, the narrator has no rightful place, no authentic posture. In constructing a version of the past in which Joe and Violet are unknowingly linked to each other through the relationships of True Belle, Golden Gray, Hunter's Hunter, and Wild, she hopes to become a part of their life, as its understanding authority perhaps, but it doesn't work. In the matrix of the values of the village Morrison works from, the narrator's alienation is not an advantage, but a handicap. And the climax of this plot is her full realization that her isolation has limited her understanding.

The parallel plots of Violet's recovery and the narrator's decline are not causally linked. There is no suggestion that the one must wane to let the other wax, nor is the narrator "unreliable," as we used to say. In *Jazz,* narrative itself is unreliable if it is performed outside a responsive relationship. The narrator

12. Morrison, *Jazz,* 137, 150, 151, 154, 160.

begins her wind-up with: "I started out believing that life was made just so the world would have some way to think about itself, but that it had gone awry with humans because flesh, pinioned by misery, hangs on to it with pleasure. Hangs on to wells and a boy's golden hair; would just as soon inhale sweet fire caused by a burning girl as hold a maybe-yes maybe-no hand. I don't believe that anymore. Something else you have to figure in before you figure it out." What's missing she begins to suggest in the opening of the next paragraph, which has been separated from the last line above by more than the usual white space: "It's nice when grown people whisper to each other under the covers. Their ecstasy is more leaf-sigh than bray and the body is the vehicle not the point. They reach, grown people, for something beyond, way beyond and way, way down underneath tissue." In her terms, they reach for the intimacy developed from memories of a shared past; in other terms, they reach for the real that is always beneath and beyond language's and the novel's grasp, its ideal in what is often figured as a silent, inexpressible materiality, underneath tissue, as though within the beloved's body itself.

This narrator has no beloved, no one next to her, within whispering distance, no body of her own, unless it is the book in which the text of her "voice" is held, the book in our hands. And that's exactly what she wants to make it. Her final paragraphs seek to realize her materially in a mode of being she doesn't have otherwise, that she cannot have merely as language. And her words, in all their particular poignancy, are also Morrison's description of the novel:

> I envy them their public love. I myself have only known it in secret, shared it in secret and longed, aw longed to show it—to be able to say out loud what they have no need to say at all: *That I have loved only you, surrendered my whole self reckless to you and nobody else. That I want you to love me back and show it to me. That I love the way you hold me, how close you let me be to you. I like your fingers on and on, lifting, turning. I have watched your face for a long time now, and missed your eyes when you went away from me. Talking to you and hearing you answer—that's the kick.*
>
> But I can't say that aloud; I can't tell anyone that I have been waiting for this all my life and that being chosen to wait is the reason I can. If I were able I'd say it. Say make me, remake me. You are free to do it and I am free to let you because look, look. Look where your hands are. Now.[13]

13. *Ibid.*, 227–28, 228–29, 229.

INDEX